Oracle Data Guard
Standby Database Failover Handbook

Oracle In-Focus Series

Bipul Kumar

RAMPANT
TECHPRESS

This book is dedicated to my sister, Anima Choudhary.

Oracle Data Guard
Standby Database Failover Handbook

By Bipul Kumar

Copyright © 2004 by Rampant TechPress. All rights reserved.

Printed in the United States of America.

Published in Kittrell, North Carolina, USA.

Oracle In-focus Series: Book 19

Series Editor: Don Burleson

Editors: Robin Haden, Janet Burleson and John Lavender

Production Editor: Teri Wade

Cover Design: Bryan Hoff

Printing History: December, 2004 for First Edition

Oracle, Oracle7, Oracle8, Oracle8i, Oracle9i and Oracle10g are trademarks of Oracle Corporation.

Many of the designations used by computer vendors to distinguish their products are claimed as Trademarks. All names known by Rampant TechPress to be trademark names appear in this text as initial caps.

Flame Warriors illustrations are copyright © by Mike Reed Illustrations Inc.

The information provided by the authors of this work is believed to be accurate and reliable. However, because of the possibility of human error by our authors and staff, Rampant TechPress cannot guarantee the accuracy or completeness of any information included in this work and is not responsible for any errors, omissions, or inaccurate results obtained from the use of information or scripts in this work.

ISBN: 0-9745993-8-7

Library of Congress Control Number: 2004096472

Table of Contents

Table of Contents

Oracle Data Guard

Using the Online Code Depot

Purchase of this book provides complete access to the online code depot that contains the sample code scripts.

All of the code depot scripts in this book are available for download in zip format, ready to load and use and are located at the following URL:

rampant.cc/data_guard.htm

If technical assistance is needed with downloading or accessing the scripts, please contact Rampant TechPress at info@rampant.cc.

Are you WISE?

Get the premier Oracle tuning tool. The Workload Interface Statistical Engine for Oracle provides unparallel capability for time-series Oracle tuning, unavailable nowhere else.

WISE supplements Oracle Enterprise Manager and it can quickly plot and spot performance signatures to allow you to see hidden trends, fast.

WISE interfaces with STATSPACK or AWR to provide unprecedented proactive tuning insights. Best of all, it is only $199.95. Get WISE. Download now!

www.wise-oracle.com

Get the Oracle Script Collection

This is the complete Oracle script collection from Mike Ault and Donald Burleson, the world's best Oracle DBA's.

Packed with over 500 ready-to-use Oracle scripts, this is the definitive collection for every Oracle professional DBA. It would take many years to develop these scripts from scratch, making this download the best value in the Oracle industry.

It's only $39.95 (less than 7 cents per script!). For immediate download go to:

www.oracle-script.com

Conventions Used in this Book

It is critical for any technical publication to follow rigorous standards and employ consistent punctuation conventions to make the text easy to read.

However, this is not an easy task. Within Oracle there are many types of notation that can confuse a reader. Some Oracle utilities such as STATSPACK and TKPROF are always spelled in CAPITAL letters, while Oracle parameters and procedures have varying naming conventions in the Oracle documentation. It is also important to remember that many Oracle commands are case sensitive, and are always left in their original executable form, and never altered with italics or capitalization.

Hence, all Rampant TechPress books follow these conventions:

Parameters - All Oracle parameters will be lowercase italics. Exceptions to this rule are parameter arguments that are commonly capitalized (KEEP pool, TKPROF); these will be left in ALL CAPS.

Variables – All PL/SQL program variables and arguments will also remain in lowercase italics (*dbms_job*, *dbms_utility*).

Tables & dictionary objects – All data dictionary objects are referenced in lowercase italics (*dba_indexes*, *v$sql*). This includes all *v$* and *x$* views (*x$kcbcbh*, *v$parameter*) and dictionary views (*dba_tables*, *user_indexes*).

SQL – All SQL is formatted for easy use in the code depot, and all SQL is displayed in lowercase. The main SQL terms (select, from, where, group by, order by, having) will always appear on a separate line.

Programs & Products – All products and programs that are known to the author are capitalized according to the vendor specifications (IBM, DBXray, etc). All names known by Rampant TechPress to be trademark names appear in this text as initial caps. References to UNIX are always made in uppercase.

Structure of the Book

This book is structured into ten chapters and two appendices. These are:

Chapter 1: Introduction gives an overview of the standby database and Data Guard technology. It lays the foundation before embarking on more detailed aspects of this subject.

Chapter 2: Data Guard Architecture presents a quick architectural synopsis of Data Guard technology.

Chapter 3: Implementing Standby Databases deals with the nitty-gritty of implementing physical and logical standby databases.

Chapter 4: Standby Database Administration covers the general techniques of standby database administration.

Chapter 5: Log Management Services presents concise information on log transport and log apply services.

Chapter 6: Switchover and Failover provides an insight into role transition services and the issues that may be encountered in Data Guard environment. This chapter marks the end of fundamentals of Data Guard technology.

Chapter 7: Performance Tuning of Data Guard Configuration deals with aspects of performance tuning in a Data Guard configuration ranging from basic performance requirements to complex tuning tips.

Chapter 8: Data Guard Broker augments the information presented on Data Guard broker in Chapter 2. Specific information on using DG broker to manage a site is available in this chapter.

Chapter 9: Recovery Manager and Data Guard explains the use of RMAN in conjunction with physical standby database.

Chapter 10: Oracle10g: New Features of Data Guard gives a detailed overview of new features of Data Guard introduced in Oracle10g.

Appendix A: Data Guard References presents the initialization parameters, dynamic performance views and PL/SQL packages relevant to Data Guard technology.

Appendix B: Troubleshooting Guide contains a set of potential problems and solutions that might be encountered when using Data Guard.

Customer feedback

The details and code in this book have been tested and verified to create a high quality product, but you may find that certain things are platform specific or just do not work as expected.

Every attempt is made to ensure the accuracy of the content of this book, but there is the occasional oversight. I am very much interested in knowing what you think of this book.

Please write to me with your feedback. I can be contacted at bipulc@btinternet.com.

Many thanks.

Bipul Kumar

Bipul Kumar
London, United Kingdom
August 08th 2004

Acknowledgements

This project would not have been feasible without the help from some key individuals. I would like to take this opportunity to thank them. My deep gratitude goes to Don Burleson, a legend in Oracle and who I'm deeply honoured to work with. I thank Don Burleson for having faith in a first time author, travelling to London to meet with me personally, and providing useful insight in the book writing process. Thanks Don!

My sincere gratitude goes to Lars Bo Vanting for reviewing each and every line of this book and providing numerous suggestions on improving the quality of this text.

Thanks to Cindy Cairns for copyediting and transforming it into a more readable form. Many thanks to Janet Burleson, Linda Webb, Robert Strickland, Andy Liles and John Lavender of Rampant Tech press for their willing and continuous support.

Most importantly, thanks to my wife, Adeepti, for encouraging me to take up this project and providing tremendous support throughout.

Thanks to folks at work: Phil Gray; Geoff Sherlock; Sebastian Glass; Steve Bowker; Stephen Waldock; and William Moore for helping me learn many technical and non-technical things. A big thank you goes to Sanjeev Vishwakarma for providing excellent feedback on the content of this book. Last but not least, thanks to all my friends. It's a pleasure to have you guys around.

With my sincerest thanks,

Bipul Kumar

Preface

In 1970, Dr. Edgar F. Codd of IBM Research published the first paper on the Relational Database. For the next nine years, no one attempted to create a commercial version of the relational database. The relational model was considered to be very slow, which meant that it would never be viable for industry. It was treated as something for the academicians.

However, in 1979, Oracle was introduced to the world as the first commercial relational database by a company called Relational Software Incorporated (RSI) which later became Oracle Corporation.

Since its inception in 1979, Oracle database software has seen many phases of improvement. When Oracle 6 was released, its online backup feature was considered to be "ground-breaking". Oracle 6 was then followed by the extremely sophisticated database of its time, Oracle 7.

These versions of Oracle and other relational databases were good tools that were to support the business of their time. They succeeded in providing good performance in their day, but the demands and nature of business have taken on a different shape as time has passed.

A few years ago, performance was the key word and the sole measure of the success of a database administrator (DBA) was the "speed of the database". Since that time, DBAs have been presented with many new challenges.

The advent of very large databases (VLDB), the internet age and e-commerce, to name a few, have radically altered the focus of database designers and administrators alike. These days, the minimum business requirement is "24X7". "Database downtime" has no place in the vocabulary of database administrators.

This book is all about the use of Oracle Data Guard for both high availability and database failover.

Best Regards,

Bipul Kumar

Introduction to Oracle Data Guard

An unrecoverable Oracle Database is a serious event!

Introduction

If a database requires 99.99% availability, how much downtime does that leave the DBA for both planned and unplanned outages in one year? The answer is a mere 52 minutes and 33 seconds.

While attempting to maintain this high level of availability, the importance of data integrity and quality cannot be compromised. Should something go wrong with a database, most if not all, businesses want the database to be recovered without the loss of a single byte of information. This adds a new dimension of disaster recovery to the realm of database administration.

When combining the two paradigms of "24X7" with regard to availability and "disaster recovery", there are not many downtime solutions left to the DBA. Thus, when high performance is added to this paradigm, it becomes the straw that breaks the DBA's back. This dilemma presents itself fully when there is a need to create a backup without shutting down the database. The problem is that the only remaining solution is for the DBA to create an online hot backup.

Online hot backup on a moderate to large size database will have significant performance implications. As a result, the savvy DBA will quickly realize that the online hot backup may not be the most suitable solution to the problem, which combines the demands of "24X7", "full protection of database" and "high performance".

To address this problem, database vendors started to explore the area of high availability (HA) solutions. Oracle Corporation has made significant advances in the Parallel Server configuration called Real Application Cluster (RAC) in Oracle 9i, Advanced Replication and Data Guard technology.

Data Guard was introduced as the Standby Database in Oracle 7.3, and has evolved significantly since then. Ideally, Data Guard provides a combined solution for the problem of high availability and disaster recovery without compromising performance.

This chapter provides an overview of Oracle Data Guard technology. It includes basic information on standby databases. This information will help DBAs decide if Oracle Data Guard is the appropriate solution, in the realm of disaster protection and high availability, for their enterprise.

Oracle Failover Options

There are four methods for achieving failover technology within the Oracle software. Each failover option has its own costs, advantages and disadvantages (Figure 1-1).

When choosing a failover option, the DBA must consider their tolerance for unplanned downtime as well as the cost per minute for downtime.

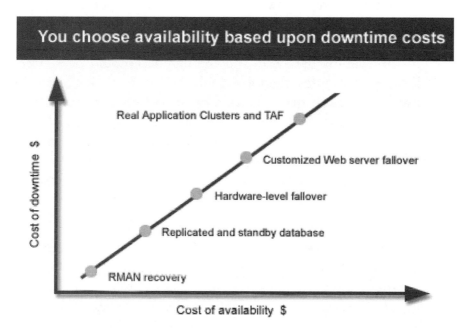

Figure 1-1 – *Oracle Failover options*

📖 **Code Depot Username = book, Password = secure**

Each of these options will incur different downtimes, configuration costs and expenses. Since Oracle introduced recovery products 12 years ago, their technologies have evolved significantly:

Traditional recovery (1990-1995) – This recovery method requires restoration of failed database files and a roll-forward using Oracle's Enterprise Backup Utility (EBU) or the Oracle8 Recovery Manager (RMAN) utility. This type of recovery could take several hours.

Manual Standby databases (1993-present) - Oracle7 introduced mechanisms that allow a standby database to be constantly in recovery mode and to be refreshed from Oracle's archived redo logs. In case of failure, the last redo log could be added to the standby database, and the database could be started in just a few minutes. Standby database is not an Oracle product, but a procedure that was used prior to Oracle Data Guard to create a standby database. Oracle7 introduced mechanisms that allow a standby database to be constantly in recovery mode and to be refreshed from Oracle's archived redo logs. In case of failure, the last redo log could be added to the standby database, and the database could be started in just a few minutes.

Oracle Parallel Server (1996-2001) - The OPS architecture allowed for several Oracle instances to share a common set of database files. In case of instance failure, the surviving instances could take over processing. There was a significant performance issue with OPS because shared RAM blocks had to be "pinged" between instances, imposing an additional processing burden on the cluster.

Replication failover – Multi-master replication can allow the standby database to be open and accepting transactions, with DML cross-feeding each instance. This requires Oracle Enterprise Edition and is only for databases with low DML rates

Real Application Clusters (2001–present) - The RAC architecture allows many instances to share a single database, but it avoids the overhead of RAM block pinging. RAC has also been enhanced to work with Oracle's Transparent Application Failover (TAF) to automatically restart any connections when an instance fails.

Oracle Streams - This is a high-speed replication solution that takes SQL directly from the *log_buffer* RAM area and replicates transactions to a remote database. During a server crash, transactions can be quickly redirected to the replicated system.

Oracle Data Guard - This is a free option with Oracle Enterprise Edition, and it provides an automated standby database. Upon server failure, a series of database procedures synchronizes the standby database and opens it to accept connections. Oracle Data Guard is free with Enterprise Edition.

Failover and Oracle licensing

Cost-conscious Oracle shops want to know how they can get Oracle failover as cheaply as possible. In addition to Data Guard, Oracle has a wealth of failover options, each with its own licensing costs. Oracle has two licensing tiers, Enterprise Edition (EE) and the far cheaper Standard Edition (SE).

- **Manual failover is** allowed in Oracle SE, but there is the risk of data loss. Also, it may take up to 30 minutes to recover the server

- **Data Guard** requires Oracle EE, but it automates the failover process to reduce downtime

- **Oracle Streams** requires Oracle10g Enterprise Edition.

The least expensive option is the Oracle manual standby database.

Manual standby database

If the goal is to save money by using Oracle Standard Edition, which does not have Oracle Data Guard included, multimaster replication and Oracle Streams, a manual approach might be the solution.

In this approach, a daemon process is written on the OS that will detect when the Oracle ARCH process has completed writing an archived redo log. Then, the daemon uses FTP or rsh to move the archived redo to the standby database server where it is automatically accepted into the standby database because it remains in RECOVER DATABASE mode.

The trick to this approach is to set the size of the online redo logs to minimize data loss. This is done by examining the log switch rate for the Oracle database at its PEAK DML load. For example, if the size of the online redo logs is set such that it has log switching every 5 minutes at peak load with an average of 15 minutes, the maximum data loss is 15 minutes.

Many shops improve this mechanism with solid-state disk (SSD) for the online redo logs and archived redo log filesystem. SSD can increase write speeds by 100 times, reducing recovery time by two orders of magnitude and reducing the maximum data loss from 15 minutes to less than one minute. In summary, the standby database approach has these issues:

- Allows the use of Oracle Standard Edition, which is far less expensive than the Enterprise Edition.

- Requires the purchase of a license to use Oracle Data Guard for the standby database.

- If standby database is geographically removed from the primary system, it also provides a disaster recovery option.

- Recovery can take up to 15 minutes.

- If the instance fails, the last redo log remains in the log buffer and online redo log files. This means that there might be a small data loss.

- Requires manual intervention to open the surviving standby database and re-direct incoming requests via *tnsnames.ora* or Apache to the new server.

Using older Oracle techniques can be dangerous

NOTE: Oracle standby servers need to be fully licensed if they are "hot standby" servers that can be used for queries. Cold standby servers used less than 10 days per year do not need to be licensed.

Now that information on the options has been presented, a closer look at the standby database method will be presented in the next section.

Standby Database Concepts

A standby database is a replica of the primary database. A standby database can be used when the primary database is not available. In a standby database configuration, usually two or more databases are involved.

The primary database is the main functional or production database, which in normal circumstances provides all or most of the database services. The primary database is also called the source database. In the standby database configuration, there will be one primary database and one or more standby databases.

The standby database is the secondary database or target database, which receives transaction details from the primary database in the form of archived redo logs. This database can be either in read-only mode or recovery mode. When in recovery mode, the transaction details from archived redo logs are applied in the standby database to keep it current with the primary database.

In addition, standby databases can be opened in read-only mode and used for reporting purposes. As long as a physical standby database is in read-only mode, it diverges from the primary database in terms of data.

In the read-only mode, logs apply service stops but the log transfer service continues. The database is synchronized again using these archived redo logs when it returns to recovery mode. A physical standby database cannot exist in both recovery and read-only modes at the same time, but a logical standby database can. Figure 1.2 shows a Data Guard environment.

More about the types of standby databases and the services involved in the synchronization of standby databases is covered later in this chapter.

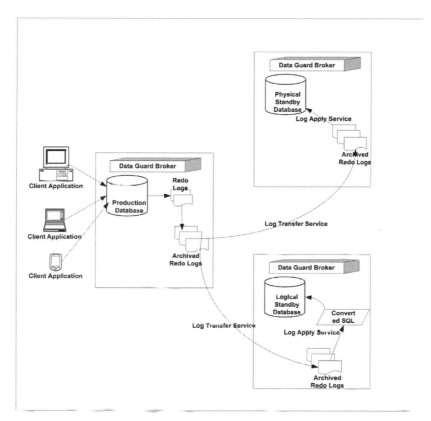

Figure 1.2 - *Data Guard Configuration*

Primarily, a standby database can be used for disaster recovery and ad hoc reporting. In addition, it can be used to offload the backup activity from the primary database to the standby database.

The work of standby databases is based on transaction details embedded in redo logs. A primary database serves the request from database clients. When a piece of information within the primary database is changed, the change detail is registered in redo logs.

When a redo log is full, the log writer starts writing to the new redo log and the old redo log is archived by the archive process (ARCH). In a standby configuration, archived logs are transferred to the standby database. If the standby database is in recovery mode, the archived logs are then applied. This process ensures that the changes made on the primary database are applied to the standby database; hence, the two databases remain in sync.

In case of an outage on the primary database, the standby database can be activated to perform the role of the primary database to minimize downtime.

History of the Standby Database

Standby databases were first introduced in Oracle 7.3. At that time, there were more limitations than features in the standby database; therefore, it was not considered to be a viable option for disaster recovery. Since then, Oracle has made many improvements in the functionality of standby databases.

The technology was made very robust and usable in Oracle8i. The existence of multiple physical standby databases, the read-only mode, and the managed recovery mode are some of the key enhancements to standby database technology included in Oracle8i.

In Oracle9i, the new features such as logical standby databases, multiple physical database, and ease of administration using the management tool called Oracle Data Guard Broker made this technology comparable with other disaster recovery options.

Chronological Development of Standby Technology

In Oracle 7.3, the newly introduced standby database technology supported only disaster recovery and was required to operate in recovery mode. Standby databases could not be opened in read-only mode for query. The transfer of archived redo logs was a manual process and required the DBA to write operating system specific scripts to transfer the logs from the primary to a standby host. In the event of primary database failure, the loss of the current redo logs would result in the loss of data.

Hence, a more robust redo logs member and group were required to minimize data loss. Since its introduction, Oracle Corporation has made improvements in standby technology.

Oracle 8i enhancement

The enhancements to standby technology that came with the release of Oracle8i include the following:

- The inclusion of a managed recovery mode which automates the process of archived redo log transfers from the primary to a standby site and the application of redo logs on the standby site. This reduced the number of manual interventions by DBAs.

- The restructuring of the standby database so that it could be opened for queries and reporting; thus, reducing some load on the primary database. During this period, the archived redo logs will be transferred from the primary site to a standby site and will be applied when the database is put back in recovery mode.

- The Recovery MANager (RMAN) could be used to back up the standby database, which can then be used for recovery of the primary database using the traditional backup/recovery method. Up to four standby databases could be configured in managed recovery mode.

The next section will introduce the Oracle9i Data Guard feature.

Introduction to Oracle9i Data Guard

Each of the two Releases of Oracle9i offered improvements that represented advancements in database technology. A summary of the changes is presented below.

Enhancements in Release 1

In Release 1 of Oracle 9i, standby database technology was renamed to Data Guard technology and Data Guard Broker was introduced. Data Guard Broker is a distributed management framework which simplifies the configuration and management of the Data Guard configuration.

Two new concepts were introduced to safeguard against data loss: no data loss and no data divergence. In no data loss mode, a transaction is not committed on the primary database until it is committed on at least one standby database. In no data divergence mode, the primary database will shut down if it cannot distribute the archive log to at least one standby database.

Standby databases could be configured to automatically detect and resolve gap sequence. In the older versions, only the failover operation was supported, which required the recreation of the standby database after the failover operation. In Oracle 9i, a new switchover operation was introduced, which does not require the rebuilding of the standby database; therefore, after a switchover operation, the primary and standby databases swap roles.

Up to nine standby databases could be created to support one primary database in managed recovery mode. In fact, Oracle9i does not mention manual recovery mode, but it can still be created.

Enhancements in Release 2

New data protection modes were introduced in Release 2. The new modes are: maximum protection for no data loss; maximum availability for no data loss; and maximum performance for minimal data loss.

The logical standby database is another new feature in Oracle9i Release 2. This feature enables the creation of a standby database that is logically similar to the primary database but does not need to be structurally exact to the primary database. Logical standby databases can assist in creating a reporting only system from the primary database.

New data dictionary views and initialization parameters were also added to improve the management of standby database.

Types of Standby Databases

Standby databases can be categorized as either a physical standby database or a logical standby database depending on the method used to propagate changes from the primary database.

A physical standby database has the identical structure of the primary database on a block-per-block basis; whereas, a logical standby database does not need to be an exact replica of the primary database. In addition to these two primary types, the standby database can be configured to act as archive log repository.

Management will judge you on Oracle's Failover performance!

Physical Standby Database

As previously mentioned, the physical standby database is an exact copy of the primary database on a block-per-block basis. The archived redo logs on a physical database are applied using the physical rowed values. Hence, all the segments in the primary and the standby database must be the same.

The physical database can be in recovery mode or read-only mode, but it cannot operate in both modes at the same time. When in recovery mode, the archived redo logs from the primary database are applied to keep it current and in sync with the primary database. When in read-only mode the standby database can be used for reporting.

The physical standby database in read-only mode can never be open for updates, because updates in a standby database will create a different rowed value; therefore, further recovery will not be possible.

In Oracle8i, there are two types of recovery mode supported: managed recovery and manual recovery. In Oracle9i, only managed recovery mode is mentioned; however, a physical standby database can still be put in manual recovery mode the same way that is was done in Oracle8i.

In managed recovery mode, the archive redo logs from the primary database are transferred automatically to the standby database provided that a Net8 connection is established between the primary and the standby database. The logs are then applied to the standby database by the log apply services; therefore, there is no need for manual intervention. The details of the processes involved in the transfer and application of redo logs to the standby database are given in Chapter 2, "Data Guard Architecture".

The manual recovery mode of Oracle8i required the manual transfer of archived redo logs from the primary to the standby database. The application of the logs was achieved manually by using SQL*Plus commands. This is a useful option if a Net8 connection between the primary and standby databases is not possible. Due to the significant number of manual tasks involved in this mode, it is not an obvious choice for disaster protection.

The read-only mode is used for ad-hoc reporting and can be very useful for offloading some of the reporting tasks from the primary database to the standby database. In this mode, the archived redo logs cannot be applied to the standby database, and at this point, the primary and the standby databases diverge. If there is only one standby database in the configuration, the DBA should be very protective about the archived redo logs as long as the standby database is in read-only mode.

The mode of operation of standby databases can be changed between recovery mode and read-only mode and vice versa; however, the standby database can only be in one mode at a time.

The physical standby database performs better than the logical standby database because it uses media recovery to apply archived redo logs. Moreover, there are fewer limitations on a physical standby database compared to a logical standby database.

Logical Standby Database

The logical standby database is a new feature in Data Guard technology introduced in Oracle9i. A logical standby database can contain all or a set of objects from the primary database. In addition, it can be a mixture of a few objects from the primary database and few objects of its own.

The data in a logical standby database is kept current using the SQL apply mode. In SQL apply mode, the SQL statements from archived redo logs are extracted using LogMiner technology and are then applied to the standby database. The main difference between physical and logical standby databases is that a logical database is always open and is recovered when it is open; whereas, a physical standby database can be either open or in recovery mode.

If a system has heavy reporting requirements, logical standby databases can be very useful. For example, with the use of a decision support system or a data warehouse a DBA can create extra indexes and materialized views in a logical standby database that do not need to be present in the primary database.

As a result, the data manipulation on the primary database will not have the overhead of updating the indexes and refreshing materialized views. These extra objects will assist in reporting and running queries on the standby database.

A logical standby database can be open in read/write mode. Database objects, which are not replicated from the primary database, can be updated. The objects to be updated by the log apply service can only be in read only mode to ensure the consistency of data between a logical standby and the primary database.

Unlike a physical standby database, a logical standby database does not support all data types. Data types such as CLOB, BFILE, LONG, ROWID, NCLOB, UROWID, LONG RAW and user-defined types are not supported in logical standby databases. During the SQL apply on a logical database, any attempt to update data in a table containing columns of an unsupported data type will return error, and the log apply service will terminate. *dba_logstdby_unsupported* view can be used on the primary database to find out if the database contains any unsupported data types.

Theoretically, a logical standby database can be used as the primary database during an outage on the true primary database. Since a logical standby database may not contain all the objects from the primary database, the switchover to the logical standby database may restrict the services offered by the true primary database. As a result, the DBA should carefully consider the objects to be replicated in a logical standby database during the configuration phase.

Archive Log Repository

Sometimes, the standby database configuration is used only as an archive log repository. In this case, the benefit is the storage of the archived redo logs on another server for a small period of time. The transfers of archived redo logs are maintained by Oracle processes using Net8. For an archive log repository configuration, data files are not required; therefore, it cannot be used for data recovery.

Benefits and Drawbacks of Data Guard

Like any technology, Data Guard has advantages and disadvantages. Data Guard configuration has following advantages:

Disaster Protection

A Data Guard configuration consists of several standby databases connected to the primary database using Oracle Net. These standby databases can be used for failover operation if the primary database is not available thereby minimizing the loss of service. Data Guard configuration provides a safeguard against physical corruption as well as prevention of user errors on the primary database. The physical corruptions of data blocks due to device failure will not be propagated via archived redo logs.

Since the information between the primary and the standby database flows in the form of redo logs, a delay can be built into the redo log application mechanism on the standby database. This built-in delay in log application service can be used to prevent propagation of user errors to the standby database as long as the errors are detected on the primary database before the application of the logs on the standby database.

Moreover, a Data Guard environment can be configured in three different modes: maximum protection, maximum availability and maximum performance. The DBA must evaluate the requirements of their enterprise to configure Data Guard in one of these modes to suit the chosen disaster recovery strategy.

In addition to disaster protection, standby databases can be used for database services during the planned outage of the primary database for maintenance work. Once the role of the standby database is switched and it starts serving as the primary database, the DBA must update the Oracle Net configuration to route the application requests to the new primary database. The details about changes in Oracle Net and alternative approach using Transparent Application Failover are described later in this book.

Load Balancing

Standby databases can contribute towards load balancing on the primary database. The ad-hoc reporting and backup operation activities can be off loaded to the standby database, reducing load on the primary database.

The physical standby database can be opened in read-only mode and will cater to the DBA's reporting requirements. Careful consideration is required when selecting the operating mode because as long as a physical standby database is open in read-only mode, it cannot be synchronized with the primary database.

As a result, the most up-to-date data will not be available for reporting. If the reporting requirements of the organization demand the most up-to-date information from the primary database or real-time data, a logical standby database will be the obvious choice. A logical standby database is always open in read-only or read/write mode and can keep the data in sync with the primary database while providing reporting services.

If the backup and recovery strategy includes a traditional online or offline backup of the database along with Data Guard configuration, the backup operation can be offloaded from the primary database to the standby database.

Automated Management

The managed recovery mode of the standby database in Oracle8i greatly reduced the amount of time a DBA needed to spend on managing this configuration. In managed recovery mode, the archived redo logs are automatically transferred from the primary database to the standby database and applied to the standby database.

The only time a DBA needs to monitor and maintain the standby database is if there are gaps in the archived redo logs on the standby site. Details about gap sequence and its resolution are provided in Chapter 2, "Data Guard Architecture."

In Oracle9i, improvements were made so that gap sequences could be automatically detected and resolved. Also, the Data Guard Broker distributed management framework significantly reduces the work needed to set up a Data Guard configuration. Data Guard Broker framework provides a graphical user interface and a command line interface that can be used to easily monitor and administer Data Guard environment.

Data Guard is not a Cheap Option

On the downside, the Data Guard option is expensive to set up. To properly configure the environment, it almost certainly requires extra servers that can be switched over in case of an outage on the primary database. Also, extra servers will require some attention from the system administration team and the database administration team for set up and regular maintenance activities. It also requires a Net8 connection between the primary and standby databases because a network connection will be required between the two sites. Sometimes, the financial implications of setting up a Data Guard environment outweigh the benefits offered by this technology.

Data Guard Operational Constraints

The following operational constraints apply to a Data Guard configuration:

- The primary database should run in ARCHIVELOG mode.

- Primary and standby databases cannot share the control file; therefore, each should have their own copy of control files.

- Servers running the primary and standby databases should have the same version of Oracle software.

- Servers running the primary and standby databases should have the same release of operating system software.

- The primary database should run in FORCE LOGGING mode to avoid any divergence of data between the primary and the standby database as a result of unrecoverable writes on the primary database.

- The Data Guard option is only available in the Enterprise Edition of Oracle Database software.

Lifecycle of a Standby Database

Lifecycle of a standby database in a Data Guard environment can be depicted using Figure 1.3.

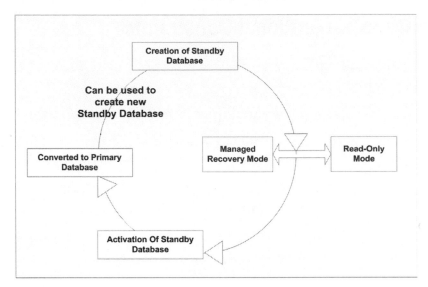

Figure 1.3 - *Lifecycle of a Standby Database*

The stages in the life of a standby database are as follows:

Creation of Standby Database

A standby database is created from the backup of the primary database. Backup database files and control files are transferred to the standby database site, where the standby database is created. A Net8 connection is established between the primary and the standby database to facilitate the transfer of archived redo logs.

Also, the initialization parameters on the primary and standby databases are configured for node identification to be used by log transfer services. Once these changes are made, the standby database can be started in recovery mode.

Recovery or read-only mode

After the creation of the standby database, the log transfer service can be started on the primary database to transfer the archived logs to the standby database. The log apply service on the standby database applies the archived redo logs to keep the database in sync with the primary database. These two services form an important part in the life cycle of the standby database.

As in the case of a physical standby database, it can be opened for read-only or query processing. During any time period where the physical standby database is open for read-only or query processing, the log apply service remains idle and does not apply the archived redo logs to the standby database; however, the log transfer service continues to transfer archived logs from the primary to the standby database. These logs are applied to the physical standby database when it is placed in recovery mode again.

Switchover or failover operation

The standby database will be activated to serve as the primary database at some point in its life cycle. There are normally two situations when this operation will be performed: a planned outage for maintenance of the primary database or disaster recovery. A switchover operation occurs when a standby database is transitioned into the primary database role and the primary database into the standby database role. In the switchover operation, no data is lost.

The switchover operation is performed for maintenance of the primary database. In case of an unplanned outage on the primary site, the standby database will be activated as the primary database. This is called failover. There are two types of failover operations: Graceful or "no-data-loss" failover and Forced or "minimal-data-loss" failover. Once the standby database is transitioned into primary database status in either switchover or failover, the life of the database as the standby ends and its service as the primary database begins.

A Sample Data Guard Configuration

This section presents a sample configuration of standby databases. In figure 1.4, NetBillProd is a production database located in New York. This database serves all the database requests for a telecom billing application. The database has two standby databases on the same local area network (LAN). These standby databases are: NetBillPhy1 and NetBillLog1. NetBillPhy1 is the physical standby database and NetBillLog1 is the logical standby database. Also, there is a physical standby database NetBillPhy2 located in London, UK.

The production database, NetBillProd, and the NetBillPhy2 standby database are connected over a wide area network (WAN). Although the production database and two of its standby databases reside on the same LAN, they do not share the same server or storage.

The first physical standby database, NetBillPhy1, is primarily used for switchover operation when the production database is undergoing maintenance operation. In this case, the backup is performed on the standby database instead of the production database.

In this example, the billing system is sending data to another module residing in same database, which is used for nightly batch reporting. In this case, the database objects used for reporting can be segregated and used to create only those objects in the logical standby database, NetBillLog1.

Additionally, NetBillLog1 will have materialized views and indexes to speed up the reporting queries. In other words, NetBillLog1 will cater to all reporting requests, and the computing resources on the production database, NetBillProd, will be utilized in the completion of other tasks.

In case of a disaster where the primary production database is destroyed, there are two options. If the physical standby database, NetBillPhy1, is unaffected by the disaster, it can be activated to act as production database. Since the production database and this particular standby database are on same LAN, there should not be any performance degradation; however, the performance factor largely depends on the computing resources of the standby database as compared to the original production database.

If the production database site is completely destroyed and all servers in the location are affected, the second standby database, NetBillPhy2 located in London, UK, can be activated to act as the production database. Since NetBillPhy2 is not on the same LAN, there may be performance related issues when it starts serving the database requests. Again, the performance depends on the nature of the application. For an internet application, the effect on performance should be minimal.

The physical standby databases can be configured in any of the three data protection modes. The main factors influencing the selection of a data protection mode are the importance of data and the network bandwidth. In a LAN environment, the maximum protection or maximum availability mode will not show any performance degradation; however, in a WAN, this can have a significant impact.

A performance benchmark should be conducted in each of the protection modes before finally selecting and setting the data protection mode in the Data Guard configuration.

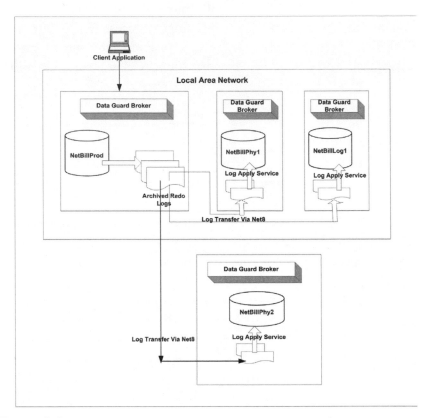

Figure 1.4 - *A Sample Data Guard Configuration*

Conclusion

This chapter introduced the concepts of standby databases and Data Guard technology. It briefly touched on much of the terminology and techniques involved in Data Guard along with historical background of this technology.

It laid the foundation for the detailed material in this book. An attempt has been made to provide sufficient information to help the DBA make good decisions regarding the implementation of the Data Guard configuration in any enterprise. The next chapter focuses on the architecture of Data Guard before embarking on implementation details.

"I'm seeking an Oracle DBA position that is commensurate with my skills."

Data Guard Architecture

Monitoring Oracle data integrity requires constant vigilance.

Introduction

As described briefly in the previous chapter, a Data Guard configuration consists of the primary database and at least one standby database. The primary database provides the usual database services. Client applications make changes to the primary database.

These changes flow between the primary and the standby database in the form of redo records. Standby databases are kept in sync with the primary database using these redo records. The

---

mechanism used for synchronization depends on the data protection mode and the type of standby database.

The Log Transport Process and Log Apply Process play an important role how Data Guard works. The log transfer service is responsible for transmitting the redo records from the primary to the standby database. The log apply service applies the redo records; reading from the redo log files onto the standby database.

Various architectural components and their interaction with each other are included in greater detail later in this chapter. The data protection modes will be explained in Chapter 5.

Figure 2.1 illustrates the general working of Data Guard. The diagram shows the flow of data in a Data Guard environment. The four main stages are identified as steps A to D:

- Step A – The client application accesses the primary database and updates data.

- Step B – The archiver process copies the online redo log file to the local archival destination.

- Step C - The log transfer process transfers the archived redo log file to the standby site.

- Step D – The log apply process on the standby site synchronizes the standby database by applying the redo records from the archived log file.

The number and type of processes involved, in the working of Data Guard, may vary slightly depending on the specified data protection mode.

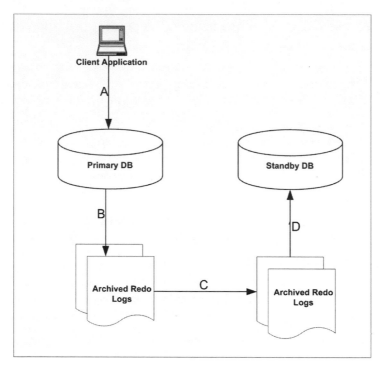

Figure 2.1 – *A general overview of a Data Guard configuration.*

Architectural Components

In this section, a detailed description of the processes and other components involved in the workings of Data Guard are presented. One of the requirements of a Data Guard configuration is that the primary database run in ARCHIVELOG mode. This ensures that all the changes made to the primary database are captured and kept in the archived redo log. The following section explains the database processes contributing to the Data Guard architecture.

Process Architecture

The Log Transport Service and Log Apply Service form the backbone of the Data Guard environment. The log transport service starts on the primary database and completes on the standby database. The following processes facilitate the log transport service on the primary and the standby site:

- **Archiver Process** – The archiver process (ARCn or ARCH) is responsible for archiving online redo logs. The archival destination could be a local destination or a remote standby database site. In the case of a Data Guard configuration, one of the archival destinations must be a standby database. The archiver process of the primary database writes the redo log file.

  For a better data protection mode, the standby redo log files can be configured on the standby database. In this case, the archiver process on the standby site will be used to archive the standby redo log files.

- **Log Writer** (LGWR) – The log writer process on the primary database writes entries from the redo log buffer to the online redo log file. When the current online redo log file is full, it triggers the archiver process to start the archiving activity. In some cases, the log writer process writes redo entries to the online redo log file of the primary database and the standby redo log file of the standby database. Usually, in this kind of arrangement the LGWR works as the log transport agent that is setup to achieve high data protection modes.

- **Remote File Server (RFS) Process** – The RFS process runs on the standby database and is responsible for communication between the primary and the standby database. For the log transport service, the RFS on the standby database receives the redo records from the archiver or the log writer process of the primary database over Oracle Net and writes to filesystem on the standby site.

- **Fetch Archive Log (FAL)** – The FAL process has two components: FAL Client and FAL Server. Both processes are used for archive gap resolution. If the Managed Recovery

Process (MRP) on the standby database site detects an archive gap sequence, it initiates a fetch request to the FAL client on the standby site. This action, in turn, requests the FAL server process on the primary database to re-transmit the archived log files to resolve the gap sequence. Archive gap sequences will be discussed later in this chapter.

Once the log transport service completes the transmission of redo records to the standby site, the log apply service starts applying the changes to the standby database. The log apply service operates solely on the standby database. The following processes on the standby site facilitate the log apply operations:

- **Managed Recovery Process (MRP)** – The MRP applies the redo entries from the archived redo logs onto the physical standby database.

- **Logical Standby Process (LSP)** – The LSP applies the redo records from archived redo logs to the logical standby database. The Oracle database log miner engine is used by the logical standby process for the SQL apply operations. Using the log miner engine, the LSP process recreates the SQL statements from redo logs that have been executed on the primary database. These statements are then applied to the standby database to keep it current with the primary database.

Figure 2.2 shows the database processes involved in Data Guard. In most cases, only a subset of these processes is used, based on the type of standby database and mode of data protection.

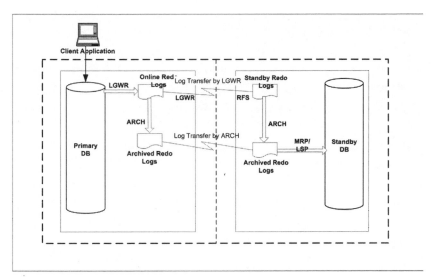

Figure 2.2 – *Processes and files involved in the Data Guard environment.*

Redo Log File

The Redo Log file is an essential structure for any Oracle database. There must be at least two redo log groups with at least one log member per group. A redo log member is a physical file that contains all the committed and uncommitted transactions. Any changes made to the database are registered to the redo log buffer inside the System Global Area (SGA) memory structure.

When the redo log buffer fills, the LGWR process writes the buffer information to the online redo log file. The redo log file contains both old and new values and can be used for media recovery. In addition, each transaction is given a unique System Change Number (SCN) that is used for media recovery.

Redo log groups are reused in a circular method in that when the current redo log file fills, the LGWR starts writing to the next redo log file group. When all of the redo log groups are filled, the LGWR starts reusing the redo log members.

Archived Redo Log File

An archived redo log file is a replica of an online redo log file. When an online redo log file group fills, the archiver process copies the online redo log file to archival destinations.

Once the archiver process completes the replication of the online redo log file to archival destinations, the online redo log file is marked for reuse. The redo thread number and log sequence number uniquely identify an archived redo log file. In case of media recovery, archived redo log files can be used to update the database files.

In a Data Guard environment, a standby database should be an archival destination. Remote archival to the standby database is achieved by a combination of the archiver process on the primary database and the remote file server process of the standby database. The archived redo log file on the standby database is exactly the same as the archived redo file written to a local archival destination.

Data Guard Apply Modes

The log apply service in a Data Guard environment keeps the standby database up to date with the primary database. The log apply mechanism differs based on the type of standby database. A physical standby database is an exact replica of the primary database; therefore, the log apply service does a block-per-block media recovery using archived redo logs of the primary database.

The log apply service on a logical standby database uses the SQL apply mode to recover the standby database. In the following two sections details on the apply mechanism will be presented.

Redo Apply Mode

The principle of the Redo Apply mode in a Data Guard environment is the same as the media recovery of any Oracle database. In the redo apply mode, the archived redo log files on the standby site are read and applied to the standby database. The redo records generated at the primary database and recorded in the archived redo log files are used to roll forward the standby database, just as it works in media recovery.

During this phase, the undo records, which are registered in the undo segment of the standby database, are also generated. These undo records are then used to roll back the standby database in order to discard any uncommitted transactions that may have been applied during the roll forward phase of recovery. The redo apply mode is used by the log apply service on physical standby databases.

SQL Apply Mode

The log apply service uses the SQL apply mode to update logical standby databases. In the SQL apply mode, the log apply service starts a LSP on the standby site, which reads redo records from archived redo log files and then converts the redo records into SQL statements.

Depending on the subset of objects to be maintained in the logical standby database, the log apply engine filters the SQL statements and then selectively applies those to the standby database. A SQL apply mode uses log miner technology to generate the SQL statements from the redo records of the archived redo log file. A brief overview of Log Miner technology is provided in the next section.

The following background processes and parallel execution servers are used in the SQL apply mode:

- **COORDINATOR** – This is the main LSP process that starts other background processes and coordinates the tasks performed by the other background processes involved in recovery.

- **READER** – Reads the redo entries from the archived redo log file.

- **PREPARER** – Redo entries in the redo log files are stored in the form of changes in Oracle blocks. This process converts the changes in blocks to changes in Oracle segments.

- **BUILDER** – Builds the completed transactions to be applied on the standby database.

- **ANALYZER** – Analyzes the SQL statements provided by builder and filters out the statement that needs to be applied on the database. The analyzer performs all dependency calculations.

- **APPLIER** – Applies the SQL statements onto the standby database. Usually, the applier process runs as a parallel execution server.

The SQL apply mode is substantially slower than the redo apply mode of standby database recovery.

Understanding Log Miner Technology

Log Miner is a redo log query engine that is provided with the Oracle database server. Log Miner was introduced in Oracle 8.1, and later releases of Oracle improved on the performance of the log miner utility. In Oracle 9i Release 2, the log miner engine is the core of the log apply service for the logical standby database.

Log Miner uses redo entries embedded in online redo log files or archived redo log files and data dictionary information to build the SQL statement. Log Miner keeps the contents of the redo log file in the fixed view, *v$logmnr_contents*. The SQL interface can be used to query this view in order to see the SQL statement executed on a database at any point in time.

Together, the column SQL_REDO and the SCN of *v$logmnr_contents,* can provide relevant information on the activity within the database. In addition, this view contains the segment name and owner which is useful in further identification of the objects being altered.

The redo log file of an Oracle database contains change vectors in the form of internally generated numerical identifiers. Moreover, the old and new values of columns are represented as hex bytes. These internally generated identifiers or hex bytes are not easy to understand.

In order to generate SQL statements in external data format, the log miner engine uses data dictionary information. This data dictionary information can be extracted to an external operating system file or redo logs using the *dbms_logmnr_d.build* procedure. As an alternative, the data dictionary can be read directly from an online catalog. In the latter case, the Log Miner engine can only provide the SQL statements using the current structure of objects within the database.

In the SQL apply mode of a Data Guard environment, the dictionary is built using the *dbms_logstdby.build* procedure, which stores the dictionary information to the redo log file. The extraction of dictionary information from the redo log file for mapping of the internal identifier is more efficient.

For the best results, a separate tablespace should be used to create the objects required by the Log Miner utility. By default, these objects are created in the system tablespace. This may slow down the overall response time of the primary database.

The *dbms_logmnr* package provides several functions to control the working of Log Miner. For more information on Log Miner, refer to Oracle documentation, "Oracle 9i Database Administrator's Guide Release 2 (9.2)".

A good Oracle DBA is always on the lookout for potential problems.

Archive Gap Sequence

An Archive Gap Sequence is a set of archived redo logs that could not be transmitted to the standby site. As a result of an archive gap, the standby database will lag behind the primary database. Usually, an archive gap sequence is created as the result of a network outage and the connection between the primary and the standby site is lost. The archive gap sequence can also occur during the creation of a standby database.

In Release 2 of Oracle 9i, Oracle Corporation has significantly improved automatic archive gap detection and resolution which reduces the chances of lag between the primary and the standby site.

Detection and Resolution

Starting with Release 2 of Oracle 9i, three methods of automatic archive gap detection became available. The following is a description of their features:

- The *archiver* process of the primary database polls the standby databases every 60 seconds. This is referred to as "heartbeat." During heartbeat, if a standby database reports an archive gap, the *archiver* of the primary database sends the archived redo log files required to fill the gap. Once the files have been transferred, the site is marked as up to date.

- Archived redo logs are transferred from the primary database to the standby database. On the primary database side, the LGWR or ARCH is responsible for sending the archived redo logs. On the standby site, the RFS process takes the archived redo log file and writes to the host machine. An archived redo log file is uniquely identified by its sequence number and thread number.

- When the RFS process receives an archived redo log file, it compares the sequence number with the sequence number of the previously received archived redo log file. If the sequence number of the current archived redo log file is greater than the sequence number of the last received archived redo log file plus one, a request is sent to the *archiver* process of the primary database that is providing a list of missing archived redo log files. The *archiver* of the primary database then retransmits these archived redo log files, thereby resolving the gap sequence.

- For a physical standby database, Oracle 9i Release 2 introduced a request-response system for gap resolution through the FAL background process. The FAL method of gap resolution is initiated by the Managed Recovery Process (MRP). If the MRP detects a gap in archived redo logs during the application of log files, it requests the *archiver* process of the primary database to resend the archived redo log files which have caused the gap sequence.

- There are two important parameters required for gap resolution through the FAL background process: *fal_server* and *fal_client*. These two parameters need to be set in the initialization parameter file of the physical standby database. *fal_server* is the service name of the primary database and *fal_client* is the service name of the standby database.

- The *fal_client* should be one of the remote archival destinations of the primary database pointing to this standby database. When MRP detects a gap sequence, it requests the *archiver* process of the primary database, identified by the *fal_server* parameter, and passes the sequence number of log files causing the archive gap. In addition, it passes the service name defined by the *fal_client* parameter to the *archiver* of the primary database. The *archiver* process of the primary database then retransmits the archived log files requested by the MRP of the standby database.

Now that the basic information on that Archive Gap Sequence has been presented, the next section contains more detailed information on the Data Guard Broker Architecture.

Data Guard Broker Architecture

Data Guard Broker is an assistance utility that is provided with Oracle Database Server software to facilitate the creation and management of Data Guard configurations. Data Guard Broker consists of server side and client side components that are used together in the implementation of a distributed computing architecture.

The server side component includes a Data Guard Monitor (DMON) process and configuration files. The client side component includes Data Guard Manager and a Command Line interface.

Data Guard Broker manages a Data Guard configuration using a broker management model. The broker management model is a hierarchal structure comprised of Configuration, Site and Database resources. Broker can manage all three layers of the management model. More information about the broker management model will be presented later in this section.

Data Guard Broker is available with Oracle 9i Release 2 or above.

Data Guard Broker can manage the primary database and up to nine standby databases in one configuration. These nine standby databases can be a mixture of physical and logical standby databases. Standby databases can be created using Data Guard broker. In addition, it can be used to add an existing standby database to a configuration.

When a standby database is created using Broker, Broker takes care of the entire set of supporting files such as SPFILE, Oracle Net configuration files, etc. If a DBA needs to add an existing standby database to a Data Guard configuration, the SPFILE and Oracle Net files must be configured manually before the standby database is added to a configuration. If Data Guard Broker is to be used for the management of standby databases, SPFILE must be used to hold the initialization parameters on all the participating databases.

Some advantages of using Data Guard Broker are as follows:

- It is a centralized management tool that can be used to manage the entire configuration using a GUI or CLI interface.

- It provides an extensive health check mechanism for the primary database, standby databases and supporting services in the configuration.

- It reduces the complexity of role management services. Switchover and Failover operations can be performed from a centralized console.

- It can be used to gather useful statistics for fine tuning the log transfer and log apply services.

In Oracle 9i, Data Guard Broker cannot be used with Oracle Real Application Cluster. RAC support is provided with Oracle 10g.

The following subsections will present the broker management model and the broker components, in brief.

Configuration, Sites and Resources

The Broker management model is a three layer hierarchical framework. The logical units of the management model are Configuration, Site and Database Resources. These three layers share a parent-child relationship as shown in Figure 2-3 below.

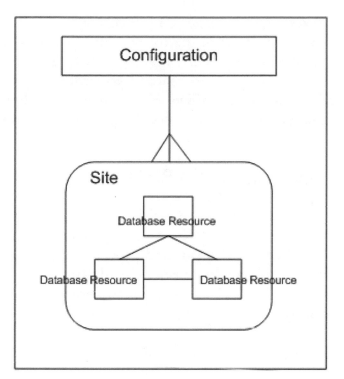

Figure 2.3 – *The relation between layers of the Broker management model.*

A Database Resource is the smallest unit managed by Data Guard Broker. In the Broker management model, a database resource represents an instance of the primary or standby database. In addition, a service such as the log apply service can be classified as a database resource in the context of a management model. The site in this model is a collection of database resources.

In other words, a site is equivalent to a host machine on which a database instance is running. Configuration is the largest unit in the Broker management model and consists of the primary site and one or more standby sites.

Data Guard Broker can manage all three layers of the management model. Any operation performed on a higher level of the model is applicable to all child objects of that layer. For example, if the status of a site is changed to offline, all the resources under that site will be offline. More information about the management model will be presented in Chapter 7 of this book.

Server Side Components of the Broker

The server side component of Data Guard Broker includes the Data Guard Monitor (DMON) process and a configuration file. The Data Guard Monitor is a background process that runs on each of the sites managed by Data Guard Broker. The configuration file is a binary file that contains the properties and status of all the sites in a configuration.

The DMON process is responsible for managing a consistent copy of the configuration file across the entire configuration. The DMON processes in a configuration communicate over Oracle Net to control the role management and log management services. In addition, the DMON process gathers statistics about the health of a site that can be used for monitoring and fine-tuning. The following diagram shows a sample Data Guard configuration managed by Data Guard broker.

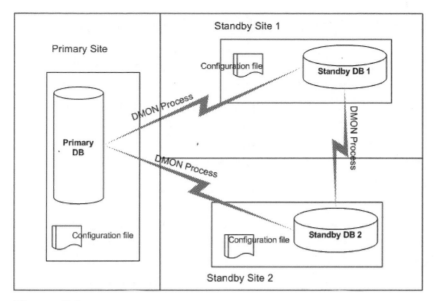

Figure 2.4 – *The server side components of Data Guard Broker.*

Client Side Components of the Broker

The Data Guard Manager and Command Line Interface (DGMGRL) make up the client side components of Data Guard Broker. Data Guard Manager is a graphical user interface that is integrated with the Oracle Enterprise Manager (OEM). It contains several wizards that are used to ease the management of a Data Guard configuration. DGMGRL or Command Line Interface provides most of the functionalities of Data Guard Manager and can be useful in writing custom scripts to automate Data Guard tasks.

Chapter 7 provides the practical details of Data Guard Broker. More information about the server side and client side components can be found in that chapter.

Role of the Transport Network Substrate

Oracle Net services play an important role in the performance of standby databases. It acts as communication channel between primary and standby databases. In order for the log transfer service, automatic archive gap resolution and role management service to work without manual intervention, an Oracle Net connection between the primary and the standby site must be maintained.

Oracle Net is not required when a standby database is running in manual recovery mode. However, given the limitations and high degree of DBA intervention required in the manual recovery mode, that particular structure would not be an obvious choice.

Oracle Net can be configured to connect sites over a LAN or a WAN. Good network bandwidth should be provided in order to achieve better performance of the log transfer service. In addition to connecting the primary site to all of its standby sites through Oracle Net, it is a good practice to connect the standby sites with each other. This will minimize the downtime during switchover or failover operations.

The Oracle Name services on the primary site should be configured such that the *archiver* process can resolve the service name for archiving to a remote standby destination. Moreover, the listener on standby sites should be configured properly to respond to the request sent by the *archiver* process of the primary site. The details about the configuration of Oracle Net services in context of Data Guard configuration are provided in the next chapter.

Conclusion

This chapter included a quick architectural overview of the Oracle Data Guard and standby databases. In general, the following topics were covered in order to build the foundation for the rest of this book:

- Detail about Oracle processes and files involved in the working of Data Guard have been presented.

- The redo log apply service for physical and logical standby databases were included, in detail.

- A brief description of Log Miner technology, which forms the backbone of the SQL apply mode, was provided.

- The concept of archive gap sequences and how they are detected and resolved in Oracle 9i Release 2 was covered in detail.

- A complete section on Data Guard Broker provided broker architecture information along with other core concepts.

- The importance of Oracle Net in the context of Data Guard has been included, in brief.

A review of the first two chapters should provide a clear picture of Data Guard and standby databases. Most of the concepts discussed in these chapters will be elaborated upon in the remainder of this book.

Implementing Standby Databases

Beware of Oracle experts who speak fluent Klingon

Introduction

The previous chapters of this book dealt with the theoretical aspect of Data Guard and standby databases. This chapter will present information on the implementation and administration of standby databases.

In this chapter, the creation of standby databases in various configurations using operating system utilities will be presented. A brief description of a physical standby database will be provided followed by details for the creation of a physical standby database. Various configurations will be presented for comparison purposes. For example, a standby database on a remote host, a standby database on a local host, and a standby database in a different directory structure will be included.

Logical standby databases will be the basis for the latter part of this chapter at which time the limitations of logical standby databases and the step-by-step process of creating a logical standby database will be presented.

A sample configuration at the end of this chapter will give insight into the real life Data Guard environment.

Physical Standby Database

Before delving into the nitty-gritty of implementation, a brief description of physical standby databases will be presented.

A physical standby database is a replica of the primary database on a block-for-block basis. Hence, the structure of a physical standby database and the primary database should be exactly same. The physical standby database is kept in sync with the primary database using media recovery from the archived redo logs. The media recovery uses the physical *rowid* of segments. Consequently, any difference in segments will cause the recovery to fail.

Physical standby databases can be grouped into three categories based on the recovery mode. These categories are manual recovery mode, managed recovery mode and read-only mode.

Manual Recovery - Physical Standby Database

A physical standby database in manual recovery mode does not have any supporting processes to automate the job of recovery. In this mode, the archived redo logs are not transferred from the primary to the standby automatically; therefore, custom scripts should be created to achieve this functionality.

Manual recover mode is not a natural choice for implementation. The only time that putting a standby database in manual recovery mode should be considered is when an Oracle Net connection between the primary and the standby node cannot be established.

Managed Recovery - Physical Standby Database

Managed recovery mode is the same as manual recovery mode in concept in that the database should be: mounted; ready for recovery; and not open. Unlike the manual recovery mode, the managed recovery mode does not require manual intervention or custom scripts to transfer and apply logs.

The archived redo logs from the primary database are transported by the log transfer service and applied automatically to the standby site by the log apply service. A background process, MRP can be used to manage the detection and application redo logs on the standby site, or the DBA can choose to start a foreground process to perform the same function. Recovery using the background process method has distinct advantages over using the foreground process method.

Read-Only – Physical Standby Database

A physical standby database can exist in recovery mode or open for read-only queries, but unlike a logical standby database, it cannot exist in both modes simultaneously. The transition from managed recovery to read-only mode is very natural in the lifecycle of a physical standby database when it will be used for reporting purposes.

When a database is in read-only mode, the log transfer services continue to transfer archived redo logs, but the log apply services rest. When the database is put into recovery mode again, the log apply service becomes active and applies all the archived redo logs accumulated during the read-only phase.

A physical standby database can be used to perform a backup operation in either recovery or read-only mode.

Creating a Physical Standby Database

In this section, all the steps involved in creating a physical standby database will be presented. A physical standby database can be created in three different configurations as follows:

- On a remote host machine other than the primary database; keeping the same directory structure.

- On the local host machine; sharing the machine with the primary database. In this case, the directory structure has to be different, otherwise the primary and the standby database files will overwrite each other.

- On a remote host machine in a different directory structure.

The first option is most common configuration created and used during the implementation of Data Guard on most sites. This configuration offers ease of administration at the cost of having to buy an additional machine. The second host machine does not need to be of same specification, in terms of hardware. For example, the primary database can reside on an 8 CPU Sun Fire V880 machine and the supporting standby database on a 2 CPU Sun Fire v220.

On the Remote Host Machine

The first step in creating a physical standby database is obtaining a copy of the backup of the primary database. The backup copy does not have to be the most recent as long as all the redo logs have been archived and can be used to recover the database to its current state. The backup of the primary database includes all the data files except the temporary data files and the control file. The backup of the control file is created using a special syntax for the standby database which is covered later in this section.

The primary database must be running in archived log mode. This is a requirement of a physical standby database, and if the primary database is not running in archive log mode, it must be put into archive log mode before creating the standby control file. However, the archiving can be enabled later.

The database should be put into FORCE LOGGING mode before the backup is made. This is required to avoid data divergence on the standby database in case any operation performed on the primary database is unrecoverable. A summary of FORCE LOGGING is presented later in this section.

Preparing To Create a Physical Standby Database

The first step is the creation of a standby database. The primary database is called *appsdb* and is running on the host named *jkpr01*. The secondary database will be created on a host called *jksp01*. The next step is to check to see that the database is running in archive log mode. To do this, start a *SQLplus session*, connect as SYSDBA, and issue the archive log list command:

```
sql> sqlplus /nolog
sql> connect sys/<sys passwd> as sysdba;
sql> archive log list;
```

The output will be similar to the following:

```
archive log list

Database log mode                No Archive Mode
Automatic archival               Enabled
Archive destination              /oracle/appsdb/arch
Oldest online log sequence       220
Current log sequence             222
```

The value for the "Database log mode" shows the mode in which the database is running. In this case, it is not running in archive log mode. To change the mode, the database must be shut down, mounted and the following statement must be issued:

```
ALTER DATABASE ARCHIVELOG;
```

If the "automatic archival" is not enabled, it can be enabled using the following statement:

```
ALTER SYSTEM ARCHIVE LOG START;
```

Change the *log_archive_start=true* parameter in the initialization file so that it will remain enabled on next startup of the database.

Once the database is in archive log mode, the next step is to put it in FORCE LOGGING mode. This will ensure that all the transactions made on the primary database will be registered in the redo logs of the primary database and can be replicated on standby databases.

FORCE LOGGING Option

The FORCE LOGGING option is the safest method to ensure that all the changes made in the database will be captured and available for recovery in the redo logs. Force logging is the new feature added to the family of logging attributes.

Before the existence of FORCE LOGGING, Oracle provided logging and nologging options. These two options have higher precedence at the schema object level than the tablespace level; therefore, it was possible to override the logging settings at the tablespace level with nologging setting at schema object level.

In Oracle9i release 2, the FORCE LOGGING option was introduced. The FORCE LOGGING option can be set at the database level or the tablespace level. The precedence is from database to tablespace. If a tablespace is created or altered to have FORCE LOGGING enabled, any change in that tablespace will go into the redo log and be usable for recovery.

Similarly, if a database is created or altered to have the FORCE LOGGING enabled, any change across the database, with exception of temporary segments and temporary tablespace, will be available in redo logs for recovery.

The FORCE LOGGING option can be set at database creation time or later using the alter database command.

To set FORCE LOGGING during the database creation, specify the following:

```
CREATE DATABASE <dbname>…..FORCE LOGGING…
```

To enable FORCE LOGGING after the database is created, use the following command:

```
ALTER DATABASE FORCE LOGGING;
```

The database or tablespaces in the database should be put into FORCE LOGGING mode before creating the backup for the standby database. Either a database or all of its tablespaces should be put into this mode but not both.

The following statement will put a tablespace in FORCE LOGGING mode:

```
ALTER TABLESPACE <tablespace name> FORCE LOGGING;
```

The FORCE LOGGING mode can be cancelled at the database level using the following statement:

```
ALTER DATABASE NO FORCE LGGING;
```

The FORCE LOGGING mode can be cancelled at the tablespace level using the following statement:

```
ALTER TABLESPACE <tablespace name> NO FORCE LOGGING;
```

Temporary tablespaces and temporary segments have no effect during FORCE LOGGING mode because these objects do not generate any redo. Undo tablespaces are in FORCE LOGGING mode by default, so they cannot be put into FORCE LOGGING mode. Oracle will generate an error if an attempt is made to put a temporary tablespace or undo tablespace into FORCE LOGGING mode.

The FORCE_LOGGING column of *v$database* view can be queried to verify that the database is in FORCE LOGGING mode. Similarly, the FORCE_LOGGINGcolumn of *dba_tablespace* view provides the same information for each tablespace.

Force logging mode is persistent across database startup, but it is not maintained when the control file is recreated unless the FORCE LOGGING clause is specified in the create *controlfile* statement. Also, a tablespace in the FORCE LOGGING mode, when transported to another database, does not maintain this mode.

In these situations, the FORCE LOGGING mode would have to be re-enabled. The primary database should remain in FORCE LOGGING mode as long as there is at least one standby database in use. Putting a database in FORCE LOGGING mode will have some performance impact.

Backup of the Primary Database

Once the preliminary tasks have been completed, it is an appropriate time to take the backup of the primary database. This is not a necessary step if a good backup of the database which can be used to create the standby database already exists.

Either a cold or hot backup of the primary database can be used for this purpose. Either the operating system utility or the recovery manager can be used for backing up the primary database. For this text, a cold backup, or consistent backup, will be made using the operating system utility.

A list of all the files required to take backup can be found in the *v$datafile* view. The following query will help so identify the files:

```
select
    name
from
    V$DATAFILE;
```

A sample output from this statement is as follows:

```
NAME
-------------------------------------------------------
/oracle/appsdb/data/system01.dbf
/oracle/appsdb/data/undotbs01.dbf
/oracle/appsdb/data/userdata01.dbf
/oracle/appsdb/data/indxdata01.dbf
```

This output does not include the name of temporary tablespace files. Backups of the files of the temporary tablespace are not necessary because the transactions in the temporary tablespace or the temporary segments do not generate any redo and are therefore not used in any recovery operation.

Shut the primary database down in normal or immediate mode. Next, take the backup of the files listed by the above query. The shutdown abort command can be used, but in this case, the instance will have to be recovered when the database is put in managed recovery or read-only mode for the first time. This approach might unnecessarily complicate the creation process.

If the DBA suspects that the shutdown immediate will take significant time, the following command can be issued issuing the shutdown immediate command:

```
ALTER SYSTEM SWITCH LOGFILE;
```

This command will clear all the uncommitted transactions and will reduce the time required by the shutdown immediate command.

Once the files have been copied into the same directory structure on the standby database, the next step is to create the control file for the standby database.

If the database has not been put in archive logging mode, the DBA *must* do so before creating the standby control file.

Issue the following statement on the primary database site to create the standby control file:

```
ALTER DATABASE STANDBY
CONTROLFILE AS '/tmp/stanbycontrol.ctl';
```

This statement can be executed when the database is mounted or open. The control file should then be transferred to the standby site using the operating system utility.

Creating a Physical Standby Database

Modifying the Initialization Parameter File

To support the standby database, initialization parameters on both the primary and the standby database will need to be modified. The changes in the primary database parameter are minor.

On the primary site, new archive log destination parameters should be added to point to the standby database. These parameters are *log_archive_dest* and *log_archive_dest_state*. Add these two parameters for each of the standby databases in the Data Guard configuration. Assume that there is only one physical standby database in the configuration and its service name is *stdby1*. The initialization parameters on primary site will look like the following:

Cache and I/O

```
DB_BLOCK_SIZE=4096
DB_CACHE_SIZE=20971520
```

Cursors and Library Cache

```
CURSOR_SHARING=SIMILAR
OPEN_CURSORS=300
```

Diagnostics and Statistics

```
BACKGROUND_DUMP_DEST=/oracle/appsdb/admin/bdump
CORE_DUMP_DEST=/oracle/appsdb/admin/cdump
TIMED_STATISTICS=TRUE
USER_DUMP_DEST=/oracle/appsdb/admin/udump
```

Control File Configuration

```
CONTROL_FILES=("/oracle/appsdb/control/control01.ctl",
              "/oracle/appsdb/control/control02.ctl",
              "/oracle/appsdb/control/control03.ctl")
```

Archive

```
LOG_ARCHIVE_DEST_1='LOCATION=/oracle/appsdb/arch'
LOG_ARCHIVE_FORMAT=appsdb_%t_%s.dbf
LOG_ARCHIVE_START=TRUE
LOG_ARCHIVE_DEST_2='SERVICE=stdby1'
LOG_ARCHIVE_DEST_STATE_2=ENABLE
```

Miscellaneous

```
COMPATIBLE=9.2.0
DB_NAME=appsdb
```

Network Registration

```
INSTANCE_NAME=appsdb
```

Pools

```
JAVA_POOL_SIZE=31457280
LARGE_POOL_SIZE=1048576
SHARED_POOL_SIZE=52428800
```

Processes and Sessions

```
PROCESSES=150
```

Redo Log and Recovery

```
FAST_START_MTTR_TARGET=300
```

Sort, Hash Joins, Bitmap Indexes

```
SORT_AREA_SIZE=524288
```

Automatic Undo Management

```
UNDO_MANAGEMENT=AUTO
UNDO_TABLESPACE=undotbs
```

Up to nine standby databases can be added in the *log_archive* list. The keyword *service* in the *log_archive_dest_2* parameter value list this indicates that the archive destination is an Oracle service, which is defined in the *tnsnames.ora* file on the primary site. *log_archive_dest_n* parameter has several options to control the behavior of the log transfer service. These options are explained later in this book.

On the standby site, the following parameters will have to be changed:

- *control_file*

- *standby_archive_dest*

- *log_archiver_format*

- *fal_server*

- *fal_client*

Moreover, setting the parameter *log_archive_trace* will be useful in troubleshooting. A brief description of *log_archive_trace* parameter is given below the example code. The following example shows the modification on the standby initialization file:

```
# Control File Configuration
CONTROL_FILES=("/oracle/appsdb/control/ standbycontrol.ctl")
# Archive
STANDBY_ARCHIVE_DEST=/oracle/appsdb/arch
LOG_ARCHIVE_FORMAT=stdby.%t_%s.dbf
LOG_ARCHIVE_TRACE=127
FAL_SERVER=primary1
FAL_CLIENT=stdby1
```

log_archive_trace

The *log_archive_trace* initialization parameter governs the output generated by archiver process *(ARCn or ARCH)*. This parameter can take a numeric value. The numeric value represents the level of output. There are 12 different levels and these are represented as 2^n where n can take the value of 0 to 11. Also, two values can be added to form a valid value. The valid values have the following meanings:

log_archive_trace values	
0	Disable archivelog tracing
1	Archival of redo log file
2	Archival status of each archivelog destination
4	Archival operational phase
8	Archivelog destination activity
16	Detailed archivelog destination activity
32	Archivelog destination parameter modifications
64	ARCn process state activity
128	FAL (fetch archived log) server related activities
256	Reserved for future releases
512	Asynchronous Log Writer activities
1024	Tracks RFS physical client
2048	Tracks the ARCn or RFS heartbeat

Table 3-1: *log_archive_trace parameter values*

The default behavior value is 0 or no archivelog tracing. A value of 7 represents tracing up to level 4. The log file will show the archival state of redo log files, the status of each archivelog destination, and the operational phases.

These parameters play an important role in the creation and working of standby databases. The standby control file created on the primary site should be copied to the directory pointed by the *contol_files* parameter. The standby database MRP builds the filename from the *log_archive_format* parameter and checks the existence of this file in the *standby_archive_dest* directory.

The *fal_server* and *fal_client* parameters are used for the gap resolution. When MRP finds that an archive log is missing during media recovery, it sends the *fal_client* information to the server identified by *fal_server* and requests *fal_server* to resend the file again. *log_archive_format* parameter on the primary and the standby site does not need to be same.

If a *spfile* is being used on either the primary or the standby database, the changes in the initialization parameter should be reflected in the *spfile* before the instance is restarted.

Some of these parameters can also be enabled using the ALTER SYSTEM command. The *spfile* must be used if the intention is to use Data Guard Broker to manage the configuration.

Oracle Net Configuration

For the standby database to work in managed recovery mode, it must receive the archived redo logs from the primary database. The archived redo logs are transferred from the primary to the standby site using Oracle Net.

For this text, assume that the Oracle Net is using the *tnsnames.ora* file for node identification. On the primary site, the *tnsnames.ora* file should be configured to include the service name for each of the standby databases.

The *listener.ora* file on the primary site does not require any modification as long as it has a listener for itself. Similarly, on the standby site the listener file will not require any change.

Configure the *tnsnames.ora* file on the standby site to include the service name for the primary database. This is required for gap resolution using the "fetch archive log" method. A sample *tnsnames.ora* file from the primary and the standby site is given in the following example.

tnsnames.ora file on the primary site:

Standby DB identification on Primary Site

```
stdby1 =
  (DESCRIPTION =
    (ADDRESS_LIST =
      (ADDRESS = (PROTOCOL = TCP)(HOST =  jrsp01  )(PORT = 1521))
    )
    (CONNECT_DATA =
      (SID = appsdb )
    )
  )
```

tnsnames.ora file on standby site

#Primary DB identification on Standby Site

```
primary1 -
  (DESCRIPTION =
    (ADDRESS_LIST =
      (ADDRESS = (PROTOCOL = TCP)(HOST =  jrpr01  )(PORT = 1521))
    )
    (CONNECT_DATA -
      (SID = appsdb )
    )
  )
```

The *host, port,* and *sid* parameters of the *tnsnames* file for the primary database on the standby site should match the *host, port,* and *sid* parameters of the listener file for the primary database on the primary site. Similarly, the *tnsnames* setting for the standby site on the primary database should match the listener setting for the standby database on the standby site.

Starting the Standby Database

After configuring the initialization parameters, Oracle Net, and copying the backup files from the primary site to the standby site, everything is ready for the starting of the standby database. The standby database will be mounted and put in managed recovery mode using the following statements in the order presented: issue the startup nomount and mount the standby database. Before issuing these commands, set the *oracle_sid* environment variable to appropriate value.

```
$ export ORACLE_SID=appsdb
$ sqlplus /nolog

sql> connect sys/<passwd> as sysdba
```

If the initialization file is in $ORACLE_HOME/dbs directory, it does not have to pass as an argument to the startup command. If the initialization file from some other location is to be used, pass it as PFILE='<file location>' argument.

```
STARTUP MOUNT
```

Mount the standby database using the following statement:

```
ALTER DATABASE MOUNT STANDBY DATABASE;
```

At this point, the standby database is up and running and ready to receive archived redo logs from the primary database even though, the logs will not be applied until the database is put in managed recovery mode.

Verify the Physical Standby Database

The complete setup can be verified by switching a log file on the primary database and checking the file on the standby database in the STANDBY_ARCHIVE_DEST directory. Moreover, the Oracle Net setup for standby locations can be verified from the *v$archive_dest* view on the primary database.

Assume that on the standby site, the listener is not running. Querying the *v$archive_dest* view will show this error.

```
Select
   Status, Error
From
   V$ARCHIVE_DEST
Where
   Dest_Name = 'LOG_ARCHIVE_DEST_2';

Status    Error
--------- -----------------------------------------------
ERROR     ORA-12541: TNS:no listener
```

This view can be a starting point for troubleshooting any problem in Data Guard configuration. The same information can be gathered from the alert log file on the primary database. The content of the alert log file will look like the following:

```
Tue Sep 23 09:02:04 2003
Errors in file /oracle/appsdb/admin/bdump/appsdb_arc0_11977.trc:
ORA-12541: TNS:no listener
```

There will not be any error seen in the alert log file of the standby database. When the listener is started on both the databases and an Oracle Net connection is established, the arch process of the primary database will transfer the archived redo logs to the standby database when the next redo log is archived on the primary database. An extract from the alert log file is given in the following example to explain this scenario:

```
Errors in file /oracle/appsdb/admin/bdump/appsdb_arc0_11977.trc:
ORA-12541: TNS:no listener
Tue Sep 23 09:12:08 2003 ← Fix the Oracle Net issue at this point

Thread 1 advanced to log sequence 226  ← archive current log file at
this point.

Current log# 1 seq# 226 mem# 0: /oracle/appsdb/redo/redo01.log
Tue Sep 23 09:12:08 2003
ARC0: Evaluating archive   log 3 thread 1 sequence 225
ARC0: Beginning to archive log 3 thread 1 sequence 225
Creating archive destination LOG_ARCHIVE_DEST_2: 'stdby1' ← At this
point, the primary database recognizes the standby site as archive
log destination and verifies that a connection can be established
between primary and standby.

Creating archive destination LOG_ARCHIVE_DEST_1:
'/oracle/appsdb/arch/appsdb_1_2
25.dbf'
```

Creating a Physical Standby Database

```
ARC0: Completed archiving  log 3 thread 1 sequence 225
Tue Sep 23 09:13:19 2003
ARC1: Begin FAL archive (thread 1 sequence 224 destination stdby1) ←
Arch process transfers the archived redo logfile to standby
destination.

Creating archive destination LOG_ARCHIVE_DEST_2: 'stdby1'
ARC1: Complete FAL archive (thread 1 sequence 224 destination
stdby1)
```

At this point, there will be archives logs on the standby site, but they will not be applied to the standby database until the primary database is put in managed recovery mode. This can be achieved by issuing the following statement:

```
ALTER DATABASE RECOVER MANAGED STANDBY DATABASE DISCONNECT FROM
SESSION;
```

There are few other options for the RECOVER MANAGED STANDBY DATABASE statement, but at this information will be limited to the options that are relevant for putting the database in the managed recovery mode its creation.

The managed recovery can be started as a foreground or background process. The *"disconnect from session"* option allows the background process to do the managed recovery. It will start a MRP process on the standby site, which is responsible for applying the archived redo logs onto the standby database. If this keyword is omitted, it will be necessary to keep a session open for the recovery.

This does not start MRP process on the standby site. In almost all scenarios, the DISCONNECT FROM SESSION option will be used to have a background process take care of recovery. This process was introduced in Oracle9i in an effort to ease the administration of the standby database.

When the MRP process starts to apply log files, it finds the log files from *standby_archive_dest* directory and created the log file name using the *log_archive_format* parameter. If it detects a missing log file from this directory, it will send a request to the primary database to transfer the file again. The name of the primary database is found from the *fal_server* parameter, and it sends the *fal_client* parameter as the destination service where the files will be resent.

The following extract from the alert log file of the standby database shows the MRP process requested the archived log files to be sent to the resolve gap:

```
Completed: alter database recover managed standby database di
Tue Sep 23 10:35:46 2003
Fetching gap sequence for thread 1, gap sequence 231-231
Trying FAL server: primary1
Media Recovery Log /oracle/appsdb/arch/stdby.1_231.dbf
Media Recovery Log /oracle/appsdb/arch/stdby.1_232.dbf
```

In this case, only the *stdby.1_232.dbf* file was available on the standby archive destination, and the *stdby.1_231.dbf* was required to complete the media recovery, so the MRP process re-fetched it. The MRP log file in the BACKGROUP_DUMP_DEST directory can be checked to verify this. Also, the alert log file on the standby site can be checked to see if the database is in managed recovery mode. It will show that the archived log name has been applied to the standby database by MRP process.

```
-- Extract from alert log file from standby site
alter database recover managed standby database disconnect from
session
Wed Sep 17 16:39:47 2003
Attempt to start background Managed Standby Recovery process
MRP0 started with pid=13
MRP0: Background Managed Standby Recovery process started
```

Moreover, *v$dataguard_status* and *v$managed_standby* views give information about the processes involved in media recovery on the standby site. The following shows the output of the *dg_stats.sql* script from the code depot. The script has been executed on the standby database.

```
-- ***************************************************
-- Copyright © 2004 by Rampant TechPress
-- This script is free for non-commercial purposes
-- with no warranties.  Use at your own risk.
--
-- To license this script for a commercial purpose,
-- contact info@rampant.cc
-- ***************************************************

Set linesize 140
column Timestamp Format a20
column Facility Format a24
column Severity Format a13
column Message Format a60 trunc

Select
   to_char(timestamp,'YYYY-MON-DD HH24:MI:SS') Timestamp,
   Facility,
   Severity,
   Message
From
   v$dataguard_status
Order by
   Timestamp;
```

Here is a sample of the output from this script:

```
TIMESTAMP            FACILITY                SEVERITY       MESSAGE
-------------------- ----------------------- -------------  ------------------------------
----------------------------
2003-SEP-26 17:00:08 Log Transport Services  Informational ARC0: Archival started
2003-SEP-26 17:00:08 Log Transport Services  Informational ARC1: Archival started
2003-SEP-26 17:00:39 Log Apply Services      Control        Attempt to start background
Managed Standby Recovery process
2003-SEP-26 17:00:45 Log Apply Services      Warning        Media Recovery Waiting for
thread 1 seq# 237
2003-SEP-26 17:03:15 Log Apply Services                    Informational  Media Recovery Log
/oracle/appsdb/arch/appsdb_1_237.dbf
2003-SEP-26 17:03:15 Log Apply Services      Warning        Media Recovery Waiting for
thread 1 seq# 238
2003-SEP-26 17:03:45 Log Apply Services                    Informational  Media Recovery Log
/oracle/appsdb/arch/appsdb_1_238.dbf
2003-SEP-26 17:03:45 Log Apply Services      Warning        Media Recovery Waiting for
thread 1 seq# 239
2003-SEP-26 17:04:00 Log Apply Services                    Informational  Media Recovery Log
/oracle/appsdb/arch/appsdb_1_239.dbf
2003-SEP-26 17:04:00 Log Apply Services      Warning        Media Recovery Waiting for
thread 1 seq# 240
```

From the severity column of the output, it appears that when the log apply service is waiting for archived redo logs from the primary database, it is treated as "Warning." This is not a problem and is expected behavior.

A similar query on the *v$managed_standby* view can be useful in tracking the processes involved in the standby recovery. When this query is executed on the primary database, it gives information about the ARCH process. When it is executed on the standby database, it provides status of ARCH, RFS and MRP processes. Use the *managed_stdby.sql* script from the code depot to see the status of various processes. The following output is from the *managed_stdby.sql* script when run on the standby and primary site:

🖫   **managed_stdby.sql**

```
-- ************************************************
-- Copyright © 2004 by Rampant TechPress
-- This script is free for non-commercial purposes
-- with no warranties.  Use at your own risk.
--
-- To license this script for a commercial purpose,
-- contact info@rampant.cc
-- ************************************************

column Process format a7
column Status format a12
column Group# format 999
column Thread# format 999
column Sequence# format 999999

Select
   Process,
   Status,
   Group#,
   Thread#,
   Sequence#
From
   v$managed_standby;
```

Output from Standby Database:

```
PROCESS  STATUS        GROUP#            THREAD#  SEQUENCE#
-------  ------------  ---------------   -------  ---------
ARCH     CONNECTED     N/A                     0          0
ARCH     CONNECTED     N/A                     0          0
MRP0     WAIT_FOR_LOG  N/A                     1        240
RFS      RECEIVING     1                       1        238
RFS      RECEIVING     2                       1        239
```

Output from Primary Database:

```
PROCESS  STATUS        GROUP#           THREAD#  SEQUENCE#
-------  ------------  ------------     ------   ---------
ARCH     CLOSING       2                     1         239
ARCH     CLOSING       1                     1         238
```

The *v$archive_log* view on the standby database gives comprehensive information on the log transfer service and the log apply service operations. The script *arch_log.sql* from code depot gives the following output showing the status of archive redo logs on the standby database:

🖫 arch_log.sql

```
-- ************************************************
-- Copyright © 2004 by Rampant TechPress
-- This script is free for non-commercial purposes
-- with no warranties.  Use at your own risk.
--
-- To license this script for a commercial purpose,
-- contact info@rampant.cc
-- ************************************************

column Sequence# format 99999
column First_Time format a20
column Next_Time format a20
column Applied format a3
Select
   Sequence#,
   First_Time,
   Next_Time,
   Applied
From
   V$ARCHIVED_LOG
Order by
   Sequence#;
```

Here is the output of *arch_log.sql*:

```
SEQUENCE#  FIRST_TIME            NEXT_TIME             APP
---------  --------------------  --------------------  ---
      231  2003-Sep-23 10:27     2003-Sep-23 10:31     YES
      232  2003-Sep-23 10:31     2003-Sep-23 10:35     YES
      233  2003-Sep-23 10:35     2003-Sep-23 16:43     YES
      234  2003-Sep-23 16:43     2003-Sep-23 17:24     YES
      235  2003-Sep-23 17:24     2003-Sep-26 12:09     YES
      236  2003-Sep-26 12:09     2003-Sep-26 12:11     YES
      237  2003-Sep-26 12:11     2003-Sep-26 17:03     YES
      238  2003-Sep-26 17:03     2003-Sep-26 17:03     YES
      239  2003-Sep-26 17:03     2003-Sep-26 17:03     YES
```

On UNIX operating systems, the process list of the O/S can be used to find the background recovery process.

$ ps -ef|grep mrp shows an ora_mrp0_<dbsid>, which indicates that the background recovery process is running.

Now, the standby database configuration is complete and is ready to receive and apply log files from the primary site. In managed recovery mode, the standby database will remain current and can be used for failover and switchover operations.

Details of failover and switchover operations will be presented later in this book. One final check should be verification that the standby database can be put in read-only mode. To do this, cancel the managed recovery mode and set it in read only mode. Remember that a physical standby database can be either in recovery or read-only mode but not both at the same time.

Use the following statement to cancel the managed recovery:

```
ALTER DATABASE RECOVER MANAGED STANDBY DATABASE CANCEL;
```

Use the following statement to cancel the managed recovery and to open the database in read-only mode:

```
ALTER DATABASE OPEN READ ONLY;
```

Ideally, to open the database in read only mode, a temporary tablespace should be created before the standby database is used for query purposes; however, it can be used without a temporary tablespace as long as all the sort operations are performed within memory specified by the *sort_area_size* parameter. As a note, the managed recovery must be cancelled when the standby database is shutdown.

On a Local Host Machine

This section contains details on the process of creating a physical standby database on the same host machine as the primary database. The initial few steps are the same as those for the creation of a physical standby database on a remote host.

The steps for creating a backup of data files and control files will not be repeated in this section. The primary database should be in archive log mode, and the FORCE LOGGING should be enabled before taking the backup.

Once a backup of the primary database data files and the control file have been created, the initialization parameter files and the Oracle Net files will have to be configured. The changes required in initialization parameters will follow in the next section.

Modifying the Initialization Parameters

The initialization parameters on the primary database will remain the same except for the archive log parameters. As explained in the previous section, the archive log destination for the standby database must be specified.

Add the following two lines in the *init.ora* file for the primary database:

```
LOG_ARCHIVE_DEST_2='SERVICE=<Name of service for standby database>
LOG_ARCHIVE_DEST_STATE_2=ENABLE
```

The changes in the initialization parameter file for the standby database are essentially the same as those presented in the previous section. However, there are three key parameters that should be added. These are as follows:

- *lock_name_space*

- *db_file_name_convert*

- *log_file_name_convert*

The *lock_name_space* parameter defines the namespace that the distributed lock manager uses to generate lock names. The value of this parameter should be set to a distinct value so that the lock names between the primary and the standby database do not collide.

The *db_file_name_convert* parameter is used to convert the filename on the primary database to a filename on the standby database. The value of this parameter should be set in a pair of strings. The first string should correspond to the filename pattern on the primary database and the next string to the filename pattern on the standby database. More than one pair can be specified if there is a need to accommodate more than one pattern in filename changes between the primary and the standby database.

The *log_file_name_convert* parameter works similarly to *db_nfile_name_convert* on the redo log files. This parameter is not required until the standby database is activated, but there is no harm in placing this parameter in the *init.ora* file so that during the activation there will be minimal work for the DBA to do.

The following is a sample *init.ora* file for the standby database. Note the change in the log file dump destinations:

Creating a Physical Standby Database **83**

Diagnostics and Statistics

```
BACKGROUND_DUMP_DEST=/oracle/stdbydb/admin/bdump
CORE_DUMP_DEST=/oracle/stdbydb/admin/cdump
USER_DUMP_DEST=/oracle/stdbydb/admin/udump
```

Control File Configuration

```
CONTROL_FILES=("/oracle/stdbydb/control/standbycontrol.ctl")
```

Archive

```
STANDBY_ARCHIVE_DEST=/oracle/stdbydb/arch
LOG_ARCHIVE_FORMAT=stdby_%t_%s.dbf
LOG_ARCHIVE_START=TRUE
LOG_ARCHIVE_TRACE=127
```

Miscellaneous

```
COMPATIBLE=9.2.0
```

Standby Related

```
DB_FILE_NAME_CONVERT=('/oracle/appsdb','/oracle/stdbydb')
LOG_FILE_NAME_CONVERT=('/oracle/appsdb','/oracle/stdbydb')
FAL_SERVER=primary1
FAL_CLIENT=stdby2
LOCK_NAME_SPACE=stdby2
```

Network Registration

```
INSTANCE_NAME=stdbydb
DB_NAME=appsdb
```

The *db_name* parameter does not change, whereas the *instance_name* parameter needs to be changed to a unique string.

Oracle Net Configuration

Service and listener must be added for the standby database. For this configuration, either an IPC or a TCP/IP connection can be created. This can be achieved by editing the *tnsnames.ora* and the *listener.ora* file or by using the Oracle Net Manager application.

The following is a sample of a *tnsnames.ora* file:

```
PRIMARY1 =
  (DESCRIPTION =
    (ADDRESS_LIST =
      (ADDRESS = (PROTOCOL = TCP)(HOST = localhost)(PORT = 1521))
    )
    (CONNECT_DATA =
      (SERVICE_NAME = appsdb)
    )
  )

STDBY2 =
  (DESCRIPTION =
    (ADDRESS_LIST =
      (ADDRESS = (PROTOCOL = TCP)(HOST = localhost)(PORT = 1521))
    )
    (CONNECT_DATA =
      (SERVICE_NAME = stdbydb)
    )
  )
```

The following is a sample of a *listener.ora* file:

```
SID_LIST_LISTENER =
  (SID_LIST =
    (SID_DESC =
      (SID_NAME = PLSExtProc)
      (ORACLE_HOME - /sw/oracle/product/9.2.0)
      (PROGRAM = extproc)
    )
    (SID_DESC =
      (SID_NAME = appsdb)
      (ORACLE_HOME = /sw/oracle/product/9.2.0)
    )
    (SID_DESC =
      (SID_NAME = stdbydb)
      (ORACLE_HOME = /sw/oracle/product/9.2.0)
    )
  )
```

Starting the Standby Database

After making these changes, restart listener to start an instance of these two services. Next, prepare the standby database to be placed in the managed recovery mode. The process of putting the standby database in the managed recovery mode is the same one described in the earlier section called "On a Remote Host Machine".

The primary database must then be restarted for the new parameters to take effect, or alternatively issue the alter system statements on the primary database to enable the new archive log parameters. Connect as SYSDBA and execute the following statements:

```
ALTER SYSTEM SET LOG_ARCHIVE_DEST_2="SERVICE=STDBY2";

ALTER SYSTEM SET LOG_ARCHIVE_DEST_STATE_2 = ENABLE;
```

Then, start the standby database in managed recovery mode using the following commands:

```
STARTUP NOMOUNT;
ALTER DATABASE MOUNT STANDBY DATABASE;
ALTER DATABASE RECOVER MANAGED STANDBY DATABASE DISCONNECT FROM
SESSION;
```

To verify the standby database, check the alert log file for the standby and the primary database. The details about the alert log files and other methods of verification are the same as provided in the section called "On a Remote Host Machine".

Accommodating the Difference in Directory Structure between the Primary and Standby Sites

It may not always be possible to configure two host machines to have the same directory structure. If a standby database is being created and the directory structure on the primary host is different from that on the standby host, the *db_file_name_convert* and *log-file_name_convert* parameters on the standby site will have to be set to accommodate the change in directory structure.

The process of creating and starting the standby database remains largely the same as explained in the previous two sections. Also, review the dump destinations in the initialization file to make sure that these directories exist on the standby host.

> WARNING - Beware that all the difference in directory structure between the primary and standby site may not be accommodated by these two parameters. The ALTER DATABASE RENAME FILENAME statement may have to be used to reflect the filename changes in the control file.

It may not always be possible to have the same directory structure between the primary and the standby host, but in most cases the same directory structure can be simulated using soft links. Keeping the same directory structure eases the management and administration of the standby database, and scripts from the script library can be used without any modification, even if the scripts rely on directory structure.

Creating a Logical Standby Database

The logical standby database is a new feature of Oracle9i Data Guard technology. It has been introduced to cater to the demands of DBAs to have a standby database that can simultaneously exist in query and recovery mode. As the name suggests, a logical standby database is not a physical replica of the primary database in that it is not structurally the same as the primary database.

Instead, it is a complete or partial set of schema objects from the primary database. A logical standby database can contain schema objects of its own that are not present in the primary database.

Logical standby databases are recovered using the LogMiner technology of Oracle RDBMS. The core of logical standby database recovery is the archived redo log file from the primary database. These log files are converted into SQL statements using LogMiner and are applied to the logical standby database using SQL apply service. Like physical standby databases, logical standby databases can participate in switchover and failover operations.

Because a logical database can be put in read-only and recovery mode simultaneously, data available in a logical standby database is always current. As a result, a logical standby database is a much better option for reporting than is a physical standby database; however, a logical standby database has many limitations which may outweigh its reporting capabilities in some scenarios.

Limitations of the Logical Standby Database

The following limitations apply to logical standby databases:

- A logical standby database does not support LONG, LONG RAW, BFILE, ROWID, UROWID, NCLOB and any of the collection data types. If the application contains any of these types, the usability of a logical standby database in that environment should be evaluated. The script, *unsup_objects.sql,* from the code depot can be used to find the tables in the database that cannot be supported in a logical standby database.

🖫   **unsup_objects.sql**

```
-- ****************************************************
-- Copyright © 2004 by Rampant TechPress
-- This script is free for non-commercial purposes
-- with no warranties.  Use at your own risk.
--
-- To license this script for a commercial purpose,
-- contact info@rampant.cc
```

```
-- **************************************************

set linesize 82
column owner format a30
column table_name format a30
column data_type format a20 trunc

Select Distinct
  Owner,
  Table_Name,
  Data_Type
From
  DBA_LOGSTDBY_UNSUPPORTED;
```

The output will be similar to the following:

```
OWNER                TABLE_NAME                 DATA_TYPE
-----------------    -------------------------  --------------
REPORTS              ITEMDESC                   LONG
```

The same view can be queried to find the offending column of the table.

- Any user-defined objects in Sys schema are not supported. Keeping user-defined tables in Sys schema is a poor design and should be avoided. If an application is well written, this limitation should not be a problem.

- *log_parallelism* should be set to 1. What does it mean? The *log_parallelism* parameter governs the concurrency of the redo allocation latch. If the database is experiencing contention on the redo allocation latch, set this parameter to a higher value to allow a parallel generation of redo. Usually, this contention is observed on high-end servers in the insert/update intensive databases. If the database is not too huge, and the database is not running on a 16 or more processor machine, this limitation should not be a problem.

- There are few DDL statements that will be skipped on a logical standby database during the SQL apply operation. Most of these operations are at system or database level.

Skipping these statements should not cause any inconsistency in the application data.

Due to these limitations, it is likely that a logical standby database will not make an attractive option for reporting and an even less attractive option for failover operations. Please note that in order to run a logical standby database in this environment, the database software will have to be upgraded to at least the 9.2.0.2 patchset level.

Requirements for the Logical Standby Database

In order to create a logical standby database, some preparatory work on the primary database has to be completed before it can be used for a logical standby database.

Archive Logging and Force Logging

As explained earlier and in much detail in the "Physical Standby Database" section, the core of the standby database are the archived redo logs from the primary database. The primary database must run in the archive log mode and the FORCE LOGGING should be enabled on the primary database to capture all changes made within the database.

Unique Identification of Rows in Tables

In the physical standby database, the recovery is achieved using the *rowid* of segments. Since a logical standby database is not structurally exact as the primary database, the *rowid* between the primary and the standby database will not be the same. For a logical standby database, the SQL apply service must use some other mechanism to uniquely identify a row in tables.

Usually, the primary key and non-null unique indexes are the best available data structure that can be used to identify a row in a table. In general, it is good practice for a database design to have a primary key or unique index on tables; however, this may not always be the case in any database.

Although having a primary key or unique index on tables will assist in recovery on a logical standby site, it is not an absolute requirement for logical standby database setup. The SQL apply service can use other scalar columns from the tables to determine the uniqueness of rows.

Normally, when a row is updated in a database, its old and new values, along with the *rowid,* are written in the redo log. The redo log does not contain any information about the primary key or unique key for that row. Since a logical standby database depends on such an identifier to uniquely identify a row, Oracle introduced a Supplemental Logging mechanism for logical standby databases.

When the supplemental logging is active on a database, the redo logs contain other columns from tables to uniquely identify a row. If the table has a primary key or unique index defined, the only columns involved in the primary key or unique index will be registered in the redo logs along with the actual column(s) that has changed.

If the table does not have any primary keys or unique index defined, Oracle will write all scalar columns from the table to identify the row. This may significantly increase the size of redo logs and will impact the log apply services on the logical standby site.

One way to resolve this issue is to define a disabled primary key RELY constraint on those tables that do not have a primary key/unique index defined. Creating a disabled primary key will not add any extra overhead in maintaining the primary key on the primary database, yet it will minimize the information required in redo logs for logical standby database recovery.

> WARNING – Before creating the Primary Key RELY constraint, it is vital that the DBA understand the application data very well. Alternatively, the application developers can help with constraints definitions.

Putting a database in Supplemental Logging mode is a requirement for a logical standby database. Even if all the tables in the database have a primary key defined, supplemental logging will have to be activated so that the primary key columns will be written to the redo logs along with the updated columns.

Oracle provides *dba_logstdby_not_unique* view that is used to find all the tables not having a primary key or unique index defined on them. The script, *not_unique.sql,* from the code depot will help in locating such tables:

🖫 not_unique.sql

```
-- ****************************************************
-- Copyright © 2004 by Rampant TechPress
-- This script is free for non-commercial purposes
-- with no warranties.  Use at your own risk.
--
-- To license this script for a commercial purpose,
-- contact info@rampant.cc
-- ****************************************************

Select
  Owner,
  Table_Name,
  Bad_Column
From
  DBA_LOGSTDBY_NOT_UNIQUE
Order by
  Owner,
  Table_Name;
```

In a sample database, there is a schema called REPORTS, which has two tables without any primary keys or unique indexes. The output from script *not_unique.sql* reveals this:

```
OWNER                         TABLE_NAME                    B
----------------------------- ----------------------------- -
REPORTS                       ITEMLIST                      N
REPORTS                       ORDERS                        N
```

The value *'N'* in the *Bad_Column* column shows that the table can be maintained in a logical standby database even though it does not have a primary key/unique index.

If any of the tables contain a CLOB or BLOB, which is supported data type for a logical standby database, but does not have a primary key/unique index defined, the value of *Bad_Column* will be *'Y'*. This means that a primary key/unique index or a disabled primary key RELY constraint needs to be defined using scalar column, i.e. non CLOB or BLOB columns for this table to be maintained in a logical standby database environment.

The primary database should be put in supplemental logging mode before creating a logical standby database. Use the following statement to enable supplemental logging:

```
ALTER DATABASE ADD SUPPLEMENTAL LOG DATA (PRIMARY KEY, UNIQUE INDEX)
COLUMNS;
```

This can be verified from the *v$database* view using the following query:

```
SELECT
   SUPPLEMENTAL_LOG_DATA_PK,
   SUPPLEMENTAL_LOG_DATA_UI
FROM V$DATABASE;
```

The following sample output shows the supplemental logging is enabled for a primary key and unique index:

```
SUP SUP
--- ---
YES YES
```

After enabling the supplemental logging on the primary database, use the alter system command to switch to a redo log file. This is required because a logical standby database does not support archived redo logs that contain redo information with and without supplemental logging.

```
ALTER SYSTEM SWITCH LOGFILE;
```

Tablespace for LogMiner Objects on the Primary Database

The metadata for a logical standby database is maintained in SYS and SYSTEM schema, which, by default, is kept in the system tablespace. These metadata are mostly related to LogMiner activity on the logical standby site. It is good practice to create a dedicated tablespace on the primary database for these objects and to move these objects from the system tablespace to the new tablespace before a backup is made to be used to create a logical standby database.

As a result, this tablespace will exist in both the primary and the standby database. Although this is an optional step in creating a logical standby database, it might save considerable time later when a switchover between the primary and the logical standby database is performed.

Oracle provides the *dbms_logmnr_d.set_tablespace* procedure to move all these log miner related objects to a new tablespace. The syntax is:

```
EXECUTE DBMS_LOGMNR_D.SET_TABLESPACE ('<New Tablespace Name>');
```

Once these preparatory tasks have been completed, the process to start the creation of the logical standby database can begin. The next section will present the step-by-step process of creating a logical standby database. For this text, it is assumed that there is no other standby database associated with this primary database.

The following is a description of the steps used to create a logical standby database.

Creating a Logical Standby Database

The first step in creating a logical standby database is to get a backup of the primary database. As mentioned in the previous section, "Creating Physical Standby Databases", this backup does not have to be the most recent backup as long as the DBA has all the archived redo logs that can be used to recover it to its current state. Either a cold backup or a hot backup can be used for the purpose of creating the logical standby database. Both the cold backup and hot backup methods will be included.

To create a logical standby database from a cold backup of the primary site, shutdown the primary database and copy the files to the standby location. This step is similar to the one presented for physical standby database creation.

The following tasks need to be performed on the primary database to create a logical standby database using a hot backup. On the primary site, the following files need to be backed up:

- Backup data files for all tablespaces, except for temporary tablespaces.

- Backup Control file.

- Backup the archived redo logs created during the tablespace backup and log miner dictionary creation phase.

- Backup the initialization parameter file to be modified and used on Standby Site.

One of the requirements for using a hot backup is that the resource manager should be running on the primary database. This is required because the DBA may need to quiesce the database to build the LogMiner dictionary. If the Resource Manager has not run since the instance startup, Alter system quiesce is restricted and the statement will fail.

> 🔔 TIP - Alter System Set Resource_Manager_Plan = < Plan Name> will change the resource plan, but the DBA will not be able to quiesce the database because resource manager was not running since instance startup. Change the parameter in *init.ora* file or SPFILE if in use, and then restart the instance.

Backup of the Primary Database

Once the DBA has ensured that the Resource Manager is running, a hot backup of the primary database can be created. To perform a hot backup, put the tablespaces in BACKUP mode one at a time and then copy the datafiles to the backup location. After all the datafiles for a tablespace are copied, take that tablespace out of BACKUP mode. ALTER TABLESPACE <TablespaceName> BEGIN BACKUP and ALTER TABLESPACE <TablespaceName> END BACKUP statements can be used for this purpose.

The control file will need to be backed up as well. To do this, mount the primary database and issue the following statement:

```
STARTUP MOUNT;
ALTER DATABASE BACKUP
CONTROLFILE TO '/tmp/logicalstdby.ctl';
```

Note the difference in syntax for a physical standby and a logical standby database. For a physical standby database, a standby control file is created; whereas, for the logical standby, a backup control file is used.

Building the LogMiner Dictionary

The next step is to build the LogMiner dictionary on the primary database. The LogMiner dictionary is used on the logical standby database during the SQL apply mode to build the SQL statements from the redo log entries. So why is it necessary to create Log miner dictionary on the primary database? The reason is that when the LogMiner dictionary is created on the primary database, the dictionary will be created on the logical standby site using the archived redo logs by the SQL apply service during the recovery.

This ensures that the dictionary will exist on both of the databases; hence, during the switchover operation, the dictionary will not have to be created on the primary database.

To build the LogMiner dictionary, connect to Oracle as SYSDBA, open the database and put the database in quiesce state. Then the dictionary can be created using the following statement:

```
ALTER DATABASE OPEN;
ALTER DATABASE QUIESCE RESTRICTED;
EXEC DBMS_LOGSTDBY.BUILD;
```

After building the LogMiner dictionary, find the latest archive log. This file should be the starting point for recovery. The following SQL query can be used to find the latest archived log:

```
Set linesize 82
Column Name Format a60
Column Completion_Time format a20

Select
   NAME,
   TO_CHAR(COMPLETION_TIME,'YYYY/MM/DD HH24:MI') COMPLETION_TIME
From
   V$ARCHIVED_LOG
Where
   DICTIONARY_BEGIN='YES'
And
   STANDBY_DEST='NO'
Order by
   COMPLETION_TIME;
```

The resulting output will be similar to the following:

```
NAME                                     COMPLETION_TIME
-------------------------------------    ----------------
/oracle/appsdb/arch/appsdb_1_248.dbf     2003/09/30 14:55
/oracle/appsdb/arch/appsdb_1_564.dbf     2003/10/03 09:54
/oracle/appsdb/arch/appsdb_1_568.dbf     2003/10/03 12:08
```

Ideally, there should only be one row in the output, but if the dictionary has been built more than once on the primary database, there will be more than one redo log having the DICTIONARY_BEGIN entry.

The DICTIONARY_BEGIN column indicates this log contains the start of LogMiner dictionary, and the *standby_dest='no'* will ensure that the query returns only the local archived files. If this query returns more than one row, select the latest log name. For example, in this case it would be *appsdb_1_568.dbf*.

Once the LogMiner dictionary is built, un-quiesce the database to start the usual services on the database.

```
Alter system unquiesce;
Alter system switch logfile;
```

The last switch logfile statement marks the end of the backup process on the primary database site.

If a cold backup of the primary database is used to create a logical standby database, the database does not need to be quiesced and unquiesced; however, the DBA might want to put the database in restricted mode in order to minimize any DML/DDL activity during the creation of the LogMiner dictionary.

Oracle Net Configuration

The next step in this process is to create Oracle Net service for the standby database on the primary site. As noted previously, the archived redo logs are transferred using Oracle Net between the primary and the standby site. Read "Creating a Physical Standby Database" section for a detailed analysis of the Oracle Net configuration, as this step is identical to the physical standby database creation process.

Modifying the Initialization Parameter File

The database initialization file on the primary site requires some modification to support a logical standby database. In this step, changes in the *init.ora* parameter file on the primary database will be required. The following example shows an extract from the *init.ora* file from the primary site, highlighting the parameters required to support a logical standby database:

```
# Archive
LOG_ARCHIVE_FORMAT=appsdb_%t_%s.dbf
LOG_ARCHIVE_START=TRUE
LOG_ARCHIVE_DEST_1='LOCATION=/oracle/appsdb/arch'
LOG_ARCHIVE_DEST_2='SERVICE=appsstdby'
LOG_ARCHIVE_DEST_STATE_2=ENABLE
```

Miscellaneous

```
COMPATIBLE=9.2.0
DB_NAME=appsdb
STANDBY_FILE_MANAGEMENT=AUTO
```

Resource Manager

```
RESOURCE_MANAGER_PLAN=SYSTEM_PLAN
```

log_archive_dest_2 should correspond to the logical standby service name configured in the *tnsnames.ora* file on the primary site.

standby_file_management=auto will ensure that all the modification of datafiles on the primary database will be reflected on the standby site.

Changes on the Logical Standby Site

This completes the tasks required on the primary database. The next stage in the process is to instantiate the logical standby database.

Connect to the standby site and copy the following files to the standby site from the primary site:

- Backup Data files
- Backup Control file
- Modified *Init.ora* file
- Latest Archive redo log generated during LogMiner dictionary build.

Modifying the Initialization Parameter File on the Standby Site

Before the logical standby database is started and mounted, the initialization parameter file will have to be modified and the Oracle Net connection setup. Modify the *init.ora* file copied from the primary site to add the parameters required to support a logical standby database.

The following is a sample *init.ora* file for a logical standby database. This is not a complete *init.ora* file, and only the logical standby database related parameters are shown here.

 TIP – All the DUMP_DEST parameters should be updated if the directory structure is different.

Diagnostics and Statistics

```
BACKGROUND_DUMP_DEST=/oracle/appsdb/admin/bdump
CORE_DUMP_DEST=/oracle/appsdb/admin/cdump
USER_DUMP_DEST=/oracle/appsdb/admin/udump
```

Control File Configuration

```
CONTROL_FILES=("/oracle/appsdb/control/logicalstdby.ctl")
```

Archive

```
STANDBY_ARCHIVE_DEST='LOCATION=/oracle/appsdb/arch'
LOG_ARCHIVE_FORMAT=appsdb_%t_%s.dbf
LOG_ARCHIVE_START=TRUE
LOG_ARCHIVE_DEST_1='LOCATION=/oracle/appsdb/archlocal'
REMOTE_ARCHIVE_ENABLE=TRUE
```

Miscellaneous

```
COMPATIBLE=9.2.0
DB_NAME=appsdb
STANDBY_FILE_MANAGEMENT=AUTO
FAL_SERVER=appsstdby
FAL_CLIENT=appsprim
```

Network Registration

```
INSTANCE_NAME=appsdb
```

The *remote_archive_enable* parameter should be TRUE. Otherwise, the log transfer process will not start writing the archived redo logs to the standby site. If the standby database is being created on the local host, set the *lock_name_space* parameter to a unique value such that the distributed lock manager can generate unique lock names. Also, change the *instance_name* parameter so that the *instance_name* of the primary and the standby database are different.

Configure Oracle Net on the Standby Site

Configure the Oracle Net on the standby site to add a listener for this logical standby database and services for the logical standby database and the primary standby database. Either the *tnsnames.ora* and *listener.ora* files can be edited or Oracle Net Assistant can be used for this purpose. For the details about Oracle Net configuration, read "Creating a Physical Standby Database" section.

Renaming the Filename on the Standby Site

On the standby site, set the *oracle_sid* environment variable and then mount the standby database:

```
STARTUP MOUNT;
```

If the directory structure on the standby site is different from the one at the primary site, the data files and log files will have to be renamed to reflect the new data files and log files name in the control file of the standby database. This can be achieved using the following statement:

```
ALTER DATABASE RENAME FILE 'filespec1' TO 'filespec2';
```

filespec1 for datafiles and log files can be obtained from the *v$datafile* and *v$logfiles* views, respectively, from the primary database. Following two queries will assist in getting that information.

Data files:

```
Select
   Name
From
   V$DATAFILE;
```

Log files:

```
Select
   Member
From
   V$LOGFILE;
```

The *db_file_name_convert* and the *log_file_name_convert* parameters will not change the datafile and logfile name in the control file. Using these two parameters in the *init.ora* file will not have any effect.

Create Online Redo Log Files

In order for a logical standby database to work, the online redo logs must be created. The redo logs can be created using the *clear logfile group* statement for each log group. Use the following statement on the primary database to find the log group #.

```
Select
   GROUP#
From
   V$LOGFILE;
```

The output will be similar to the following:

```
GROUP#
--------
       1
       2
       3
```

In this case there are three log groups.

```
ALTER DATABASE CLEAR LOGFILE GROUP 1;
ALTER DATABASE CLEAR LOGFILE GROUP 2;
ALTER DATABASE CLEAR LOGFILE GROUP 3;
```

These statements will create three redo logs of the same size as those defined on the primary database site.

Prepare to Start the Log Apply Service

Before the log apply service can be started on a logical standby database, the logical standby database must be recovered to bring it to a point where the SQL apply mode can start reading and applying the changes from the redo logs onto the database. This starting point for the SQL apply mode should be the next SCN after the LogMiner dictionary is created on the primary database.

In order to apply all the changes up to this SCN, the logical standby database should be manually recovered using the archived logfile that was created just after building the LogMiner dictionary.

 TIP – If a cold backup of the primary database is used to create a logical standby database, there is no need to manually recover and this step can be skipped. Open the database using the resetlogs and continue from changing the dbname.

In this case, the archived redo logfile is *appsdb_1_568.dbf*. The following statement will start recovery using *appsdb_1_568.dbf* logfile:

```
ALTER DATABASE RECOVER LOGFILE
'/oracle/appsdb/arch/appsdb_1_568.dbf';
```

This may give an error that a previous archived redo log is required for recovery. Copy this file to the standby site and continue recovery using this log:

```
ERROR at line 1:
ORA-00279: change 393493 generated at 10/03/2003 12:03:12 needed for
thread 1
ORA-00289: suggestion : /oracle/appsdb/arch/appsdb_1_567.dbf
ORA-00280: change 393493 for thread 1 is in sequence #567
ORA-00278: log file '/oracle/appsdb/arch/appsdb_1_567.dbf' no longer
needed for
this recovery
ORA-00308: cannot open archived log
'/oracle/appsdb/arch/appsdb_1_567.dbf'
ORA-27037: unable to obtain file status
SVR4 Error: 2: No such file or directory
Additional information: 3
```

Copy the *appsdb_1_567.dbf* file and recover using this logfile followed by the recovery using next logfile:

```
Alter database recover logfile
'/oracle/appsdb/arch/appsdb_1_567.dbf';

alter database recover logfile
*
ERROR at line 1:
ORA-00279: change 393816 generated at 10/03/2003 12:07:58 needed for
thread 1
ORA-00289: suggestion : /oracle/appsdb/archlocal/appsdb_1_568.dbf
ORA-00280: change 393816 for thread 1 is in sequence #568
ORA-00278: log file '/oracle/appsdb/arch/appsdb_1_567.dbf' no longer
needed for this recovery
```

And then the archived log file, which is created after log miner dictionary creation.

```
Alter database recover logfile
'/oracle/appsdb/arch/appsdb_1_568.dbf';

alter database recover logfile
*
ERROR at line 1:
ORA-00279: change 393836 generated at 10/03/2003 12:07:59 needed for
thread 1
ORA-00289: suggestion : /oracle/appsdb/archlocal/appsdb_1_569.dbf
ORA-00280: change 393836 for thread 1 is in sequence #569
ORA-00278: log file '/oracle/appsdb/arch/appsdb_1_568.dbf' no longer
needed for this recovery
```

This will recover the logical standby database to the point where the log miner dictionary was created. Archived logs generated after this point can be registered with the standby database to be recovered by the log apply service. After applying the archived log, open the database using resetlogs.

```
ALTER DATABASE OPEN RESETLOGS;
```

Change the DBNAME of the Standby Database

The dbname of the standby database can be changed using the *nid* utility. The database will need to be shutdown and mounted again:

```
nid target=sys/change_on_install dbname=lappsdb setname=yes
```

The following output will appear. The command will prompt for input on the following question:

```
"Change database name of database <old dbname> to  <new dbname>?
(Y/[N]) => "
Type Y and press enter.

---------------Output of nid command--------------
DBNEWID: Release 9.2.0.4.0 - Production
Copyright (c) 1995, 2002, Oracle Corporation.  All rights reserved.

Connected to database APPSDB (DBID=659867667)

Control Files in database:
    /oracle/appsdb/control/logicalstdby.ctl

Change database name of database APPSDB to LAPPSDB? (Y/[N]) => Y

Proceeding with operation
Changing database name from APPSDB to LAPPSDB
    Control File /oracle/appsdb/control/logicalstdby.ctl - modified
    Datafile /oracle/appsdb/data/system01.dbf - wrote new name
    Datafile /oracle/appsdb/data/undotbs01.dbf - wrote new name
    Datafile /oracle/appsdb/data/userdata01.dbf - wrote new name
    Datafile /oracle/appsdb/data/indxdata01.dbf - wrote new name
    Datafile /oracle/appsdb/data/logstdby.dbf - wrote new name
    Control File /oracle/appsdb/control/logicalstdby.ctl - wrote new
name
```

```
Database name changed to LAPPSDB.
Modify parameter file and generate a new password file before
restarting.
Successfully changed database name.
DBNEWID - Completed successfully.
--------------End of nid output----------------------------
```

Change the *db_name* parameter in *init.ora* file and restart the database.

Setting Data Guard On

The next step is to turn the Data Guard on and create the temporary tablespace datafiles. The temporary tablespace is required because the log apply service uses the temporary tablespace during the SQL apply mode. The Data Guard can be enabled using the following statement:

```
ALTER DATABASE GUARD ALL;
```

The guard status can be verified from the *v$database* view:

```
Select
    Name,
    Guard_Status
From
    V$DATABASE;


NAME        GUARD_S
---------   -------
LAPPSDB     ALL
```

Create a Temporary Tablespace

To create temporary tablespace files, find the temporary tablespaces from the *dba_tablespaces* view. For all of the temporary tablespaces defined in the primary database, datafiles will need to be added in the logical standby database. This is because the temporary tablespace files are not backed up or copied to the standby site:

```
Select
   Tablespace_Name
From
   DBA_TABLESPACES
Where
   Contents = 'TEMPORARY';

TABLESPACE_NAME
------------------------------
TEMP
```

The following statement will add a 200MB temporary tablespace file:

```
Alter tablespace temp add tempfile '/oracle/appsdb/data/temp01.dbf'
size 200M REUSE;
```

This statement can be edited to suit the environment and temporary tablespace size required.

Starting the Logical Standby Database

At this point, the logical standby database is ready and the automatic log apply service can be started. Register the archived redo log, which is generated after the LogMiner dictionary creation on the primary database, and start the SQL apply service. To register the archived redo log use the following statement:

```
ALTER DATABASE REGISTER LOGICAL LOGFILE
'/oracle/appsdb/arch/appsdb_1_568.dbf';
```

Use the following statement to start applying the log files:

```
ALTER DATABASE START LOGICAL STANDBY APPLY INITIAL;
```

At this point, Oracle will start a process called LSP0. This process will facilitate the recovery process using log miner on the standby site. This step can be verified in the alert log file:

```
ALTER DATABASE START LOGICAL STANDBY APPLY
with optional part
INITIAL
LSP0 started with pid=11
Fri Oct  3 16:14:47 2003
Attempt to start background Logical Standby process
Completed: ALTER DATABASE START LOGICAL STANDBY APPLY INITIAL
Fri Oct  3 16:14:48 2003
LOGSTDBY event: ORA-16111: log mining and apply setting up
```

The last line in the alert log file shows an Oracle error 16111. This is normal and it indicates that the log apply service is waiting for the redo from the primary database.

Since the primary database was running before the logical standby database was created and the *init.ora* file of primary database has *log_archive_dest_state_2 = ENABLE*, it will try to transfer the log files to the standby site.

However, at that time, the listener on the standby site was not running, and as a result the log transfer service on the primary site will throw error [TNS: No Listener] and invalidate the *log_archive_destination*. The *v$archive_dest* view can be queried on the primary database to check this.

Once the listener is started on the standby site and the tnsnames on both the standby and the primary site is configured to establish connection between the primary and the standby database, the *log_archive_dest* can be validated again using the following statement executed on the primary site:

```
ALTER SYSTEM SET LOG_ARCHIVE_DEST_STATE_2 = ENABLE;
```

Query the *v$archive_dest* view again to verify that the archive destination pointing to standby site is valid:

```
Select
    DEST_NAME,
    STATUS,
    ERROR
From
    V$ARCHIVE_DEST;
```

Switch a logfile on the primary database to initiate the log transfer. After a log file on the primary database is switched, the log transfer service will transmit all the archived log files created after the LogMiner dictionary was built. For example, all the log files created after logfile will be transmitted. Check the *standby_archive_dest* location on the standby database to verify this. If any log is missing, a gap sequence will be created.

Verify the Logical Standby Database

A couple of SQL statements should be run on the primary database and the standby database to verify that the data on both databases are in sync. Alternatively, a sample table can be created on the primary database. Populate a few rows in it, commit the changes, and do a log switch. After few moments, the new tables and rows should appear in the standby database. This will prove that the logical standby database is running and is being updated with the changes on the primary database.

Although, verifying the application data between the logical and the primary database is the best method to check the consistency of data on standby database, this may not always be the most appropriate method. There are few views in the Oracle data dictionary that can be queried to find the status of the various processes involved in the log transfer and log apply services. In this section, two views that will show the log transfer process and the overall progress of the log apply service will be presented.

Once logs are transferred from the primary site to the standby site, they need to be automatically registered with the logical standby database before the log apply process (lsp0) can read and apply the SQL statements.

The *dba_logstdby_log* view provides information on the archived logs registered at the standby site. The script, *reg_log.sql,* from the code depot shows the logs registered with the logical standby database.

💾 reg_log.sql

```
--  ***************************************************
--  Copyright © 2004 by Rampant TechPress
--  This script is free for non-commercial purposes
--  with no warranties.  Use at your own risk.
--
--  To license this script for a commercial purpose,
--  contact info@rampant.cc
--  ***************************************************

Set linesize 100
Column Sequence# Format 99999
Column File_Name Format a60
Column Timestamp Format a20

Select
   Sequence#,
   File_Name,
   to_char(Timestamp,'YYYY/MM/DD HH24:MI:SS') Timestamp
From
   DBA_LOGSTDBY_LOG
Order by
   Sequence#;
```

A sample output from the *reg_log.sql* script shows the archived redo logs and the time it was registered with the standby database:

```
SEQUENCE# FILE NAME                                TIMESTAMP
--------- ------------------------------------     --------------------
-
      527 /oracle/appsdb/arch/appsdb_1_568.dbf     2003/10/05 19:14:17
      528 /oracle/appsdb/arch/appsdb_1_569.dbf     2003/10/05 19:18:41
      529 /oracle/appsdb/arch/appsdb_1_570.dbf     2003/10/05 19:18:41
      530 /oracle/appsdb/arch/appsdb_1_571.dbf     2003/10/05 19:18:42
      531 /oracle/appsdb/arch/appsdb_1_572.dbf     2003/10/05 19:17:22
```

A few log switches can be performed on the primary site and then checked to see if this query is showing the new archived logs as registered.

Another view, *dba_logstdby_progress,* shows the overall progress of the log apply service on the standby site. See the script *log_progress.sql* from code depot. This script is a query on *dba_logstdby_progress* view and shows the received, read, and applied SCN by the standby database.

🖫 log_progress.sql

```
-- ****************************************************
-- Copyright © 2004 by Rampant TechPress
-- This script is free for non-commercial purposes
-- with no warranties.  Use at your own risk.
--
-- To license this script for a commercial purpose,
-- contact info@rampant.cc
-- ****************************************************

Set linesize 100
Column Applied_Scn Format 999999
Column Read_Scn Format 999999
Column Newest_Scn Format 999999

Select
   Applied_Scn,
   Read_Scn,
   Newest_Scn
From
   DBA_LOGSTDBY_PROGRESS;
```

The following is a sample output from *log_progress.sql* script:

```
APPLIED_SCN   READ_SCN NEWEST_SCN
----------- ---------- ----------
     168011     167225     168133
```

newest_scn shows the most recent SCN available on the standby site. When all the changes from the primary site have been applied on the standby site, the value of *applied_scn* and *newest_scn* will be equal.

Sample Configuration

To put all the bits and pieces explained in this chapter together and to give a complete idea about a working standby database, a sample Data Guard configuration will be created. This sample configuration involves two host machines and two primary databases. The hostnames are jrpr01 and jrpr02, and the databases are "appsdb" and "meddb".

The name "appsdb" is the production or the primary database on jrpr01, and "meddb" is the primary database on jrpr02. The standby database for "appsdb" is created on jrpr02, and the standby database for "meddb" is created on jrpr01. Figure 3.1 illustrates this configuration.

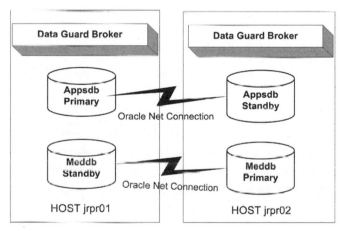

Figure 3.1 – *Sample Data Guard configuration*

This two-node cross-host configuration will provide a high degree of fault tolerance for both databases. In case of failure of one of the host machines or one primary database, the corresponding standby database can be activated to perform as the primary node. For example, if the host jrpr01 is not available for planned maintenance or due to unplanned outage, the standby database for "appsdb" on jrpr02 host can be activated.

To make this activation process as quick as possible, a symmetrical initialization parameter file will be used for this configuration. This means having the same initialization parameters file for the primary and the standby database. The initialization file does not have to be changed during switchover or failover operations.

The *init.ora* file, in this case, will contain a superset of parameters specific to both the standby and the primary database. For example, the *standby_archive_dest* parameter is not required for the primary database and the *log_archive_dest_2* parameter is not required for the standby database during their normal operations, but the symmetrical *init.ora* file will contain both of these parameters.

What happens to the parameters that are not required? The answer is that the non-essential parameters are ignored. Therefore, the *stanby_archive_dest* parameter will be ignored when the database is behaving as the primary, and the *log_archive_dest_2* will be ignored when the database is acting as the standby. There will not be any errors or warnings in the alert log file about the parameters that have been ignored.

The following example shows a symmetrical *init.ora* file for database meddb:

Diagnostics and Statistics

```
BACKGROUND_DUMP_DEST=/oracle/meddb/admin/bdump
CORE_DUMP_DEST=/oracle/meddb/admin/cdump
USER_DUMP_DEST=/oracle/meddb/admin/udump
```

Control File Configuration

```
CONTROL_FILES=("/oracle/meddb/control/control01.ctl",
               "/oracle/meddb/control/control02.ctl",
               "/oracle/meddb/control/control03.ctl")
```

Archive

```
STANDBY_ARCHIVE_DEST='LOCATION=/oracle/meddb/arch'
LOG_ARCHIVE_FORMAT=meddb_%t_%s.dbf
LOG_ARCHIVE_START=TRUE
LOG_ARCHIVE_DEST_1='LOCATION=/oracle/meddb/arch'
LOG_ARCHIVE_DEST_2='SERVICE=medstdby'
LOG_ARCHIVE_DEST_STATE_2=ENABLE
```

Miscellaneous

```
COMPATIBLE=9.2.0
DB_NAME=meddb
STANDBY_FILE_MANAGEMENT=AUTO
```

Network Registration

```
INSTANCE_NAME=meddb
FAL_SERVER=medstdby
FAL_CLIENT=medprim
```

The *init.ora* parameters for the appsdb database are similar except for the changes in the directory structure, *db_name* and *instance* parameters. In this configuration, an assumption has been made that the DBA is able to create the standby database in same directory structure on remote host. If it must be created it in a different directory structure, include the *db_file_name_convert* and *log_file_name_convert* parameters in the *init.ora* files.

Also, the Oracle Network files are similar on the two hosts. The *listener.ora* file on jrpr01 machine should contain entries for appsdb primary instance and meddb standby instance. Similarly, on jrpr02 host, it should have a listener for appsdb standby and meddb primary instance. The *tnsnames.ora* on both the servers will be the same and should contain the service names for all four databases. The *listener.ora* file from jrpr01 server is shown in the following example:

```
LISTENER =
  (DESCRIPTION_LIST =
    (DESCRIPTION =
      (ADDRESS_LIST =
        (ADDRESS = (PROTOCOL = IPC)(KEY = EXTPROC))
      )
      (ADDRESS_LIST =
        (ADDRESS = (PROTOCOL = TCP)(HOST = jrpr01)(PORT = 1521))
      )
    )
  )

SID_LIST_LISTENER =
  (SID_LIST =
    (SID_DESC =
      (SID_NAME = appsdb)
      (ORACLE_HOME = /sw/oracle/product/9.2.0)
    )
    (SID_DESC =
      (SID_NAME = meddb)
      (ORACLE_HOME = /sw/oracle/product/9.2.0)
    )
  )
```

And the *tnsnames.ora* looks like

```
appsstdby =
  (DESCRIPTION =
    (ADDRESS_LIST =
      (ADDRESS = (PROTOCOL = TCP)(HOST =  jrpr01  )(PORT = 1521))
    )
    (CONNECT_DATA =
      (SID = appsdb )
    )
  )

appsprim =
  (DESCRIPTION =
    (ADDRESS_LIST =
      (ADDRESS = (PROTOCOL = TCP)(HOST =  jrpr02  )(PORT = 1521))
    )
    (CONNECT_DATA =
      (SID = appsdb )
    )
  )

medprim =
  (DESCRIPTION =
    (ADDRESS_LIST =
      (ADDRESS = (PROTOCOL = TCP)(HOST =  jrpr01  )(PORT = 1521))
```

```
      )
    (CONNECT_DATA =
      (SID = meddb )
      )
    )

medstdby =
  (DESCRIPTION =
    (ADDRESS_LIST =
      (ADDRESS = (PROTOCOL = TCP)(HOST =  jrpr02  )(PORT = 1521))
      )
    (CONNECT_DATA =
      (SID = meddb )
      )
    )
```

The "appsprim" and "appsstdby" services are for the primary "appsdb" database and standby "appsdb" database respectively. Similarly, the "medprim" service corresponds to the primary "meddb" database, and the "medstdby" service is for the standby "meddb" database.

Once these files are configured and in place, the primary and the standby databases on both the servers can be started using the procedure explained in "Creating Physical Standby Database on a Remote Host" section. Verify the standby databases after switching a few redo log files on each of these primary databases. The verification procedures remain the same as explained before.

Conclusion

A complete treatise on creating a physical and logical standby database has been presented in this chapter. The salient features of this chapter are as follows:

- Different physical database recovery modes were introduced along with the methodologies of creating physical standby databases in various configurations.

- Limitations of logical standby databases were presented and were followed by a step-by-step guide for creating logical standby databases.

- Sample configurations were provided that gave insight into real world examples of Data Guard configuration.

In the subsequent chapters, the management and administration of standby databases will be presented.

"We need Data Guard in order to be safe.
Please find out what Data Guard is"

Standby Database Administration

Not all Managers understand Oracle Data Guard technology

Introduction

This chapter details the administration and management of standby databases. It is divided into sub-sections for physical and logical standby databases. The focus in each of these sub-sections is general administration and monitoring. Information will be presented on the changes of the primary database that need to be manually propagated to the standby site, the use of the *dbms_logstdby* package to manage a logical standby database explained in detail, and a brief description of the cascaded standby database.

Administration of Physical Standby Databases

Although physical standby databases are very much self-managed, it will be necessary to monitor them at times. If the standby database is to be used for reporting purposes, the database mode will have to be cycled between managed recovery and read-only. Moreover, there are some operations, involving changes in data files, which will not be reflected on the standby database and requires the intervention of the DBA to propagate these changes. The text in this section describes such events and the actions required to make changes on the standby site; beginning with the general administration tasks.

General Administration Tasks

Physical standby databases run in three modes: managed recovery mode, read-only mode, and manual recovery mode. Starting with Oracle9i, there will be very few scenarios the database will need to run in manual recovery mode. Most of the time, databases will be run in managed recovery mode or read-only mode. The general administration tasks include controlling various modes of recovery, starting up, and shutting down the standby database.

Controlling the Managed Recovery Process

To start the database in managed recovery mode; mount it first, and then start the managed recovery. This is a three-step process involving:

- Starting up the database using:
  ```
  STARTUP NOMOUNT;
  ```
- Mounting the standby database using:
  ```
  ALTER DATABASE MOUNT STANDBY DATABASE;
  ```
- Starting the recovery process using:
  ```
  ALTER DATABASE RECOVER MANAGED STANDBY DATABASE;
  ```

These statements should be executed by a user having SYSDBA privileges.

The RECOVER MANAGED STANDBY DATABASE statement has several options for controlling the recovery process. Either a foreground or a background recovery process can be started. The above-mentioned statement will initiate a foreground recovery process, and a session open will need to remain open. If recovery is started in a foreground session, use the TIMEOUT clause to stop recovery after the time specified by TIMEOUT.

For example:

```
ALTER DATABASE RECOVER MANAGED STANDBY DATABASE TIMEOUT 5;
```

This clause will stop the recovery process, if a new archive log does not arrive within five minutes.

A better option is to run the recovery process in background. The DISCONNECT FROM SESSION clause of the RECOVER MANAGED STANDBY DATABASE starts recovery in a background session. A complete statement to start recovery in background is:

```
ALTER DATABASE RECOVER MANAGED STANDBY DATABASE DISCONNECT FROM
SESSION;
```

If the database is DML intensive, a multiple parallel recovery process can be started on the standby site to spread the load during the log apply operation. The parallel clause is a request to start five parallel processes. Oracle may decide to choose to start a different number of parallel processes depending on the resources available on the host machine. The following statement

---

will start five parallel recovery processes to apply archived redo logs on the standby site:

```
ALTER DATABASE RECOVER MANAGED STANDBY DATABASE DISCONNECT FROM
SESSION PARALLEL 5;
```

To stop the managed recovery, the Cancel command can be issued on the standby database. The complete statement is:

```
ALTER DATABASE RECOVER MANAGED STANDBY DATABASE CANCEL;
```

This statement will stop the MRP. There are several other options for the RECOVER MANAGED STANDBY DATABASE statement, which can be found in the Oracle documentation.

Opening the Standby Database in Read-only Mode

As explained before, a physical standby database can be toggled between recovery and read-only mode. If the database is currently in managed recovery mode, in order to open it for reporting, cancel the recovery and open it as read-only. The following statements summarize the steps involved:

- Stop the managed recovery process using:
  ```
  ALTER DATABASE RECOVER MANAGED
  STANDBY DATABASE CANCEL;
  ```

- Open database as read only:
  ```
  ALTER DATABASE OPEN READ ONLY;
  ```

If the database is shutdown, in order to open it as read-only, mount the database as standby and then open it as read-only. The following statements illustrate this:

- Startup the database using:
  ```
  STARTUP NOMOUNT;
  ```

- Mount the standby database using:

```
ALTER DATABASE MOUNT STANDBY DATABASE;
```

- Open the database in read only mode using:

```
ALTER DATABASE OPEN READ ONLY;
```

To start recovery again on the standby site, terminate all active user sessions and issue the following statement:

```
ALTER DATABASE RECOVER MANAGED STANDBY DATABASE DISCONNECT FROM
SESSION;
```

The *v$session* dynamic performance view can be used to find the active user sessions in the database.

When the database is open in read-only mode for reporting and query purposes, it is very likely that sorting operations will take place. In any database, sorting operations occur in memory specified by the *sort_area_size* or on a disk in a temporary tablespace. Ideally, all sorting operations should occur in memory, but that is not always possible, so temporary tablespaces are required.

If the temporary tablespace was not created during the creation of the physical standby database, it must be created before queries can be executed on the standby database. There are few things that must be considered about a temporary tablespace in the standby database:

- A temporary tablespace cannot be created on the standby database. Tempfiles can only be associated with a temporary tablespace. Therefore, the temporary tablespace should be present on the primary database before creating the standby database, or it should be created on a standby database through the recovery mechanism.

- The temporary tablespace should contain only temporary files.

- The temporary tablespace should be locally managed.

To add a temporary file to a temporary tablespace, open the standby database in read-only mode and add the tempfile. The following statement adds a tempfile to the temporary tablespace temp on the standby database:

```
ALTER TABLESPACE TEMP
ADD TEMPFILE '/oracle/appsdb/data/temp01.dbf'
SIZE 200M REUSE;
```

Manual Recovery of Standby Databases

Starting with Oracle9i, manual recovery may not be the natural option for recovering a standby database, but this mode formed the foundation of standby database technology back in the days of Oracle7.x. Apart from the historical importance, there are other good reasons to learn manual recovery. The knowledge of manual recovery can prove to be very handy when the managed recovery is not working. Moreover, in some cases it may not be possible to establish an Oracle Net connection between the primary and the standby node, and in this situation manual recovery is the only option.

To start manual recovery of a standby database, mount the database, and start recovery. During the recovery process, the archive logs will be read from the default location specified by the *log_archive_dest_n* initialization parameter. However, the location of the archived logs can be specified in the RECOVER …DATABASE statement to override the location designated by the *log_archive_dest_n* parameter.

The following statements start the manual recovery process. It assumes that the *oracle_sid* is set correctly and the initialization file is in the $ORACLE_HOME/dbs directory. Also, the archived logs are copied from the primary database onto the *log_archive_dest_1* location on the standby site:

- Startup the database:

  ```
  STARTUP NOMOUNT;
  ```

- Mount as standby database:

  ```
  ALTER DATABASE MOUNT STANDBY DATABASE;
  ```

- Start recovery process:

  ```
  RECOVER STANDBY DATABASE;
  ```

If the archive logs are not located in the directory specified by the *log_archive_dest_1* parameter, the following statement can be used to start recovery reading the log files from other locations:

```
RECOVER FROM 'archive_log location' STANDBY DATABASE;
```

Figure 4.1 shows the manual recovery process.

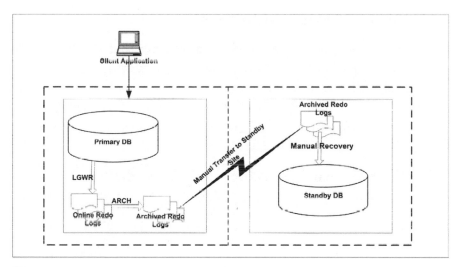

Figure 4.1 – *Manual Recovery Process*

Shutting Down the Standby Database

Before shutting down the standby database, exclude this standby site from the archival operation on the primary database. As long as the standby database is down, the log transfer service will not attempt to write any new archived log files to this standby destination. This parameter can be updated dynamically using the ALTER SYSTEM statement followed by switching a log file on the primary site.

On the standby site, ensure that the managed recovery process is not running. Find the status of the managed recovery process using the *v$managed_standby* dynamic view. If the managed recovery process is running, cancel the recovery before shutting down the database.

If the database is open in read-only mode, find the active sessions in the database and close the active sessions before issuing the shutdown statement. The following steps show the shut down procedure of the standby database:

- Defer the log transfer service, assuming that this standby site is designated as second destination on the primary database:

```
ALTER SYSTEM SET
LOG_ARCIVE_DEST_STATE_2=DEFER;
```

- Switch a log file on the primary database:

```
ALTER SYSTEM SWITCH LOGFILE;
```

- Check the managed recovery process on the standby site:

```
Select
    Process,
    State
From
    V$MANAGED_STANDBY;
```

- Cancel the recovery process on the standby site:

```
ALTER DATABASE RECOVER MANAGED
STANDBY DATABASE CANCEL;
```

- Shutdown the database:

  ```
  SHUTDOWN IMMEDIATE
  ```

The next section describes the monitoring procedures for the physical standby database.

Monitor Physical Standby Databases

Periodically, the Data Guard configuration will have to be monitored to check the health of standby databases. In this section, the tools for monitoring the physical standby database and finding the progress of the recovery process will be presented.

Tools for Monitoring Standby Databases

The following tools can be used to monitor a physical standby database:

- Alert log file on the primary and the standby site.
- Dynamic performance view on the primary and the standby database.
- Static view on the primary database.

Using Alert Log to Monitor

The alert log file on the primary database keeps a wealth of information related to the changes taking place on the primary site. All of the information available in the alert log file may not be relevant from the standby database perspective, but the DBA can mine the alert log file to find the operations that can affect the standby database. Some of these operations include:

- Changes in the Control file.
- Changes in Redo Log files.

- Changes in Data files.

- Changes in Tablespace status.

In addition, the alert log on the standby site holds useful information pertaining to standby database operations. The *log_archive_trace* parameter controls the level of information related to standby operations that will be available in the alert log file and other associated trace files. The usual setting of *log_archive_trace* is 127 and will produce messages related to the log transfer and the log apply service in the alert log file.

Using Dynamic Performance View to Monitor

The other effective method use to monitor the standby database is querying the fixed views. These views hold information about the changes on the primary database as well as on the standby database. The following fixed views are useful for monitoring the events affecting the standby database:

- *v$log*

- *v$logfile*

- *v$thread*

- *v$recover_file*

- *v$datafile*

- *v$database*

Using Static Views to Monitor

The static views are *dba_** views. These are specifically useful for finding changes in tablespaces and datafiles on the primary database. When the standby database is in recovery mode, the static views cannot be queried. The following static views on the primary database can be queried in order to find the changes in datafiles and tablespaces:

- *dba_tablespaces*

- *dba_data_files*

Recovery Progress on Standby Sites

Determining the progress of the recovery process is essential before switchover to a standby database. Moreover, the recovery progress should be monitored periodically in order to find the lag between the primary database and the standby database.

If the standby database is showing a regular backlog of archived logs required to be applied on the standby database, the recovery process will have to be tuned in order to synchronize it with the primary database. Otherwise, during the failover operation, it will take longer for the log apply service to catch up before the standby database can be activated.

As mentioned earlier, the alert log file will assist the determination of the progress of recovery; however, querying the dynamic performance views will provide the same level of information without going to the trouble of reading thousands of lines in the alert log file. In this section, the use of dynamic views to find the overall recovery progress and the status of various processes involved in recovery will be presented. The following views are particularly important in determining the status of managed recovery:

- *v$managed_standby*

- *v$archived_standby*

- *v$archive_dest_status*

- *v$log_history*

To find the overall progress of the recovery process on the standby database, *v$archive_dest_status* on the standby site can be queried to find the last archived log received and applied on this site. The following query, when executed on standby database, will provide this information:

```
Select
    ARCHIVED_THREAD#,
    ARCHIVED_SEQ#,
    APPLIED_THREAD#,
    APPLIED_SEQ#
From
    V$ARCHIVE_DEST_STATUS;
```

The following sample output from the query shows the standby database is eight logs behind the primary database:

```
ARCHIVED_THREAD# ARCHIVED_SEQ# APPLIED_THREAD# APPLIED_SEQ#
---------------- ------------- --------------- ------------
              1           594               1          586
```

The difference between the ARCHIVED_SEQ# and APPLIED_SEQ# column is the number of logs available on the standby site that need to be applied to synchronize it with the primary database. The above query only shows the difference between logs available and applied on the standby site. There may be a scenario when all the logs from the primary database are not transferred to the standby site. In this case there may be more logs that are required to synchronize the standby database.

The archived logs can be found by comparing the ARCHIVED_SEQ# column from the above output with the last log archived on the primary database. The last archived log on the primary site can be obtained from the SEQUENCE# column of *v$log_history*. The following query can be executed on the primary database for this purpose:

```
Select
    max(SEQUENCE#) Latest_Archive_Log
From
    V$LOG_HISTORY;
```

The *v$archived_log* view shows details of the progress of the managed recovery process for individual archived logs. The following query can be used to see the status of an individual archived log on the standby site. 'RFS' in the REGISTRAR column shows that these logs are transferred from the primary site by log transfer services.

```
Select
    THREAD#,
    SEQUENCE#,
    APPLIED,
    REGISTRAR
From
    V$ARCHIVED_LOG;

    THREAD#   SEQUENCE# APP REGISTR
---------- ---------- --- -------
         1         585 YES RFS
         1         586 YES RFS
         1         587 NO  RFS
         1         588 NO  RFS
         1         589 NO  RFS
```

 TIP - The archived logs that have REGISTRAR='RFS' and APPLIED='YES' can be safely removed from the archive log location of standby site.

In the managed recovery operation, there are various processes involved at the standby site. The *v$managed_standby* view gives the status of these processes. A sample output from the following query will show the status of ARCH, RFS, and MRP process:

```
Select
    PROCESS,
    SEQUENCE#,
    STATUS
From
    V$MANAGED_STANDBY;
```

```
PROCESS   SEQUENCE#  STATUS
-------   ---------- ------------
ARCH            0 CONNECTED
ARCH            0 CONNECTED
MRP0          595 WAIT_FOR_LOG
RFS           595 ATTACHED
RFS           594 RECEIVING
```

Propagating Unrecoverable Operations to Standby Databases

There are few operations on the primary database which cannot be recovered on the standby site using the managed recovery process; therefore, the DBA needs to intervene to propagate these changes to the standby database.

The *standby_file_management* initialization parameter plays an important role in the recovery process when the attributes of the data files are modified on the primary site. For the ease of administration, this parameter should be set to AUTO in the *init.ora* file on the standby site.

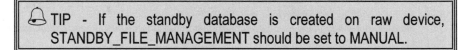

TIP - If the standby database is created on raw device, STANDBY_FILE_MANAGEMENT should be set to MANUAL.

When this is set to AUTO, adding a tablespace or datafile on the primary database will automatically propagate to the standby database. As a part of the recovery, Oracle will create the required operating system files.

The following section presents details of events that require intervention of the DBA and the possible solution to reflect these changes to the standby site.

Changes in the Tablespaces or Datafiles

In this section, information on the steps required to update the standby database when the tablespace or datafiles on the primary database are changed and the automatic file management is not enabled on the standby database. It is assumed that the standby database is running in managed recovery mode.

Creating Tablespace and Datafiles in the Primary Database

If a tablespace or a datafile has been added to an existing tablespace in the primary database, the following steps must be performed in order to synchronize the standby site. The following steps should be performed on each physical standby site:

- After altering the tablespace on the primary site, take it offline:

  ```
  ALTER TABLESPACE <tablespace name> OFFLINE;
  ```

- If it is a new tablespace, copy all the datafiles associated with this tablespace to the standby site. If datafiles have been added to an existing tablespace, only copy the new datafiles.

- Bring the tablespace online on the primary database:

  ```
  ALTER TABLESPACE <tablespace name> ONLINE;
  ```

- Switch a logfile on the primary database so the data dictionary on the standby site will be updated by the managed recovery process:

  ```
  ALTER SYSTEM SWITCH LOGFILE;
  ```

The new datafiles can be verified from the *v$datafile* view on the standby database.

Removing a Tablespace on the Primary Database

When a tablespace is dropped on the primary database, the managed recovery process will update the data dictionary on the standby site when it applies the next log file; however, this will not remove the file from the operating system. To keep the file system clean, manually remove the datafiles associated with this tablespace. The following steps are required to update the standby database when the DBA drops a tablespace on the primary database:

- Drop the tablespace on the primary database using this statement:

  ```
  DROP TABLESPACE <tablespace name>;
  ```

- Switch a logfile on the primary database so the changes in the data dictionary will be reflected on the standby site:

  ```
  ALTER SYSTEM SWITCH LOGFILE;
  ```

- Verify that the managed recovery process has applied the latest archived log to the standby database.

- Remove the datafiles associated with this tablespace on the standby site.

- Remove the datafiles associated with this tablespace on the primary site.

Reset Online Redo Logs on the Primary Database

If the RESETLOGS statement is issued on the primary database either as a part of recovery or to create a controlfile, it will reset the online logs. Resetting the online logs will invalidate the standby database because the next archive log sequence from the primary database will start from one; therefore, it will not match with the archive log sequence in the standby control file. In this case, the standby database will have to be recreated.

If an online log is cleared on the primary database before it is archived using the statement ALTER DATABASE CLEAR UNARCHIVED LOGFILE, it will invalidate all the associated standby databases.

Datafile Name Changes on the Primary Database

Any change in the name of the datafile of the primary database will not be propagated to the standby database by the log apply service. This change is not required until the standby database control file is refreshed, and it is recommended that the standby database be updated manually to reflect the new datafile name at the earliest opportunity.

If the datafile name in the primary and the standby database is not same, refreshing the control file on standby site will result in error. In order to update the datafile name, perform the following steps:

- After renaming the file on the primary site, connect to the standby site. Stop the managed recovery process and shutdown the standby database.

- Rename the file on the host using operating system utility.

- Start and mount the standby database.

- Use ALTER DATABASE RENAME FILE statement to rename the datafile in the controlfile of the standby database.

- Start the managed recovery process.

The ALTER TABLESPACE ...RENAME DATAFILE statement cannot be used on the standby site to rename the datafile because this statement will generate redo which is not allowed on the physical standby database.

Changing the Initialization Parameter on the Primary Standby Database

For the normal functioning of the standby database, it is not essential to mirror all the changes in initialization parameters from the primary to the standby site. The mirroring is recommended and will save time during the failover or switchover operations. The changes in initialization parameters on the primary database can be replicated either by dynamically changing the parameter on the standby site or updating the *init.ora* file and restarting the standby database.

Physical Standby Databases with Time Lag

In order to protect the database from user errors or log corruption, a Data Guard environment may need to be configured in which the archived redo logs from the primary database are not immediately applied to one or all of its physical standby databases.

Oracle Data Guard provides functionality to manage the time lag between delivery of the archived log file on the standby site and the application of these archived logs. In essence, it builds a delay between the log transfer and the log apply service on the physical standby database.

To configure a physical standby database with time lag, nothing has to be changed on the physical standby database; instead, the initialization parameter of the primary database will have to be altered. On the primary site, change the *log_archive_dest_n* parameter to include the DELAY attribute.

The following example will put a delay of 60 minutes between the log transfer and the log apply services on the physical standby database identified as *appsdbstdby*:

```
ALTER SYSTEM SET LOG_ARCHIVE_DEST_3='SERVICE=appsdbstdby DELAY=60';
```

The timer starts on the standby database after the archived log is received by the standby site.

Resolving Archive Gap Sequence on Physical Standby Databases

Oracle9i has introduced many new features designed to detect and resolve gap sequences. One of the main improvements is the new Fetch Archive Log service using *fal_server* and *fal_client* parameters. In spite of these automated process, there are certain scenarios when the gap sequence cannot be avoided, and the DBA needs to intervene to resume the managed recovery on the physical standby database.

Usually, a stalled managed recovery process is the indication of gap sequence. If the recovery process on the physical standby site is stopped, query the *v$archive_gap* view to find the gap sequence. The query *find_gap.sql* from code depot will assist in finding out if there is any archive log gap in the database.

🖫 **find_gap.sql**

```
-- ************************************************
-- Copyright © 2004 by Rampant TechPress
-- This script is free for non-commercial purposes
-- with no warranties.  Use at your own risk.
--
-- To license this script for a commercial purpose,
-- contact info@rampant.cc
-- ************************************************

Select
   THREAD#,
   LOW_SEQUENCE#,
   HIGH_SEQUENCE#
From
   V$ARCHIVE_GAP;
```

A sample output from *find_gap.sql* is:

```
THREAD#        LOW_SEQUENCE#        HIGH_SEQUENCE#
--------       -------------        --------------
    1              606                   609
```

If the LOW_SEQUENCE# is less than the HIGH_SEQUENCE# in the output, the database is having a gap sequence, and the difference in value is the number of archive logs that must be applied to resolve the gap. In the above output, the standby database is three logs behind the primary database.

The next step in gap resolution is to identify the archived logs on the primary database that are missing on the standby database. The *v$archive_log* view can be used to find the location of logs in the local archive destination. This step can be skipped if the DBA is familiar with the naming convention of archive logs in the database and can identify the SEQUENCE# from the logfile name.

It is recommended that this procedure be used to find the logs required to resolve gap. Substitute the values for THREAD# LOW_SEQUENCE# and HIGH_SEQUENCE# from previous query in the following query and execute to find the location of the missing archived logs on the primary database:

```
Select
    NAME
From
    V$ARCHIVED_LOG
Where
    THREAD#=<Thread# from previous query>
And
    DEST_ID=<Destination id of local archive destination>
And
    SEQUENCE# BETWEEN <Low Sequence# from previous query>
And <High Sequence# from previous query>;
```

Once the archived logs required for gap resolution have been identified, the logs should be copied into the directory specified by the *standby_archive_dest* initialization parameter on the standby site. Also, if the *log_archive_format* on the standby and the primary database are not same, these files must be renamed to match the format specified by the *log_archive_format* parameter of the standby database.

The file can be renamed using the operating system utility. Since these logs were not transferred by the log transfer service, the managed recovery process will not have any information about these logs. These logs will need to be manually registered with the managed recovery process before they will be applied by the log apply service. To register the logs with the MRP, use the following statement:

```
ALTER DATABASE REGISTER LOGFILE 'filespec';
```

For example:

```
ALTER DATABASE REGISTER LOGFILE
'/oracle/appsdb/arch/stdby_1_607.dbf';
```

At this point, the managed recovery process will start applying this archive log file.

Administration of Logical Standby Databases

The usual administration of logical standby databases involves:

- Startup and Shutdown of the database.
- Starting and Stopping the log apply service.
- Monitoring the logical standby database.
- Managing schema objects and transactions on the logical standby database.

- Manually propagating changes to the logical standby site.

In addition to these administrative tasks, this section will briefly describe how to manage logical standby databases with time lag.

Starting Up and Shutting Down Logical Standby Databases

The startup and shutdown procedure of a logical standby database is similar to the primary database. Be sure to stop the log apply service before shutting down the database. In order to avoid gap sequence, it is recommended to keep the logical standby database up when the primary database is running and sending the archive logs to the standby site. That is, before shutting down the logical standby database, stop the log archive services to the logical standby site.

Starting and Stopping the Log Apply Service

Once the logical standby database is started, then start the log apply service to keep it in sync with the primary database. The log apply service can be started using:

```
ALTER DATABASE START LOGICAL STANDBY APPLY;
```

The INITIAL keyword is required only when the log apply service is started for the first time after the creation of the logical standby database.

Log apply services can be stopped using the following statement:

```
ALTER DATABASE STOP LOGICAL STANDBY APPLY;
```

The status of the log apply service can be verified using the *v$logstandby* view. After executing the STOP statement, the DBA should not see any rows in the *v$logstdby* view.

Monitoring Logical Standby Databases

Once a logical standby is setup, it does not require a great deal of monitoring. However, keep an eye on the recovery progress to ensure that the data in the logical standby database is as current as in the primary database. A backlog in the recovery process will leave the logical standby database unusable for reporting, and will cause delay during activation if the DBA opts to failover or switchover to this logical standby site. In this section, details on the recovery progress and the tools available for monitoring will be presented.

Tools to Monitor Logical Standby Sites

Like physical standby databases, the following means can be used to monitor the recovery progress of logical standby databases:

- Alert Log file
- Dynamic Performance View
- Static view *(dba_*)* Views

The alert log file on the logical standby site contains useful information about the changes in the logical site. It also contains messages about the transactions that could not be applied on database. The output in the alert log file is controlled by the *log_archive_trace* parameter. If there is a problem in the database, set this parameter to produce an extensive output. The disadvantage of the alert log is that the information is not organized, and the DBA will have to search through a vast number of messages to find the needed information. Nevertheless, when no other tool such as database views can be used, the alert log is the only companion the DBA has.

Dynamic performance views are the most commonly used tool for monitoring. The following dynamic views have special purpose in the monitoring process:

- *v$logstdby* – This view provides information on individual processes involved in the SQL Apply operation.

- *v$logstdby_stats* – This view holds the statistics about the log apply service particularly related to LogMiner activities.

- *v$dataguard_status* – This view has information about the overall processes of the standby database. For example, RFS, FAL etc.

Since, unlike the physical standby database, the logical standby database is open for query during the recovery process, there is an option to query static views to extract information about logical standby processes. The following three views can be used for this purpose:

- *dba_logstdby_progress* – This view holds the information about the overall progress of the log apply service on the standby site.

- *dba_logstdby_log* – This view has extensive information about individual archived logs. The timestamp column of the view shows the time when archived log file was received on the standby site. It can be used in diagnosing issues with the log transfer service.

- *dba_logstdby_events* – Events affecting the SQL Apply operations are recorded in this view. This should be the starting point in diagnosing problems with the SQL Apply operations. This view holds 100 records by default. The default number of records can be changed using the *dbms_logstdby* package.

In addition to the above-mentioned views specially designed for the logical standby database, the dynamic performance views holding information about LogMiner activities can be used to find out if the SQL Apply operation is performing as expected.

Monitoring Overall Progress of the SQL Apply Operation

A quick query on the *dba_logstdby_progress* view shows the overall progress of the SQL Apply operation on the standby site. The *applied_scn* column holds the system change number, which has been read and applied on the database, and the *newest_scn* has the latest system change number that has been received on the standby database. An equal value in the *applied_scn* and *newest_scn* indicates that all the logs received by the standby site have been applied on the database.

The script *log_progress.sql* from code depot can be used to find the overall progress:

🖫 **log_progress.sql**

```
-- **************************************************
-- Copyright © 2004 by Rampant TechPress
-- This script is free for non-commercial purposes
-- with no warranties.  Use at your own risk.
--
-- To license this script for a commercial purpose,
-- contact info@rampant.cc
-- **************************************************

Set linesize 100
Column Applied_Scn Format 999999
Column Read_Scn Format 999999
Column Newest_Scn Format 999999

Select
   Applied_Scn,
   Read_Scn,
   Newest_Scn
From
   DBA_LOGSTDBY_PROGRESS;
```

The following is a sample output from the *log_progress.sql* script:

```
APPLIED_SCN   READ_SCN  NEWEST_SCN
-----------  ----------  ----------
     168011      167225      168133
```

This script shows there are few changes still to be applied on the logical standby database in order for it to be consistent with the primary database.

Monitoring Log Apply Services

The *v$logstdby* and *v$logstdby_stats* views provide comprehensive data about the various processes involved in the SQL Apply operations. As mentioned earlier in the "Data Guard Architecture" chapter, the SQL Apply operation is facilitated by LogMiner technology. The *v$logstdby* view can be queried to find the state of the individual process of LogMiner. The following simple query on *v$logstdby* will give sufficient information needed to analyze any problem with the log apply service:

```
Select
    PID,
    TYPE,
    STATUS
From
    V$LOGSTDBY
Order by
    HIGH_SCN;
```

The following is a sample output, from the above query showing the status of the log apply service:

```
PID     TYPE        STATUS
------  --------    ------------------------------------
1479    ANALYZER    ORA-16116: no work available
1475    BUILDER     ORA-16127: stalled waiting for additional
                    transactions to be applied
1477    PREPARER    ORA-16116: no work available
1471    COORDINATOR ORA-16116: no work available
1473    READER      ORA-16127: stalled waiting for additional
                    transactions to be applied
1481    APPLIER     ORA-16116: no work available
```

The *v$logstdby_stats* view contains the performance statistics on the log apply service. The records from this view will be cleared when the log apply service is not running. The following query can be used for performance monitoring purposes:

```
Select
    NAME,
    VALUE
From
    V$LOGSTDBY_STATS;
```

The output from the *v$logstdby_stats* view is as follows:

```
NAME                                  VALUE
-----                                 ---------
number of preparers                       1
number of appliers                        1
maximum SGA for LCR cache                 2
parallel servers in use                   5
maximum events recorded                 100
transaction consistency                FULL
record skip errors                        Y
record skip DDL                           Y
record applied DDL                        Y
coordinator state                  APPLYING
transactions ready                        2
transactions applied                      2
coordinator uptime                        4
preparer memory alloc waits               2
builder memory alloc waits             2346
attempts to handle low memory          2346
successful low memory recovery            1
pageout avoided                           0
pageout avoided by rollback               0
pageouts                                  0
memory low watermark reached              0
recovery checkpoints not taken            0
recovery checkpoints taken                0
available work units                    155
prepared work units                       0
committed txns ready                      0
un-committed txns ready                   0
committed txns being applied              0
un-committed txns being applied           0
```

Details about this view and interpretation of the data will be revisited in the "Performance Tuning of Standby Databases" chapter.

The *dba_logstdby_events* view records the activity of the log apply service. If there is a halted SQL Apply operation, query this view to find the cause of the halt. The EVENT and STATUS columns of this view hold the last executed SQL statement on the logical standby database and its result.

Additionally, it displays the current and committed SCN numbers. In case of any failure, the CURRENT_SCN column can be used to find the name of the archived log file that contains the statement causing the failure. The query *arch_log_name.sql* from code depot can assist in finding such log files. It requires the CURRENT_SCN from *dba_logstdby_events* view as input, and prints the name of the archived logs file that contains this SCN.

🖫 **arch_log_name.sql**

```
-- ****************************************************
-- Copyright © 2004 by Rampant TechPress
-- This script is free for non-commercial purposes
-- with no warranties.  Use at your own risk.
--
-- To license this script for a commercial purpose,
-- contact info@rampant.cc
-- ****************************************************

Column Archive_Log_Name format a30
Column Thread format 99
Column Status_Code format a10
Select
   l.FILE_NAME Archive_Log_Name,
   l.THREAD# Thread,
   e.STATUS_CODE Status_Code
From
   DBA_LOGSTDBY_LOG l,
   DBA_LOGSTDBY_EVENTS e
Where
   l.SEQUENCE# = &CURRENT_SCN;
```

Managing Schema Objects

A logical standby database can contain schema objects that are not present in the primary database. Additionally, the DBA might want to create some supporting data structures such as index or materialized views in a logical standby database to speed up the reporting queries. In order to alter or create a schema object in logical standby database, the appropriate user access should be instated. The database guard controls the user access in a logical standby database. The access levels that can be established are as follows:

- **NONE** – In this mode, the logical database is not protected by database guard. Any user can alter any objects in the database as long as the SQL Apply operation is not running.

- **STANDBY** – In this mode, only users with SYS privilege can modify the objects maintained by the log apply service. All users subject to the usual security policies can modify other schema objects.

- **ALL** – In this mode, only users with SYS privilege can modify any object in the database.

> 🔔 TIP - Users cannot issue any DDL or DML statement when the log apply service is running on the standby database. Once the SQL Apply operation starts, the DATABASE GUARD mode changes to ALL by default

The ALTER DATABASE GUARD statement can be used to set the access control on the database. For example, the following statement will set the access control to STANDBY:

```
ALTER DATABASE GUARD STANDBY;
```

The *v$database* view can be queried to see if DATABASE GUARD is on, and the access control level is as shown below:

```
Select
   GUARD_STATUS
From
   V$DATABASE;
```

In addition to controlling the user access to objects in the database, the access of the SQL Apply operation to objects and statements in the logical standby database can be controlled. An object or a DDL statement can be set so that it will be skipped by the SQL Apply operations. The skipping and un-skipping of schema objects are achieved by using the *dbms_logstdby* package.

Triggers and constraints in the logical standby database do not behave the same way as they do in the primary database. The triggers on tables are never executed in the standby database because they have already been executed in the primary database and the data to be applied on the standby site is the combined result of the direct DML and the data modified by the trigger.

Similarly, constraints are evaluated on the primary database and the data is posted only if it satisfies the constraints. To reduce the amount of work performed by the log apply service, the constraints are not re-evaluated on the logical standby site. As a result, if one of the tables from a referential integrity chain is skipped, the result may be inconsistency in the data on the logical standby database. The SQL Apply operation will not complain about the inconsistency, but the reports using these tables will not be correct.

Managing Tables in Logical Standby Databases

This section will detail the requirements and processes for altering a table in a logical standby database. In particular, information will be provided on performing DDL on a table that is maintained by the SQL Apply operation and the re-building or adding of a table to a logical standby database from the primary database. Also described in this section is the SKIP and UNSKIP procedure of the *dbms_logstdby* package that can be used to add and remove tables from the set of objects maintained by the SQL Apply operation.

Executing DDL Statements on Tables

Performing DDL statements on tables maintained by the SQL Apply operation is a four step process. The Database Guard will have to be bypassed before any statement can be issued against the tables. The DBA should be logged in as a user having privilege to alter objects when the guard is set to ALL or STANDBY. The following example shows the step-by-step process used to add a column to the existing table ADDRESS in the REPORTS schema:

- Stop the log apply service using:

  ```
  ALTER DATABASE STOP LOGICAL STANDBY APPLY;
  ```

- Bypass the Database Guard using the *dbms_logstdby* Package:

  ```
  EXEC DBMS_LOGSTDBY.GUARD_BYPASS_ON;
  ```

- Issue the DDL statement. For example:

  ```
  ALTER TABLE ADDRESS ADD
  AREA_CODE VARCHAR2(10);
  ```

- Enable the Database Guard using:

  ```
  EXEC DBMS_LOGSTDBY.GUARD_BYPASS_OFF;
  ```

- Start the log apply service using:

  ```
  ALTER DATABASE START LOGICAL STANDBY APPLY;
  ```

Instantiating a Table

Using the *instantiate_table* procedure of the *dbms_logstdby* package, the DBA can re-build or add a new table in the logical standby database. The DBA will need to re-build a table or refresh its data in the logical standby database, if any unrecoverable statement is issued on the primary database against that table. The unrecoverable transaction will not be recorded in the archive log file, so it will be missing from the standby database. However, setting the FORCE LOGGING option on the primary database will avoid any unrecoverable operation. Also, the DBA may need to re-build a table when it is desirable for this table to be managed by the SQL Apply operation. Either add a new table from the primary database or un-skip a previously skipped table.

Prior to executing the *instantiate_table* procedure, a dblink between the primary and the standby site must be created. The user specified in the database link should exist on the primary database. Moreover, the role LOGSTDBY_ADMINISTRATOR must be granted to the user used in the database link. The *dba_logstdby_skip* view contains operations being skipped on a table.

If a previously skipped table is being added to the set of objects managed by the SQL Apply operation, query this view to find the list of operations that are being skipped. All of these operations will have to be set as valid in order to be applied on the table after re-building it. The following steps show how to re-build a table on the standby site:

- Stop the log apply service using:

  ```
  ALTER DATABASE STOP LOGICAL STANDBY APPLY;
  ```

- Recreate the table using:

  ```
  EXEC DBMS_LOGSTDBY.INSTANTIATE_TABLE
  ('Schema_Name','TableName','DblinkName');
  ```

- Un-skip all the operations determined from the *dba_logstdby_skip* view for this table as explained above. The *dbms_logstdby.unskip* procedure can be used to UNSKIP a previously set filter.

- Start log apply service using:

  ```
  ALTER DATABASE START LOGICAL STANDBY APPLY;
  ```

Skipping a Table

The SQL Apply operation can be set to skip one or more tables from the set of objects maintained by the log apply service. This will be useful if there is a need to modify a subset of objects in the logical standby database independently of the primary database.

The Database Guard should be set to STANDBY for the log apply service to maintain only a subset of objects from the primary database. The following steps are required to set a table to be skipped by the log apply service. As an example, the table ITEM in the REPORTS schema will be excluded from the list of tables maintained by the log apply service:

- Stop the log apply service using:

  ```
  ALTER DATABASE STOP LOGICAL STANDBY APPLY;
  ```

- Set the Database Guard to STANDBY using:

  ```
  ALTER DATABASE GUARD STANDBY;
  ```

- Use the DBMS_LOGSTDBY.SKIP procedure to DML on the table:

  ```
  EXEC DBMS_LOGSTDBY.SKIP('DML','REPORTS','ITEM');
  ```

- Start the log apply service using:

  ```
  ALTER DATABASE START LOGICAL STANDBY APPLY;
  ```

UnSkipping a Table

The *unskip* procedure of the *dbms_logstdby* package to add a previously skipped table to the list of objects maintained by the SQL Apply operation. The steps required for this are similar to skipping a table. They are as follows:

- Stop the log apply service.

- Use the *dbms_logstdby.unskip* procedure to remove the filter. For example:

  ```
  EXEC DBMS_LOGSTDBY.UNSKIP
  ('DML','REPORTS','ITEM');
  ```

- Start the log apply service.

Query the *dba_logstdby_skip* view to verify the result of the UNSKIP operation.

There are several other statement options for the *dbms_logstdby.skip* and *unskip* procedure. They will be explained in detail in Chapter 10, *Data Guard PL/SQL Packages*.

Logical Standby Databases with Time Lag

As explained in the section, "Physical Standby Database with Time Lag", the time lag between the log transfer and the log apply service can be built using the DELAY attribute of the *log_archive_dest_n* initialization parameter on the primary database. This delay timer starts when the archived log is completely transferred to the standby site. The default value of the DELAY attribute is 30 minutes, but this value can be overridden as shown in the following example:

```
LOG_ARCHIVE_DEST_3='SERVICE=logdbstdby DELAY=60';
```

This parameter can be set using the ALTER SYSTEM statement or by restarting the primary database. The time lag specified by the initialization parameter can be overridden using the following procedure:

```
DBMS_LOGSTDBY.APPLY_SET('APPLY_DELAY',<TimeLag>)
```

The *dbms_logstdby* package provides another procedure called *apply_unset*, which can be used to cancel the time lag in case of failover to the logical standby database.

When Oracle does not failover, the DBA is the first target!

Resolving Archive Gap Sequence on Logical Standby Databases

Finding and resolving an archive gap sequence on a logical standby database is a similar process to the one used on the physical standby database. The SQL script, *find_gap.sql*, from the code depot can be used to get the missing sequence numbers. Once the name of the archived redo logs that are missing on the standby site are obtained, they can be transferred from the primary database local archive destination to the standby site and registered with the log apply service using the following statement. The log file name might need to be renamed to match the *log_archive_format* parameter on the standby site.

```
ALTER DATABASE REGISTER LOGICAL LOGFILE 'filespec';
```

For example:

```
ALTER DATABASE REGISTER LOGICAL LOGFILE
'/oracle/appsdb/arch/logstdby_1_607.dbf';
```

Repeat this statement for all missing archived log files.

Cascaded Standby Databases

The term "Cascaded Standby Database" is used to describe a setup where a standby database can feed its own set of standby databases. In this configuration, there are three layers of databases: the original primary database; standby databases originating from the primary database; and the cascaded standby databases. Using this setup, one primary database can have a maximum of 90 standby databases.

Although the creation of 90 standby databases may never be required for one primary database, this functionality can be fairly useful for offloading either reporting or backup activities to databases remotely located in a WAN without having the overhead of the primary database to transfer the archived log files to these standby databases over WAN. Figure 4.2 illustrates the cascaded databases configuration.

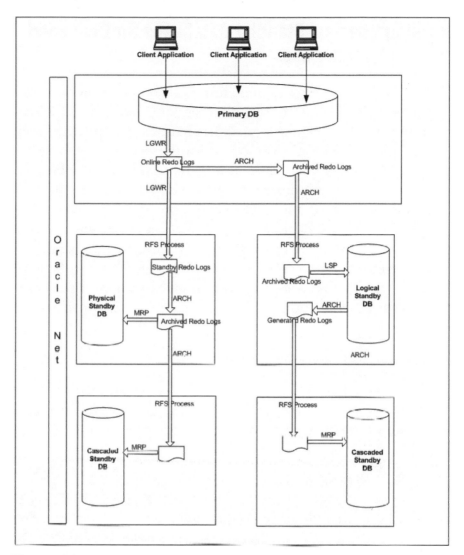

Figure 4.2 – *Cascaded Standby Database*

Cascaded standby databases can be setup from either a physical standby database or a logical standby database.

Using Physical Standby Databases for Cascaded Standby Databases

The *log_archive_dest_n* parameters will need to be set in the initialization file of the physical standby database to send the archived redo logs to cascaded destinations. The physical standby database will receive redo logs from the primary database in the form of standby redo logs and not archived redo logs. Hence, the log writer on the primary database will need to be set to write standby redo logs to this physical standby database. Also, standby redo logs will need to be created on the standby site so that the LGWR of the primary database can write to the standby redo logs using RFS process. The following statement can be used to create standby redo logs on the physical standby site. This will create a standby redo log group and add a log file of size 4 MB to it:

```
ALTER DATABASE ADD STANDBY LOGFILE GROUP 1
('/oracle/appsdb/redo/redo01.log') SIZE 4096K;
```

The same number of standby redo log groups and members as are present in the primary database must be created.

 WARNING - If the standby redo log on a physical standby database is full and is not archived, the primary database may wait or shutdown, depending on the protection mode setting. This will disrupt the database services provided by the primary database.

When the standby database is using standby redo logs, it will try to transfer, on log switch, the archived redo logs to all the destinations specified in the *init.ora* file using the *log_archive_dest_n* parameter. This may include other physical standby databases and the primary database along with cascaded archival destinations, if a symmetrical *init.ora* parameter file is being used.

The archival destination related to the cascaded standby database should be set to DEFER the in *init.ora* file on the primary database. For example, the following *init.ora* file specifies four archival destinations.

Destinations identified by service C_apps is pointing to the cascaded destination. The *log_archive_dest_state_4* is set to DEFER, so that the primary database will not try to send directly to this destination. After switchover, where the primary database will swap the role with standby database, this parameter can be altered to ENABLE, so that archiving to the cascaded destination can begin. The *log_archive_dest_2* is a physical standby database, which is supporting the cascaded standby databases. The log transfer method for this destination is set to LGWR.

The following is the *init.ora* file on the primary database:

```
#Archive
STANDBY_ARCHIVE_DEST='LOCATION-/oracle/appsdb/arch'
LOG_ARCHIVE_FORMAT=appsdb_%t_%s.dbf
LOG_ARCHIVE_START=TRUE
LOG_ARCHIVE_DEST_1='LOCATION=/oracle/meddb/arch'
LOG_ARCHIVE_DEST_2='SERVICE=appsstdby1 LGWR'
LOG_ARCHIVE_DEST_STATE_2=ENABLE
LOG_ARCHIVE_DEST_3='SERVICE=appsstdby2'
LOG_ARCHIVE_DEST_STATE_3=ENABLE
LOG_ARCHIVE_DEST_4='SERVICE-C_apps'
LOG_ARCHIVE_DEST_STATE_4=DEFER
```

Initialization parameter file on the physical standby database shows that the *log_archive_dest_state_4* parameter is set to ENABLE. As a result, the ARCH process on the standby site will transfer the archived redo logs to the cascaded destination.

The following is the *init.ora* file on a physical standby database:

```
#Archive
STANDBY_ARCHIVE_DEST='LOCATION=/oracle/appsdb/arch'
LOG_ARCHIVE_FORMAT=appsdb_%t_%s.dbf
LOG_ARCHIVE_START=TRUE
LOG_ARCHIVE_DEST_1='LOCATION=/oracle/appsdb/arch'
LOG_ARCHIVE_DEST_2='SERVICE=appsstdby1 LGWR'
LOG_ARCHIVE_DEST_STATE_2=ENABLE
LOG_ARCHIVE_DEST_3='SERVICE=appsstdby2'
LOG_ARCHIVE_DEST_STATE_3=ENABLE
LOG_ARCHIVE_DEST_4='SERVICE=C_apps'
LOG_ARCHIVE_DEST_STATE_4=ENABLE
```

Upon switchover or failover, this parameter should be changed to DEFER to stop the archival to the cascaded destination. As an option, the state can be set to DEFER for other standby databases connected to the primary database. To have a symmetrical *init.ora* file, the name of Oracle Net services should be consistent on all the sites.

Using Logical Standby Databases for Cascaded Standby Databases

The setup for transmitting archived redo logs from a logical standby database to the cascaded archive destination is similar to the one explained above for the physical standby database with the exception that a logical standby database cannot have standby redo logs. Therefore, the ARCH process from the primary database sends archived redo logs to the standby site. In this case, if the *init.ora* file of the logical standby database contains any archive destination pointing to other standby databases created directly from the primary database, these should be set to DEFER.

The archived redo logs produced by the logical standby database contain only the filtered data that has been generated and applied by SQL Apply operation. Because two layer of filtering are being introduced when a cascaded logical standby database is created from a logical standby database, the cascaded logical standby database may contain a very small set of objects from the primary database. Similarly, a cascaded physical standby database created from a logical standby database may not represent the actual primary database in its entirety.

Conclusion

This chapter dealt with the administration of standby databases. The topics covered in detail are as follows:

- General administration of physical and logical standby databases.

- Manually applying changes on standby databases that cannot be transmitted using log management services.

- Monitoring of log management services on standby databases.

- Determining and resolving archive gap sequence.

- Cascaded standby databases.

The next chapter will present log management services in detail.

Failure to recover is a major emergency!

Log Management Services

The personality of your Oracle database can change quickly

Introduction

The log management service is an integral part of Data Guard architecture. It is comprised of two components: Log Transport service and Log Apply service. The concept of Log Transport and Log Apply services are similar for a physical and logical standby database; however, there are differences at the detailed level of the working of log management for these two types of standby databases.

The processes involved and the architectural details of log transport and log apply services were provided in Chapter 2, "Data Guard Architecture". This chapter will mainly focus on the characteristics of these two services, influence of log transport service on the disaster recovery policies, and the implementation of various protection modes in Data Guard configuration.

In addition, it will briefly introduce the protection modes available in Release 1 of Oracle9i database for the benefit of a DBA running databases on Oracle9i Release 1.

Log Transport Services

The log transport service is responsible for the successful transmission of redo data from the primary database to a standby database over Oracle Net. In brief, the log transport service involves the log writer (LGWR) or archiver (ARCH or ARCn) process on the primary database site and the Remote File Server (RFS) on the standby database for transmission of data changes on the primary database in the form of redo records.

The choice of log writer or archiver on the primary database as the log transfer agent depends on the data protection mode. The standby database should be started and mounted in order for the log transport service to deliver archived redo log files to it. The DBA can opt to send either a complete archived redo log file or individual redo entries as these are generated on the primary database. For the latter, standby redo logs will have to be created on the standby site. The details on the method and form of redo transmission will be described in detail later in this chapter.

The log destination can be a physical standby database, a logical standby database or an archive log repository without any database files. The archive log destination without an underlying database is used as an alternate repository for archived logs from the primary database.

In some configurations, a common archive log repository can be set up to cater to more than one standby database as shown in Figure 5.1. In this scenario, the common archival destination receives archived redo logs from the primary database and transmits them to standby sites using Oracle Net. This setup can be very useful if the standby databases are remotely located over WAN, and the DBA does not want to put the performance of the primary database at risk while transferring archived redo logs.

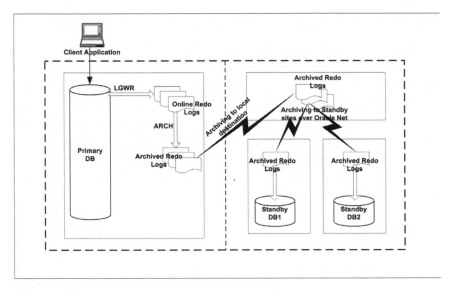

Figure 5.1 – *Log Archival to a common archive destination*

Log Apply Services

The other part of log management is the log apply service. The log apply service reads archived log files from the directory specified by the *standby_archive_dest* initialization parameter and in the format specified by the *log_archive_format* parameter. The concept of log application is very different between the two types of standby databases.

On the physical standby database, the log apply service uses the block-per-block media recovery method to apply the changes. The logical standby database utilizes the concept of LogMiner technology introduced in Oracle8i to convert the redo data into SQL statements and then applies those to the standby database using SQL Apply operation. In the following section, the log apply services on physical and logical standby databases will be detailed.

Physical Standby Database

On the physical standby database, the log apply service reads and applies redo logs when the database is in managed recovery mode. In this mode, a process called the Managed Recovery Process (MRP), which takes care of the complete recovery process, is initiated by the database. The MRP can be started using the following statement:

```
ALTER DATABASE RECOVER MANAGED STANDBY DATABASE DISCONNECT FROM
SESSION;
```

The RECOVER MANAGED STANDBY DATABASE statement was presented, in detail, in Chapter 3, *Standby Database Administration*.

The following diagram shows various processes of log management services on the physical standby database. In this diagram, log writer is used to transfer redo log entries from the primary to the standby database. Also, standby redo logs are created and used at the standby site. A log switch on the primary database triggers archiving on the standby database.

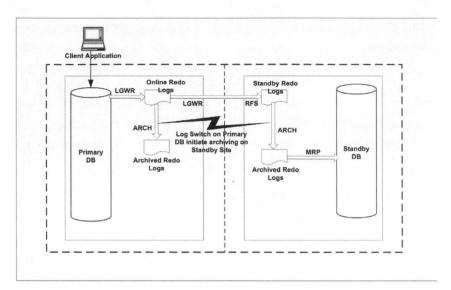

Figure 5.2 – *Log management service on physical standby database*

Logical Standby Database

The logical standby database provides a unique feature in which a database can coexist in recovery and query mode simultaneously. The log apply service on a logical standby database uses the LogMiner engine of Oracle database. When the log apply service is initiated on the standby database, the LogMiner engine reads the archived redo logs from the *standby_archive_dest* directory and converts these redo logs into SQL statements. These statements are then applied to standby database by SQL Apply operations. The log apply service can be started using:

```
ALTER DATABASE START LOGICAL STANDBY DATABASE APPLY;
```

When this statement is executed in the standby database, it starts a Logical Standby Process (LSP) which controls the MRP on the standby site.

The following diagram shows the complete log management service on a logical standby database. In this case, LGWR is configured for log transport.

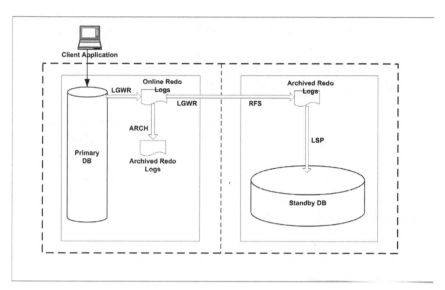

Figure 5.3 – *Showing Log Management Services on Logical Standby Database*

Log Management Policies

Log management policies play an important role in the disaster recovery strategy. These policies are largely guided by the importance of data in the database and the ability to recover the data using other sources like re-loading data from flat files, etc.

In a Data Guard environment, the log management policies are implemented using attributes of the *log_archive_dest_n* parameter. The attributes like MANDATORY, REOPEN, and ALTERNATE can be used to control the transmission of archived redo data. In this section, the attributes of the *log_archive_dest_n* and *log_archive_dest_state_n* parameters will be presented.

Factors Influencing Log Transport Policies

The *log_archive_dest_n* parameter has a vast number of attributes to control the working of log transfer services. The following attributes are important for setting up policies of log management services:

Online Redo Logs Reuse Policy

Online Redo logs on the primary database will be taken up for reuse based on the status of archiving to the log archive destinations. The archiving destinations can be set as MANDATORY or OPTIONAL destinations. For MANDATORY destinations, archiving should be completed before the online redo logs of the primary database can be marked for reuse. On the contrary, for OPTIONAL destinations, the log writer on the primary database will not wait for archiving to finish.

Setting the remote archiving destination to MANDATORY may have adverse effects on the primary database. If archiving to the mandatory destination fails or takes longer to complete, the primary database will suspend. This attribute setting should be evaluated in conjunction with the performance requirement of the database. This attribute can be set as shown below:

```
LOG_ARCHIVE_DEST_2 = 'SERVICE=appsstdby1 MANDATORY'
LOG_ARCHIVE_DEST_3 = 'SERVICE=appsstdby2 OPTONAL'
```

The default value is OPTIONAL for all types of archival destination. All 10 archive log destinations can be set as OPTIONAL, but it is recommended to keep at least one local archive destination as a MANDATORY location. Column BINDING of *v$archive_dest* view provides the information on this attribute.

Retrying Archiving to a Failed Destination

The *log_archive_dest_n* parameter has two attributes called REOPEN and MAX_FAILURE. These attributes can be set so that the archiver on the primary database will try to re-transmit the archived redo logs to the archive destination if the previous attempt of archival failed. The value of MAX_FAILURE specifies the number of times the archiver will try to re-transmit the log file before marking the destination as NOREOPEN. The value of REOPEN specifies the delay, in seconds, before the archiver makes another attempt to send log files. The REOPEN and MAX_FAILURE attributes can be specified as shown in the following example:

```
LOG_ARCHIVE_DEST_2 = 'SERVICE=appsstdby1 MANDATORY REOPEN=90
MAX_FAILURE=5'
```

The default value of REOPEN is 300 seconds. These parameters are not related to any specific type of failure. A heartbeat process on the primary database keeps polling the physical standby database. The frequency of polling is 60 seconds by default. When the REOPEN attribute is set, the heartbeat polling frequency changes to the REOPEN value. The minimum value of REOPEN can be 0 seconds, but the heartbeat will still poll the physical standby site every 60 seconds even if the REOPEN is set to less than 60 seconds. Hence, setting it to less than 60 seconds does not have any effect.

 WARNING – MAX_FAILURE attribute did not work in release 9.2.0.2 due to Bug 2449124. Check the metalink site for any bug fixes on this issue if the attribute is not working in the existing environment.

Archiving to an Alternate Destination

Using the ALTERNATE attribute of *log_archive_dest_n* and *log_archive_dest_state_n* parameters, an alternate archival destination can be setup. When log archiver on the primary database is unable to archive to the original archival destination, it attempts to write to alternate destinations. Moreover, if the REOPEN and MAX_FAILURE attribute is used, the alternate destination will not be enabled unless archiver completes the MAX_FAILURE number of attempts of archiving redo logs to the original destination.

In the following example, the log destination specified by *appsstdby1* has an alternate destination specified by the *log_archive_dest_4* parameter. If the archiver on the primary database is not able to archive logs to the *appsstdby1* standby database on two successive attempts at an interval of 90 seconds, it will write the log file in local file system */oracle/appsdb/arch_2* directory.

```
LOG_ARCHIVE_DEST_2='SERVICE=appsstdby1
REOPEN=90 MAX_FAILURE=2 ALTERNATE=LOG_ARCHIVE_DEST_4'
LOG_ARCHIVE_DEST_STATE_2=ENABLE
LOG_ARCHIVE_DEST_4=
'LOCATION=/oracle/appsdb/arch_2'
LOG_ARCHIVE_DEST_STATE_4=ALTERNATE
```

The primary database will not reuse the online redo log file if the log is archived to an alternate location for an archive destination defined as MANDATORY. If a destination is specified as listed below and the *appsstdby1* service is not accessible, the archiver will archive the redo file into the destination specified by *log_archive_dest_4*. The online redo log file, however, will not be marked as archived; therefore, it will not be re-used by log writer.

```
LOG_ARCHIVE_DEST_2='SERVICE=appsstdby1 MANDATORY REOPEN=0
ALTERNATE=LOG_ARCHIVE_DEST_4'
```

Dependence relationship between archival destinations

In some Data Guard configurations, the DBA may want to keep only one repository of archived redo logs and feed all the standby databases from this repository. In this kind of scenario, the physical archival of log files to one common location needs to be configured. Upon the successful archival of the log file, inform the dependent standby databases so that the recovery process on the standby databases can continue.

This is more like parent-child relationships between the log archival destinations. Using the DEPENDENCY attribute of the *log_archive_dest_n* parameter, such a parent-child relationship can be set. The validity of the child destination depends upon the success of archival in the parent archive destination. Also, the *standby_archive_dest* parameter needs to be updated on the standby databases to point to the location where the physical archiving will take place. The *log_archive_format* on the standby databases and the primary database should be the same; otherwise, the MRP process on the standby databases will not be able to identify the logs required for recovery.

In the following example, the redo logs will not be physically archived to the standby database pointed by *appsstdby1* service name. Instead, this destination is dependent on *log_archive_dest_1*. When a log file is archived to the */oracle/appsdb/arch* location, the name of archived redo log is registered in the standby database and the recovery process on the standby database reads the log file from the */oracle/appsdb/arch* directory:

```
LOG_ARCHIVE_DEST_1='LOCATION=/oracle/appsdb/arch
MANDATORY'
LOG_ARCHIVE_DEST_STATE_1=ENABLE
LOG_ARCHIVE_DEST_2='SERVICE=appsstdby1
DEPENDENCY=LOG_ARCHIVE_DEST_1'
LOG_ARCHIVE_DEST_STATE_2=ENABLE
```

Setting Time Lag between log transfer and log apply services

In order to minimize the risk of user error or data block corruption to the standby site, a time lag between log transfer and log apply services can be set. This can be achieved using the DELAY attribute of *log_archive_dest_n* parameter. The delay timer starts when the archived redo log is transferred to the standby destination. For example:

```
LOG_ARCHIVE_DEST_2='SERVICE=appsstdby1
DELAY=30'
```

The delay attribute is specified in minutes.

A Sample Log Management Policy

Combining the various attributes of the *log_archive_dest_n* parameter, a comprehensive log management policy can be built for a Data Guard environment. In this section, a sample policy for a configuration that includes a primary database and two standby databases will be presented. One standby database is on a local host and other is on a remote host in the LAN. Assume that the names of the databases are *appsdb*, *appsstdby1* and *appsstdby2*. Standby database *appsstdby1* is on the local host and *appsstdby2* is on the remote host. The following initialization parameters of the primary database show the log archival attributes:

```
#Init.ora file of primary database appsdb
LOG_ARCHIVE_DEST_1='LOCATION=/oracle/appsdb/arch MANDATORY
REOPEN=90 MAX_FAILURE=2 ALTERNATE=LOG_ARCHIVE_DEST_4'
LOG_ARCHIVE_DEST_STATE_1=ENABLE
LOG_ARCHIVE_DEST_2='SERVICE=appsstdby1
DEPENDENCY=LOG_ARCHIVE_DEST_1'
LOG_ARCHIVE_DEST_STATE_2=ENABLE
```

```
LOG_ARCHIVE_DEST_3='SERVICE=appsstdby2 REOPEN=90 MAX_FAILURE=5'
LOG_ARCHIVE_DEST_STATE_3=ENABLE
LOG_ARCHIVE_DEST_4='LOCATION=/oracle2/appsdb/arch'
LOG_ARCHIVE_DEST_STATE_4=ALTERNATE
```

According to this policy, the primary database physically archives the log file to the local destination on volume */oracle* and to the standby database identified by the service name *appsstdby2*. The local archival destination #1 is a mandatory destination. The primary database will halt if archival to this destination does not succeed. The log transfer service on the primary database will make two attempts to archive the redo log files to this destination as indicated by the *max_failure* parameter.

These attempts will be made at an interval of 90 seconds. If the archival is not successful, the log transfer service will try to archive the log files on volume */oracle2*. The standby database on the local host is dependent on the success of archival in archive destination #1 as specified by the DEPENDENCY attribute. Archival to the standby database on the remote host is optional; however, the log transfer service will make five attempts to archive the redo logs to this destination.

Depending on the data protection mode and the performance requirement of the environment, the DBA can choose from the list of attributes available for the *log_archive_dest_n* parameter and build a log management policy that suits the environment.

Standby Redo Logs

Standby redo logs are equivalent to online redo logs on a physical standby database. When standby redo logs are created on the standby site, the log transfer service updates the standby redo logs, which is then archived in the form of archive redo logs by the archiver process running on the standby site. Hence, the

ARCH or ARCn process must be started on the standby database if the standby redo logs are in use.

The way that the recovery process works is much the same. The Managed Recovery Process reads the archived redo log and applies the changes on to standby database. For maximum protection and maximum availability data protection mode, the standby redo logs must be created and the log writer configured on the primary database to participate in the log transfer. The data protection modes are explained in detail in the next section.

In order to avoid any wait in reuse of standby redo logs, it is recommended that one more standby redo log group be retained than the number of online redo log groups configured on the primary database. The maximum number of standby redo log groups and members per group can not exceed the *maxlogfiles* and *maxlogmembers* parameters specified during the creation of the primary database. Additionally, the size of standby redo logs should be same as that of online redo logs of the primary database; otherwise, RFS on the standby site will not use the standby redo logs.

Standby redo logs are not created automatically during the standby database creation, so they should be created when the data protection mode is changed to maximum protection or maximum availability. Executing the following SQL statement on standby database can create these logs:

```
ALTER DATABASE ADD STANDBY LOGFILE GROUP <n>
'filespec' SIZE 'size' K|M;
```

filespec is the full filename of log member, *size* is the size of log file, and *<n>* is the log group number.

A redo log member can be added to the existing standby redo log group using the following statement:

```
ALTER DATABASE ADD STANDBY LOGFILE MEMBER 'filespec' TO GROUP <n>;
```

After adding the standby log file, the script, *stdby_log.sql*, from code depot can be used to verify it:

🖫 stdby_log.sql

```
-- **************************************************
-- Copyright © 2004 by Rampant TechPress
-- This script is free for non-commercial purposes
-- with no warranties.  Use at your own risk.
--
-- To license this script for a commercial purpose,
-- contact info@rampant.cc
-- **************************************************

Set linesize 90
Column Group# Format 99
Column Filename format a50 Trunc
Column Logtype format a7
Column Status format a7
Column SizeinBytes format 999999999
Select
    s.GROUP# Group#,
    l.MEMBER Filename,
    l.TYPE Logtype,
    s.STATUS Status,
    s.BYTES SizeinBytes
From
    V$STANDBY_LOG s,
    V$LOGFILE l
Where
    s.GROUP# = l.GROUP#;
```

The following is a sample output from *stdby_log.sql* script.:

```
GROUP# FILENAME                           LOGTYPE STATUS     SIZEINBYTES
------ ---------------------------------- ------- ---------- -----------
     4 /oracle/stdbydb/redo/redo004.log STANDBY UNASSIGNED     1048576
     5 /oracle/stdbydb/redo/redo005.log STANDBY UNASSIGNED     1048576
```

In the next section, information other attributes of log transfer service that are useful for the configuration of various data protection modes will be presented.

Description of *remote_archive_enable* Parameter

The *remote_archive_enable* initialization parameter controls the transfer and acceptance of redo data in standby database configuration. It can take four different values: TRUE; FALSE; SEND; and RECEIVE.

The TRUE value allows both transmission and acceptance of redo data, whereas FALSE disables any redo exchange between the primary and the standby database. The parameter can be set to SEND or RECEIVE to selectively allow transmission or reception of redo respectively. Usually, it can be set to SEND on the primary database and RECEIVE on the standby database for the normal functioning of standby configuration. For a cascaded standby database environment, it should be set to TRUE on the standby site.

Log Transport Service Transmission Attributes

In addition to the attributes specific to log management policies, the *log_archive_dest_n* parameter has other characteristics that influence the data protection mode. In fact, the text in this section builds the foundation of standby database protection modes, which will be covered in the next section. This section covers information on the transmission and reception of redo records from the primary to the standby database and attributes of the *log_archive_dest_n* parameter that controls the data protection modes. The following can be specified using *log_archive_dest_n* parameter:

- Process to transfer redo data.

- Network characteristics to be used for redo transmission.

- Acknowledging disk I/O operations on the standby database during redo data transfer.

The following sections include information on each of these characteristics in detail.

Process to Transfer Redo Data

Log writer (LGWR) or archiver (ARCH) can be configured on the primary database site to transfer the redo data to the standby database. When LGWR is specified as the process responsible for transferring redo records, the standby database receives redo data as it is being generated on the primary database. In case of ARCH, the archived redo logs are transferred when a log switch occurs on the primary database.

For a no-data-loss environment, the LGWR should be used to transfer redo to the standby site even though the default process for the log transfer service is ARCH. The following example shows sample settings for LGWR and ARCH in *init.ora* file:

```
LOG_ARCHIVE_DEST_3='SERVICE=appsstdby1 LGWR'
LOG_ARCHIVE_DEST_4='SERVICE=appsdtby2 ARCH'
```

It is possible to switch between ARCH and LGWR for the log transfer service using the ALTER SYSTEM statement. The change will not take effect until a log switch occurs on the primary database, so for an immediate change, the current log file should be archived.

Network Characteristics Influencing Redo Transmission

In addition to the process for the log transfer service, the network attribute for the data transfer over Oracle Net layer can be specified. This option is only available when log writer is used to transfer redo to the standby site. The DBA can choose between the SYNC and ASYNC attributes of the *log_archive_dest_n* parameter.

SYNC is the synchronized transfers of redo data from the primary to the standby site. When synchronous transfer is in use, the LGWR does not write any redo entry in the online log file of the primary site until the initiated log transfer has passed the network layer successfully. The LGWR will not wait for acknowledgment receipts of the disk I/O operation of redo data on the standby site.

If more than one standby site is in use and LGWR is serving all of these for log transfer, a synchronous transfer mode will cause the LGWR to wait until all of the archival destinations receive data over the network layer. This may cause a severe performance issue on the primary database.

To ease the performance problem, Oracle has provided the option of setting the PARALLEL or NOPARALLEL synchronous data transfer to multiple standby sites. The recommended option is to use the PARALLEL transfer mode, which will initiate synchronous but parallel data transfer.

For example, if there are three standby sites and LGWR is sending redo data to these three standby sites in SYNC mode, setting the SYNC=PARALLEL will start three parallel slave processes to these three standby sites. LGWR on the primary site will resume writing to the online log file when the last parallel slave completes the log transfer. NOPARALLEL, as the name suggests, will initiate serial transfer of redo data to multiple standby databases.

ASYNC mode provides better performance of the primary database at an expense of small memory within the primary database. The ASYNC attribute is specified with a memory size in the System Global Area of the primary database that is used to buffer the redo data before sending to the standby site. Log writer sends the buffered redo to the standby site in one of the following events:

- A log switch occurs on primary database.

- Buffer to keep redo data is full and LGWR needs to clear it to write new redo data.

- The primary or standby database is shutdown normally.

In this mode, the log writer does not wait for the network I/O operation to complete before generating new redo on the primary site. This buffer is written at the same time as the log buffer of the primary database and not the online redo log files. In case of abnormal shutdown, data from this buffer as well as the log buffer will be discarded and a no-data-loss environment will be maintained. The value of ASYNC attribute is specified in terms of db blocks. The default value is 2048 blocks and the maximum can be 20480 blocks. The default setting for network I/O attribute of the *log_archive_dest_n* parameter is SYNC.

The following examples show settings of SYNC and ASYNC:

```
LOG_ARCHIVE_DEST_3='SERVICE=appsstdby1 LGWR SYNC=PARALLEL'
LOG_ARCHIVE_DEST_4='SERVICE=appsstdby2 LGWR ASYNC=4096'
```

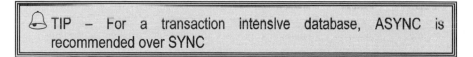

🔔 TIP – For a transaction intensive database, ASYNC is recommended over SYNC

Acknowledging Redo Disk I/O Operation on the Standby Database

A log transfer service can be built that waits for redo data to be written completely and successfully on the standby site before it will allow the primary database to make any further modifications. This guarantees that the data on the primary database is available on the standby site. The AFFIRM attribute of the *log_archive_dest_n* parameter can be used with LGWR for this purpose, but it will affect the performance of the primary database. This attribute is compliant with both LGWR and ARCH process for log transfer.

When AFFIRM is used with LGWR, the log writer will wait for the disk I/O to complete on the standby site before the control is returned to application. Similarly, when it is used with ARCH, the archiver will not release online redo logs for LGWR to reuse until the redo log is completely and successfully archived on the standby site. The default setting is NOAFFIRM. The following example shows a sample setting:

```
LOG_ARCHIVE_DEST_3='SERVICE=appsstdby1 LGWR AFFIRM'
```

The script, *log_dest_attr.sql*, from code depot to see the attributes of the log transfer service in the operating environment. A sample output of this script is shown below:

🖫 **log_dest_attr.sql**

```
-- ****************************************************
-- Copyright © 2004 by Rampant TechPress
-- This script is free for non-commercial purposes
-- with no warranties.  Use at your own risk.
--
-- To license this script for a commercial purpose,
-- contact info@rampant.cc
-- ****************************************************

Set pagesize 100
Set linesize 95
Column DEST_NAME format a20 TRUNC
Column BINDING format a9
Column REOPEN_SECS format 999
Column ALTERNATE format a20 TRUNC
Column DEPENDENCY format a20 TRUNC
Column TRANSMIT_MODE format a12
Column ASYNC_BLOCKS format 99999
Column AFFIRM format a3
Select
    DEST_NAME,
    BINDING,
    REOPEN_SECS,
```

```
   ALTERNATE,
   DEPENDENCY,
   TRANSMIT_MODE,
   Decode(TRANSMIT_MODE,'ASYNCHRONOUS',ASYNC_BLOCKS,0)
         ASYNC_BLOCKS,
   AFFIRM
From
   V$ARCHIVE_DEST;
```

```
DEST_NAME      BINDING   REOPEN_SECS ALTERNATE  DEPENDENCY TRANSMIT_MOD ASYNC_BLOCKS AFF
----------     --------  ----------- ---------- ---------------------- ------------ ---

LOG_ARCHIVE_DEST_1 OPTIONAL 300        NONE       NONE       SYNCHRONOUS  0            NO
LOG_ARCHIVE_DEST_2 OPTIONAL 300        NONE       NONE       SYNCHRONOUS  0            NO
LOG_ARCHIVE_DEST_3 OPTIONAL 300        NONE       NONE       ASYNCHRONOUS 2048         NO
```

In the following section, the combined use of these three characteristics to build various levels of the data protection mode is presented.

Standby Database Protection Modes

Protecting data of the primary database in case of any disaster is the whole purpose of Data Guard technology. Data Guard provides different levels of protection modes that can be configured to suit the need. Importance of data in the database and the ability to recover it from other sources are vital factors in deciding the protection mode. The higher the level of data protection, the more the performance of the primary database will be affected. Therefore, the performance requirement of the environment is another factor to consider.

The database protection mode is established using the attributes of log transport services which has already been covered in detail. This section will present the combined usage of those attributes to implement a data protection strategy. The protection modes have changed significantly between Oracle 9i Release 1 and Release 2, and will be described separately in this section.

Protection Modes in Oracle9i Release 1

The data protection modes in Release 1 of Oracle9i can be categorized into the following four classes:

- Guaranteed Protection
- Instant Protection
- Rapid Protection
- Delayed Protection

These four protection modes offer varying degrees of synchronization between the primary and the standby database and the amount of data loss during disaster recovery.

Guaranteed Protection Mode

The guaranteed protection mode falls in the category of 'no-data-divergence'. In this case, a transaction on the primary database is not acknowledged as complete until one of the participating standby databases has received the redo data for recovery. The primary database shuts down if the redo data cannot be transmitted to at least one participating standby database. This mode offers the highest level of data protection at the expense of performance and availability of the primary database. The following attributes of the *log_archive_dest_n* parameter should be used to setup log transfer service for guaranteed protection mode:

```
LOG_ARCHIVE_DEST_3='SERVICE=appsstdby1 LGWR SYNC AFFIRM';
```

Moreover, create standby redo logs need to be created on the standby database so it can receive redo data synchronously from the primary database. The following statement should be executed on the primary database to set the failure resolution policy:

```
ALTER DATABASE SET STANDBY DATABASE PROTECTED;
```

Instant Protection Mode

This protection mode offers a 'no-data-loss' environment with enhanced availability of the primary database. The primary database will not shut down if it cannot transmit redo data to the participating standby database. Instead, the data on the primary database will temporarily diverge from the standby database. During this period, the protection mode is lowered to the Rapid Protection mode.

Once the connectivity to a standby database is reestablished, the archived redo logs are transmitted to the standby site. It can be argued that some data may be lost in this mode if the primary database crashes when the standby database has been lowered to the rapid protection mode. In addition, un archived redo logs could be lost during the primary database crash.

The *log_archive_dest_n* parameter settings and standby redo log requirements are the same as the one for guaranteed protection mode. The failure resolution policy is unprotected which allows data divergence when the last participating standby database is unreachable for archiving. The following statement can be used to set the failure resolution policy:

```
ALTER DATABASE SET STANDBY DATABASE UNPROTECTED;
```

Rapid Protection Mode

In this mode, the primary database does not wait for the acknowledgements of the redo data transfer to any standby database. This offers a high level of performance and availability of the primary database. This constitutes a 'minimal-data-loss'

Data Guard environment. A sample setting for the log transport service for rapid protection is shown in the following example:

```
LOG_ARCHIVE_DEST_3='SERVICE=appsstdby1 LGWR ASYNC=2048 NOAFFIRM';
```

Standby redo logs are required at the standby site because the log writer transfers redo data from the primary database. The failure resolution policy should be set to unprotected.

Delayed Protection Mode

This offers another 'minimal-data-loss' Data Guard configuration. The archiver process transmits archived redo logs from the primary database to the standby database. The *log_archive_dest_n* setting is very simple and is shown below:

```
LOG_ARCHIVE_DEST_3='SERVICE=appsstdby1'.
```

Standby redo logs are not needed on the standby site. The failure resolution policy should be set to unprotected.

Protection Modes in Oracle9i Release 2

Although the types of data protection mode have been reduced in number from four to three in Release 2 of Oracle9i, there has been no significant conceptual change in the protection modes. It supports the same two important 'no-data-loss' and 'minimum-data-loss' protection levels.

The 'no-data-loss' level has two protection modes called MAXIMUM PROTECTION and MAXIMUM AVAILABILITY. MAXIMUM AVAILABILITY is not strictly a 'no-data-loss' protection level and can be categorized in either of the two classes.

MAXIMUM PROTECTION

The MAXIMUM PROTECTION mode, as the name suggests, guarantees a 'no-data-loss' configuration in any scenario. MAXIMUM PROTECTION mode can be only established using a physical standby database. A logical standby database cannot be used for maximum protection. A transaction on the primary database is not considered complete until it has been posted to at least one of the standby databases that satisfy all the attribute requirements for this mode.

The primary database halts if the transaction cannot complete on at least one standby database that is participating in providing this protection level.

The following attribute of the *log_archive_dest_n* parameter is required in order to include a physical standby database in maximum protection configuration:

```
LOG_ARCHIVE_DEST_3='SERVICE=appsstdby1 LGWR SYNC=PARALLEL AFFIRM';
```

In the above example, the assumption is that the *appsstdby1* service is pointing to a physical standby database. The PARALLEL attribute of SYNC is not required but will be useful if more than one physical standby database is included in maximum protection configuration.

In addition to the setting on the primary database, standby redo logs need to be created on all standby sites participating in maximum protection configuration. The following statement can be used to switch a primary database into MAXIMUM PROTECTION mode. The primary database should be mounted but not open to execute this statement:

```
ALTER DATABASE SET STANDBY DATABASE TO MAXIMIZE PROTECTION;
```

WARNING – Performance and availability of the primary database is at risk in MAXIMUM PROTECTION mode if adequate network bandwidth and computing resources cannot be provided for the standby database.

MAXIMUM AVAILABILITY

MAXIMUM AVAILABILITY is another 'no-data-loss' protection mode. It can be argued that it can be placed somewhere between the 'no-data-loss' and 'minimal-data-loss' category. The setup of maximum availability protection is the same as maximum protection. In MAXIMUM AVAILABILITY mode, the primary database does not halt if it cannot transmit redo data to at least one participating standby database. During this period the protection mode is switched to MAXIMUM PERFORMANCE, the lowest level of data protection.

When Data Guard is in MAXIMUM PERFORMANCE mode, data can potentially be lost if the primary database crashes and the redo logs have not been transferred to any archival destination. The protection mode is upgraded to MAXIMUM AVAILABILITY on next log switch if the log transfer service has resumed transmission of the redo data to at least one standby database participating in maximum availability configuration and all the archive gap sequences have been resolved.

A logical standby database can also participate in MAXIMUM AVAILABILITY mode. Only the availability of the primary database is enhanced in this mode. The performance issues are the same as for MAXIMUM PROTECTION mode. The following statement should be executed on the primary database to put it in a maximum availability Data Guard configuration. The primary database should be mounted but not open to execute this statement:

```
ALTER DATABASE SET STANDBY DATABASE TO MAXIMIZE AVAILABILITY;
```

MAXIMUM PERFORMANCE

This is the lowest data protection mode. In this mode, service on the primary database is independent of the redo log transfer to standby databases. The performance of the primary database is not affected because the primary database does not wait for the log transport service to complete. MAXIMUM PERFORMANCE mode is the default mode. The DBA can choose between LGWR and ARCH for the transfers of redo logs.

The network I/O attribute should be ASYNC when LGWR is writing redo logs on the standby database. Also, the disk I/O attribute should be NOAFFIRM to minimize any performance impact on the primary site. The following examples show the MAXIMUM PERFORMANCE mode settings:

```
LOG_ARCHIVE_DEST_2='SERVICE=appsstdby1 LGWR ASYNC NOAFFIRM'
```

Or:

```
LOG_ARCHIVE_DEST_2='SERVICE=appsstdby1 ARCH'
```

Or simply:

```
LOG_ARCHIVE_DEST_2='SERVICE=appsstdby1'
```

The following statement will put the primary database in MAXIMUM PERFORMANCE mode:

```
ALTER DATABASE SET STANDBY DATABASE TO MAXIMIZE PERFORMANCE;
```

The script, *db_protection.sql,* from the code depot can be used to find the current protection mode of the database. This should be

---

Standby Database Protection Modes

executed on the primary database. The *protection_level* column in the output shows the aggregated protection level for all the standby databases in the configuration:

🖫 db_protection.sql

```
-- ****************************************************
-- Copyright © 2004 by Rampant TechPress
-- This script is free for non-commercial purposes
-- with no warranties.  Use at your own risk.
--
-- To license this script for a commercial purpose,
-- contact info@rampant.cc
-- ****************************************************

Select
    NAME,
    PROTECTION_MODE,
    PROTECTION_LEVEL
From
    V$DATABASE;
```

A sample output from the script shows the current protection level:

```
NAME       PROTECTION_MODE      PROTECTION_LEVEL
---------  -------------------- --------------------
APPSDB     MAXIMUM PERFORMANCE  MAXIMUM PERFORMANCE
```

Conclusion

This chapter on log management service presented concise information regarding log transport and log apply services. In particular, the following topics were covered:

- Applying redo logs on logical and physical standby databases.

- Attributes of log transport services and designing log management policy for Data Guard environment.

- Standby redo logs concept and implementation.

- Characteristics of the log transport service influencing the data protection modes.

- Data protection modes concept and implementation in Release 1 and Release 2 of Oracle9i.

- Small SQL scripts provided to assist in gathering information about log management service.

The next chapter will present details on switchover and failover to standby databases.

Switchover and Failover

"I think it might be a network problem."

Introduction

A standby database in a Data Guard configuration is created and maintained to transition into the role of the primary database in case of an emergency. In addition to a disaster recovery situation, the DBA may want to transition a standby database into the primary role in order to perform certain types of maintenance activities on the original primary database. This process of role transition is facilitated using switchover and failover operations. This chapter will describe the role transition process in detail.

In brief, the switchover operation is a planned transition to allow maintenance work on the primary database. The failover is performed to re-establish database services if the primary database becomes unavailable and cannot be recovered within a reasonable period of time. Before deciding to activate a standby database using failover, the effects of the transition on your Data Guard configuration, the amount of time it will require for the transition, and the potential loss of data should be carefully examined.

In most cases, it is easier and more advantageous to recover the primary database than to use role transition. However, it should be noted that Data Guard technology is designed and intended to help in a disaster recovery situation. Evaluate the failure scenario to determine if it requires a disaster recovery or if it can be repaired using traditional recovery operations.

The following figures show a graphical representation of role transition in a Data Guard environment. Figure 6.1 shows the usual working relationship between the primary and standby databases in the Data Guard environment. Figure 6.2 shows the transient state when the primary database is being switched over to a standby database, Standby DB1. Figure 6.3 shows the Data Guard environment after the switchover operation.

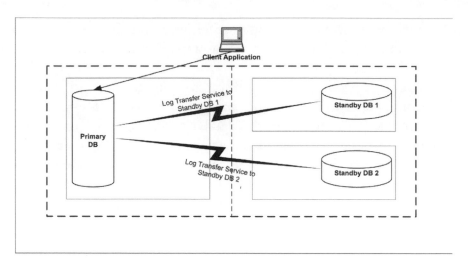

Figure 6.1 – *One primary and two standby databases in Data Guard Environment*

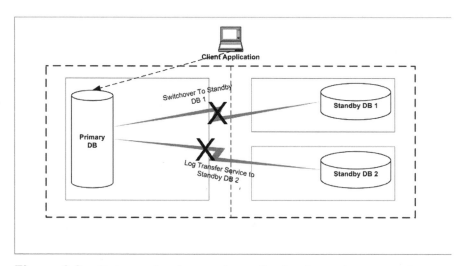

Figure 6.2 – *Primary database and standby databases during switchover*

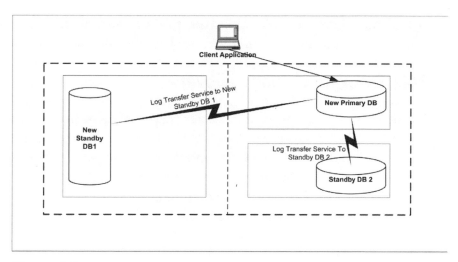

Figure 6.3 – *Data Guard environment after switchover*

Types of Database Role Transitions

Oracle9i supports two types of role transitions: *switchover* and *failover*. The failover transition can be further categorized into *graceful* failover and *forced* failover depending on the amount of data lost during the failover operation. The following sections will present these role transitions in detail.

Role Transition Using Switchover

A switchover operation is a smooth transition of a standby database into the primary role and the primary database into a standby role. This is a two-way activity. During a switchover operation, no data is lost; however, the database services may be affected for the period of time that the databases are switching their roles.

Switchover operation is ideal for performing maintenance activities on the original primary database. These maintenance activities cannot include an upgrade of Oracle software because in a Data Guard configuration, the primary and all the standby databases should be running the same Oracle software release.

Role Transition Using Failover

A failover operation is a true disaster recovery operation. Failover to one of the standby database in Data Guard configuration is performed when the original primary database is damaged beyond easy and timely recovery. Contrary to switchover, a failover operation is a one-way operation that transforms the standby database into the primary database.

After the failover, the original primary database is removed from the Data Guard configuration. Other standby databases may or may not be affected depending on the type of failover. Based on the amount of data loss and the impact on other standby databases in the Data Guard configuration, the failover operation can be classified into two categories.

Graceful Failover

A graceful failover is similar to a switchover operation except that in a graceful failover the original primary database is discarded. Graceful failover reduces the amount of data loss and the impact on other standby databases. A graceful failover is ideally suited for physical standby databases, in which standby redo logs can be created and maintained. Graceful failover supports the recovery of all possible redo data from the standby redo log file or the archived redo log file before switching the standby database over to the primary database.

Depending on the type of protection mode, failover can occur with no data loss or minimal data loss. In some cases, even if the primary database is running in maximum protection mode, it may not be possible to recover all the redo data from the standby redo log file. One such situation is a corrupt standby redo log file during the disaster of the primary database. Fortunately, the probability of these two events occurring simultaneously is negligible. Details of graceful failover will be presented later in this chapter.

Forced Failover

A forced failover operation can result in data loss. However, the amount of data loss can be minimized by copying the online log files and the archived redo log files from the original primary database and registering with the standby database. As a result, the amount of data that can be saved depends on the kind of failure on the primary database.

If archived redo logs and online redo logs are damaged in the primary database failure, a certain amount of data loss is unavoidable. The forced failover operation is achieved using the ALTER DATABASE ACTIVATE STANDBY DATABASE statement. If forced failover is used, the other standby databases in the configuration should be re-created from the new primary database. The forced failover option in the failover to a logical standby database section will be revisited later in this chapter.

> Always perform a graceful failover when failing over to a physical standby database irrespective of the data protection mode of the original primary database.

Standby Database for Role Transition

One of the most important tasks in the failover scenario is to find the best suitable standby database in the Data Guard configuration to be used for failover. The rules governing the best suitable standby database largely depend on the business requirements and the trade off between loss of data and the amount of time allowed for failover. In general, the following guidelines can be used to determine a suitable standby database:

- **Rule 1:** A physical standby database should be always given precedence over a logical standby database. This usually minimizes the loss of data and the impact on other standby databases in a Data Guard configuration.

- **Rule 2:** A physical standby database with the highest level of data protection should have higher preference. This will ensure minimal loss of data.

- **Rule 3:** Choose the physical standby database that the most recent archived redo logs have been applied. This will ensure minimal time for recovery.

- **Rule 4:** A logical standby database should be chosen only if there is no physical standby database in a Data Guard configuration or a physical standby database cannot be used for some other reason. Rule#2 and #3 remains the same for a logical standby database.

Disadvantages of Transitioning to a Logical Standby Database

A logical standby database provides the extraordinary feature of simultaneous recovery and reporting in a Data Guard environment. However, it is not recommended to transition to a logical standby database due to the following reasons:

- There are limitations on a logical standby database in terms of permissible data types and database operations. Information on these limitations is presented in Chapter 3. As a result, it is very likely that a logical standby database is not a true copy of the primary database; therefore, transitioning to a logical standby database may only provide a subset of functionality as delivered by the primary database.

- If there are any physical standby databases in the configuration, the physical standby database needs to be created from the new primary database after the transition.

- Usually, role transition to a logical standby database takes longer than transition to a physical standby database.

Switchover Operation

In this section, the detailed procedure for switching over to a physical or logical standby database will be presented. Preparation on both the primary and the standby database site must be completed in order to minimize the impact on service during role transition.

Preparing the Primary Database for Switchover

A switchover operation begins on the primary database and ends on the standby database. At the end of the switchover, the original primary database assumes the role of the standby site and vice versa. There are a few things that should always be checked before initiating a switchover. These checks can be categorized in the following three classes:

- Check for initialization parameters - A symmetrical initialization parameter file should always be used on the primary and all standby databases. A symmetrical *init.ora* file is explained in Chapter 3. For example, the *init.ora* file from the primary database is shown below.

- In this example file, there are only two archival destinations. A local destination and a remote destination specified by service name "stdby2". The *fal_server* and *fal_client* parameters will be used only after the role transition:

```
STANDBY_ARCHIVE_DEST='LOCATION=
/oracle/appsdb/archstd'
LOG_ARCHIVE_FORMAT=appsdb_%t_%s.dbf
LOG_ARCHIVE_START=TRUE
LOG_ARCHIVE_DEST_1='LOCATION=/oracle/appsdb/arch'
LOG_ARCHIVE_DEST_2='SERVICE=stdby2'
LOG_ARCHIVE_DEST_STATE_2=ENABLE
LOG_ARCHIVE_TRACE=255
REMOTE_ARCHIVE_ENABLE=TRUE
FAL_SERVER=stdby2
FAL_CLIENT=appsprim
```

- Check that the Oracle Net connection can be established between the primary and the standby database.

- Check the protection mode of the primary database by using the script, *db_protection.sql,* from code depot,. If the protection mode is anything other than MAXIMUM PERFOMANCE, use the following statement to change the protection mode:

```
ALTER DATABASE SET STANDBY DATABASE TO MAXIMIZE PERFORMANCE;
```

- Check the switchover status of the primary database by using the following statement. The switchover status should be "TO STANDBY":

```
SELECT
    SWITCHOVER_STATUS
FROM
    V$DATABASE;
```

Preparing the Standby Database for Switchover

The preparation of the standby database is explained in the following two sections:

Physical Standby Database

On the physical standby database, the following checks should be performed before starting the switchover operation:

- If a symmetrical initialization parameter file is not being used, update the initialization parameter file on the physical standby database to include all other standby databases and the original primary database as the log archive destination.

- The database should be mounted as the standby database. The standby database can be in managed recovery mode or open for read only. If the database is open for query, the switchover operation will take longer to complete.

- Verify that the standby database is in ARCHIVELOG mode. The standby database should be placed in ARCHIVELOG mode before switching over the role.

- If any delay in the log apply service has been set for the physical standby database to be switched over as the primary, reset the delay to ZERO.

Logical Standby Database

Before switching over to a logical standby database, the following checks should be performed to ensure a minimal impact on service during the switchover operation:

- The initialization parameter file should be updated to include the other logical standby databases and the original primary database as the archival destination so that the new primary database will start transmitting the redo data after the switchover operation.

- The logical standby database to be converted into the primary database should be open and the log apply service should be running.

- The logical standby database should be running in ARCHIVELOG mode.

- All delays in the log apply service should be removed using the DBMS_LOGSTDBY package. The following statement can be used to remove the delay in the log application:

```
DBMS_LOGSTDBY.APPLY_UNSET ('APLY_DELAY');
```

- Ensure that the logical standby database is in sync with the primary database. This will minimize the overall time required for the switchover operation.

Switchover to a Physical Standby Database

After performing the initial verifications on the primary and the standby database, the switchover operation is ready to be performed. The switchover operation involves changing the original primary database role to standby and one of the physical standby databases to primary. During this operation, the database service will be unavailable for the period of time when the primary is converted to standby but the standby has not yet changed roles. Creating redo logs on the standby database prior to the switchover operation can minimize the downtime. Make sure there are no users connected to the database during the switchover operation. Connect to the primary site and execute the following steps:

- Convert the primary database to the standby database using following statement:

```
ALTER DATABASE COMMIT TO SWITCHOVER TO PHYSICAL STANDBY;
```

- Shutdown the original primary database and mount it as a standby database using the following statement:

```
SHUTDOWN IMMEDIATE;
STARTUP NOMOUNT;
ALTER DATABASE MOUNT STANDBY DATABASE;

ALTER DATABASE RECOVER MANAGED STANDBY DATABASE DISCONNECT FROM
SESSION;
```

- Connect to the physical standby database that is taking the role of the new primary database and execute the following statement to verify the switchover status:

```
Select
    Switchover_status
From
    V$DATABASE;
```

Output:

```
SWITCHOVER_STATUS
------------------
TO PRIMARY
```

- On the standby database, after the primary database is switched over, the switchover status of TO PRIMARY indicates that the standby database is ready for role transition.

- Execute the following statement to transition the role of the standby database to the primary:

```
ALTER DATABASE COMMIT TO SWITCHOVER TO PRIMARY;
```

- This statement will convert the standby database to the primary role. The online log files were not created during the standby database creation, this statement will create the physical files for the online redo logs. The time taken to complete the transition depends on the size of the online redo logs of the original primary database. Once this step is complete, the new primary database is ready to be restarted.

- If the standby database and the primary database reside on the same host machine and the *lock_name_space* parameter is being used for the standby database, the following warning will appear in the alert log file when restarting the new primary database:

 "WARNING: Setting LOCK_NAME_SPACE on non-standby database can be very dangerous. It may even cause database corruption. Use it with caution"

- It is recommended that this parameter be used on the new standby database and also removed from the new primary database. In addition to the *lock_name_space* parameter, the *instance_name* parameter of both the databases involved in the switchover and the Oracle Net entries will need to be updated to reflect the correct instance names. This is not required if the primary and standby databases involved in the switchover are located on two different hosts.

Switchover to a Logical Standby Database

This section will provide the steps required to perform switchover to the logical standby database. A logical standby database should only be considered in situations when there are no physical standby databases in the Data Guard configuration, or there is only one physical standby database that shares the host machine with the primary database. The host machine will become unavailable for some time after the switchover for maintenance. The following steps should be executed to switchover to a logical standby database:

- Before starting the switchover process, stop all connections to the primary database. A quiet database always speeds up the switchover operation.

- The first step in the switchover process is to commit the primary database as the logical standby database. Connect to the primary database as a user having SYSDBA privilege and execute this statement:

```
ALTER DATABASE COMMIT TO SWITCHOVER TO LOGICAL STANDBY;
```

- The next step is to convert the logical standby database into the primary database. Connect to the logical standby database as a user having SYSDBA privilege and execute the following statement:

```
ALTER DATABASE COMMIT TO SWITCHOVER TO PRIMARY;
```

- Optionally, the entire archive log destination can be disabled on the original primary database using ALTER SYSTEM statements.

- Create a database link on all other logical standby databases in the Data Guard configuration and link the original primary database to the new primary database. The *dbms_logstdby* package can be used to temporarily bypass the database guard on logical standby databases to create the database link. On the new primary database, grant the SELECT_CATALOG_ROLE to the database user account to be used for the database link. The database link is required for future switchover operations; therefore, this step is optional at this time.

 Switchover to a logical standby database will invalidate all the physical standby databases in the Data Guard configuration.

Verify Switchover Operation

A successful switchover operation will initiate transmission of redo data from the new primary database to standby databases, including the original primary database in the Data Guard configuration. To verify the switchover operation, archive the current log file on the new primary database and check the STANDBY_ARCHIVE_DEST directory on the standby databases.

If Oracle Net is configured properly, the new archived log should appear in this directory on all the standby databases. Query a standby database to verify that the recent changes on the new primary database are propagated and applied to the standby databases.

If the switchover was to a logical standby database, only check the other logical standby database and the original primary database for new archived log files.

Failover Operation

A failover operation is a true disaster recovery operation. A failover operation should only be considered when all of the alternative options for primary database recovery are not feasible. This section will detail the step-by-step procedure for failover operation to the physical and logical standby database.

Failover to a Physical Standby Database

A failover to a physical standby database is considered a 'graceful' failover. This is similar to a switchover operation except that the original primary database will have to be discarded after the failover. Depending on the protection mode of the primary database, the graceful failover can recover all data resulting in minimal or no data loss. The next step is to study the overall procedure for a graceful failover to a physical standby database. Use the following procedure when the data protection mode is in MAXIMUM PROTECTION or MAXIMUM AVAILABILITY:

- Before starting the failover operation, update the initialization parameter file on the physical standby database that is used for failover. Include other standby databases in the Data Guard environment used as the archival destination so that after the failover, the redo data can be archived from the new primary database to other standby databases.

- In order to initiate the failover operation, the target physical standby database should be placed in MAXIMUM PERFORMANCE data protection mode using the following statement:

```
ALTER DATABASE SET STANDBY DATABASE TO MAXIMIZE PERFORMANCE.
```

- Allow the MRP to finish applying the redo data from the archived redo log file and the standby redo log files. If the database was running in MAXIMUM PROTECTION or

MAXIMUM AVAILABILITY mode prior to loss of the primary database, there should be no requirement to manually transfer and register any archived or partial online log file from the primary database. Issuing the following statement will cause the MRP to terminate when it has applied all the available redo data:

```
ALTER DATABASE RECOVER MANAGED STANDBY DATABASE FINISH;
```

- If the standby redo log files on the target physical standby database are corrupt, or it is not desirable to apply the changes that are in the standby redo log file, MRP can be completed by skipping the standby redo logs by using the following statement:

```
ALTER DATABASE RECOVER MANAGED STANDBY DATABASE FINISH SKIP
STANDBY LOGFILE;
```

- One such scenario is when the DBA want to recover from application or user error and the data within the standby log file contains the error and the DBA does not want to post it in the database.

- Once the MRP has finished applying all the redo data, issue the following statement to transition the physical standby database to the primary role. Status of managed recovery process can be obtained from the *v$managed_standby* view or from the alert log file.

```
ALTER DATABASE COMMIT TO SWITCHOVER TO PRIMARY;
```

- On all other standby databases, both physical and logical, register the standby redo log file from the new primary database. The following statement will register a log file with a database, and if the recovery process is running on a database, the redo data from the log file will be applied:

```
ALTER DATABASE REGISTER LOGFILE 'filespec';
```

- Finally, restart the new primary database to enable the read/write operation. Update the Oracle Net configuration so

---

that the new primary database will start serving the requests from applications.

If the primary database was running in MAXIMUM PERFORMANCE mode prior to failure, the procedure of failover is slightly different. In this case the following issues should be evaluated:

- Since the protection mode is MAXIMUM PERFORMANCE, the physical standby database may not have standby redo logs configured. After the loss of the primary database, there may be an archive gap on the standby database. These gaps should be resolved before transitioning the standby into the primary role.

- If possible, manually copy the online redo logs from the original primary database to the target physical standby database and register the online redo log files using the ALTER DATABASE statement. After registering the online redo log files, check the alert log file to verify the recovery process has applied the redo from these log files.

The failover to a physical standby database is similar to a switchover operation. Oracle provides the functionality of converting a physical standby database into the primary database without considering any of the above mentioned data recovery options. This is kind of intentional data loss failover and can be achieved using the following statement:

```
ALTER DATABASE ACTIVATE STANDBY DATABASE;
```

If a standby log file has been created on the physical standby database, issuing the above-mentioned statement will result in an Oracle error. The activation of the physical standby database can be force by skipping the standby log files:

```
ALTER DATABASE ACTIVATE STANDBY DATABASE SKIP STANDBY LOGFILE;
```

Failover to a Logical Standby Database

Conceptually, the failover operation to a logical standby database is similar to failover to a physical standby database in that it involves the following steps: verify the status of the recovery process; recover as much data as possible on the target logical standby database; and then transition to the primary database role.

This section describes these steps, in detail, and is accompanied by the SQL statements required to perform the failover operation:

- The initialization parameter file on the target standby database should be updated to include the other logical standby database as the archival destination. All the physical standby databases will be invalidated after the role transition, so do not include the physical standby databases.

- Remove any previously set delay in the log apply service using the DBMS_LOGSTDBY package as explained in "Preparing a Logical Standby Database for Switchover" section.

- Manually copy the archived redo logs from the primary database or any other physical standby database, if the primary database local archival destination is damaged in order to resolve any gap sequence on the target logical standby database. The archive gap sequence can be obtained using the script, *find gap.sql*, from the code depot.

- Once the archived redo logs have been manually copied to the target logical standby database, register them using the following statement:

  ```
  ALTER DATABASE REGISTER LOGICAL LOGFILE 'filespec';
  ```

- If the DBA has access to the online redo log files of the original primary database, these should be copied to the target

---

logical standby site and registered using the above-mentioned statement.

- Verify the overall progress of the log apply service on this logical standby database using the script, *log_progress.sql,* from the code depot. Once all the redo data has been applied by SQL apply operation, stop the recovery process on the standby site and activate it as the primary database using the following statements:

```
ALTER DATABASE STOP LOGICAL STANDBY APPLY;
ALTER DATABASE ACTIVATE LOGICAL STANDBY DATABASE;
```

- At this point, the logical standby database has been converted to the primary database and Oracle Net should be configured to send all the application requests to the new primary database.

- As explained in the "Switchover to a Logical Standby Database" section, create a database link on the other logical standby database in the Data Guard environment to support future switchover operations.

Verify Failover Operation

The verification of failover operation remains the same as the switchover operations. That is, after completing the failover, the current redo log on the new primary database should be archived. Then the contents of the STANDBY_ARCHIVE_DEST directory of the other standby databases should be checked.

Existence of the most recent archived log file in this directory will prove the log transfer service is working properly after the failover. Additionally, check the content of the alert log file on both the new primary and the standby sites to verify the status of the log apply services.

If the failover is to a logical standby database, check for oracle error ORA-16109 in the alert log file of the remaining logical standby databases. If this error is present in the alert log file of the logical standby database, this logical standby database should be created from the new primary database.

Impact on Other Standby Database in Configuration

Typically, a Data Guard configuration consists of more than one standby database. A role transition from the original primary to a standby database can affect the other standby databases in the environment. The impact depends on the type of database selected for role transition.

If a physical standby database is used for role transition, all other standby databases will not be affected. In fact, the other standby databases in the Data Guard environment do not need to be restarted and should operate without any issue. If the role transition is to a logical standby database, all the physical standby databases will be invalidated. Other logical standby databases may or may not be affected.

Sometimes, Oracle error *ORA-16109* will be encountered when the log apply service is started using the archived redo logs from the new primary database. In this case, the logical standby database should be recreated from the new primary database.

Transparent Application Failover

Transparent Application Failover (TAF) is a functionality offered by Oracle Net to re-establish a failed connection to another database instance. TAF can be used with the Data Guard configuration to provide complete end-to-end failover functionality. Oracle Net configuration files, *tnsnames.ora* or

Oracle Name server can be configured to avail TAF functionalities.

There are various configurations that can be used for TAF. In this section, information will be presented on a connect-time failure configuration. For more information on TAF refer to Oracle9i Net Services Administrator's Guide Release 2 (9.2).

A connect-time failure configuration requires inclusion of the *failover_mode* parameter in the *tnsnames.ora* file. A sample *tnsnames.ora* file is shown in the following example:

```
Appsdb =
 (DESCRIPTION=
 (FAILOVER=ON)
  (ADDRESS=
        (PROTOCOL=tcp)
        (HOST=jrpr01)
        (PORT=1521))
  (ADDRESS=
        (PROTOCOL=tcp)
        (HOST=jrbk01)
        (PORT=1521))
  (CONNECT_DATA=
     (SERVICE_NAME=appsdb)
     (FAILOVER_MODE=(TYPE=session)(METHOD=basic))
  ))
```

In the above connection string, client connection will be tried on host jrpr01 or jrbk01 for service "appsdb". The original primary database runs on jrpr01. As long as the original primary database is active, the client requests will go to "appsdb" database on jrpr01. After a failover, the database on jrpr01 will not respond, and the client connection requests will be routed to "appsdb" database on jrbk01 host.

Conclusion

Role transition is an integral part of the Data Guard environment. In this chapter, the concept behind role transitions and the implementation specifics was presented in detail.

The following topics were covered in detail to assist in the case of disaster recovery or a switchover needed to allow the DBA to do routine maintenance activities:

- Concepts of switchover and failover were presented followed by a quick list of disadvantages of role transition to a logical standby database.

- A brief description of how to determine the best standby database for role transition.

- The nitty-gritty of role transitions to physical and logical standby databases.

- Verification of role transition.

- A role transition should always be accompanied with changes in Oracle Net configuration to route the requests from applications to the new primary database. A limited amount of information on the Transparent Application Failover provides an alternate approach in configuring Oracle Net to handle such situations.

More information regarding role transitions can be found in Oracle manuals and from the Metalink site at metalink.oracle.com. This chapter marks the end of the basic concept and administration of standby databases. By now the techniques used to create and manage a simple Data Guard environment should be familiar.

The upcoming chapters will deal with advanced concepts like Performance Tuning, Using Oracle Data Guard Broker and Recovery Manager for Standby Databases.

I am Princess Mubojubo of Nigeria.
Why did you not answer my e-mails?

Performance Tuning of Data Guard Configuration

"Nah, it couldn't possibly be a network issue."

Introduction

Standby databases and a Data Guard environment can be very useful for the disaster recovery policy of any enterprise. On the other hand, if the Data Guard environment is not set up correctly, it can significantly impact the performance of the primary database.

The first six chapters of this book concentrated on creating and managing standby databases in a Data Guard environment. This

---

chapter will provide guidelines on the performance tuning of Data Guard components such as Log Transport and Log Apply services. The overall goal is to minimize the impact on database services provided by the primary database.

Understanding Tuning Requirements

Before undertaking performance tuning, it is important to understand the objective of performance tuning. In absence of any clearly defined goals, it will be difficult to evaluate the success of any tuning efforts. The end goal should be quantitative and not qualitative.

In other words, it is not the best practice to start the performance-tuning task with the thought; "I have to make it faster". The DBA that thinks that way will soon get lost in the process and will never be able to measure the success of the tuning exercise. The other issue will be determining when to stop tuning.

For the tuning of the Data Guard environment, the DBA can setup a clearly defined quantitative objective. The bottom line is, "data in all the standby databases in the Data Guard environment should be identical to the primary database". How will this be quantified? A Data Guard configuration involves log transfer and log apply services on individual sites to manage the standby database. Log transfer and log apply services on all the sites should be performing well enough that a redo log file should be archived and applied to the standby database in near real-time.

For example, assume that the primary database is an insert/update intensive database. This high rate of redo generation is resulting in an archive redo log file every five minutes during the peak activity period. In this case, the log management service should transfer and apply the redo logs onto standby databases within five minutes. Failing to do so will result in a backlog of archived redo log files on standby sites that will slow down the role transfer process.

Moreover, if a logical standby database is being used to serve reporting requirements, any extra delay in log management will impact the service. For this example, the goal should be to tune the entire Data Guard environment such that it will be able to finish the end-to-end log management process within five minutes.

The DBA needs to understand the redo generation rate of the primary database before the tuning objective can be quantified. Oracle alert log file and dynamic performance views can assist in the calculation of the redo generation rate in the environment. Later in this chapter, the techniques on calculating the peak redo generation rate will be presented.

Monitoring Data Guard Performance

Data Guard functionality is accomplished by two key components; log transfer services and log apply services. Any performance issue in either of these services will affect the overall performance in the Data Guard environment. Oracle provides several views to monitor the progress of log transfer and log apply services. In addition to the system views, operating system utilities can be used to diagnose the performance issues in the log transfer process. The following views are useful for monitoring purposes:

- **v$archived_log** – This view can be queried to find the delivery status of archived redo logs to remote log archive destinations. Moreover, it provides the size of archived redo log files, which can be used to calculate the optimal network bandwidth required for timely transfer of log files to remote destinations across Oracle Net. The column *completion_time* is particularly useful finding identifying any Oracle Net related issues that may cause delay in the delivery of archived redo logs to remote destinations.

- **v$archive_dest_status** – This view contains useful data on the status of the log management service on standby databases. It should be queried on the standby database and not on the primary database. Information such as the lag between log apply service and log transfer service can be found for a particular standby site from this view.

- **v$managed_standby** – On the physical standby database, the *v$managed_standby* view contains information related to individual processes involved in the log management service. The log transfer service uses the Archiver (ARCH) and the Remote File Server (RFS) processes to obtain and write redo records on the standby site. The log apply service uses Managed Recovery Process (MRP) to apply the redo records on the physical standby database. This view can give the status of these processes. The status column can be very useful in diagnosing a performance issue.

- **dba_logstdby_progress** – The two columns, APPLIED_SCN and NEWEST_SCN, of this view give an overall measure of progress of the log apply service on a logical standby database. The associated time columns provide an estimate of time when the SCN has been applied on the database.

- **v$logstdby** – Performance statistics related to the individual process facilitating the application of redo records onto a logical standby database can be obtained from this view. The HIGH_SCN column of this view against each of the process shows the progress of the individual process. This view should be queried on the logical standby database.

- **v$logstdby_stats** – The SQL operation on a logical standby database uses log miner technology to build the SQL statements from redo records. This view provides the log miner engine related statistics on a logical standby site.

In addition to these views, operating system utilities like *iostat* can be used to find the I/O related statistics on remote archival destinations. Oracle Net tracing utility can assist in determining any bottlenecks caused by the Transparent Network Substrate.

Tuning the Log Transfer Service

The previous section presented a list of views that can provide data to diagnose performance issues in a Data Guard environment. In this section, the details on collecting and interpreting statistics for the log transfer process will be presented. Additionally, determining an optimal network bandwidth using these statistics will be covered in this section. A few tips that can be used to tune the Oracle Net and I/O system for better response time during the transfer of archived logs to standby destinations will also be included.

Gathering Log Transfer Related Statistics

Most of the log transfer related statistics can be obtained from the *v$archived_log* dynamic performance view. The script, *Find_Archive_Time.sql*, from the code depot will show the size of archived redo log files and their archival timing on local and remote archive destinations. A sample output from this script is shown below:

🖫 Find_Archive_Time.sql

```
-- *******************************************************
-- Copyright © 2004 by Rampant TechPress
-- This script is free for non-commercial purposes
-- with no warranties.  Use at your own risk.
```

```
--
-- To license this script for a commercial purpose,
-- contact info@rampant.cc
-- **************************************************
--
-- Desc: Script to find out the size of archived redo log file
--       And the archival time on local and remote achiving
--       Destinations.
--
Set linesize 100
Column DESTINATION format a25 trunc
Column THREAD# format 99
Column SEQUENCE# format 999999
Column SizeOfFile format 9999999
Column COMPLETION_TIME format a20

Select
   d.DESTINATION||'('||d.TARGET||')' DESTINATION,
   l.THREAD#,
   l.SEQUENCE#,
   l.BLOCK_SIZE*(l.BLOCKS+1) SizeOfFile,
   to_char(l.COMPLETION_TIME,'YYYY-MON-DD HH24:MI:SS')
COMPLETION_TIME
From
   V$ARCHIVED_LOG l,
   V$ARCHIVE_DEST d
Where
   l.DEST_ID = d.DEST_ID
Order by
   THREAD#,SEQUENCE#,STANDBY_DEST;
```

Output from *Find_Archive_Time.sql* script:

```
DESTINATION                THREAD# SEQUENCE# SIZEOFFILE COMPLETION_TIME
-----------                ------- --------- ---------- ----------------
/oracle/appsdb/arch(PRIMA    1      1854       552448 2004-JAN-24 14:29:58
stdby2(STANDBY)              1      1854       552448 2004-JAN-24 14:29:58
appsstdby(STANDBY)           1      1854       552448 2004-JAN-24 14:53:24
/oracle/appsdb/arch(PRIMA    1      1855         1536 2004-JAN-24 14:31:19
stdby2(STANDBY)              1      1855         1536 2004-JAN-24 14:31:19
appsstdby(STANDBY)           1      1855         1536 2004-JAN-24 14:53:24
/oracle/appsdb/arch(PRIMA    1      1856        13312 2004-JAN-24 14:51:59
stdby2(STANDBY)              1      1856        13312 2004-JAN-24 14:51:59
appsstdby(STANDBY)           1      1856        13312 2004-JAN-24 14:51:59
```

This sample output reveals a problem in the log transfer to the
appsstdby standby site for Sequence# 1854. It appears that there
was some gap in the archive sequence for this standby destination
due to the fact that sequence# 1856 was transferred before 1854
and 1855. In general, the difference between the archival
completion time to the local destination and a remote destination

represents a performance issue in the log transfer service to this remote destination.

Ideally, the completion time to the local archival destination and to the remote archival destination in the local area network should be nearly the same.

The other important piece of data is the size of the archived redo log files. The sizes presented are the actual size of files that need to be transferred to the archival destination and not the size of redo logs defined on the primary database. This information will be used in calculating a suitable network bandwidth for log transfer in the next section.

The view, *v$archived_log,* has a column named APPLIED, which shows the log apply status on standby sites. It appears that the data in this column does not always reflect the actual applied status of archived logs on logical standby sites.

Determining Optimal Network Bandwidth

In a Data Guard environment, archived redo logs from the primary database are transferred to standby sites using Oracle Net. To ensure a timely delivery of archived redo log files, a suitable network connection between the primary site and all remote archival destinations must be provided.

The issue of having an optimal network bandwidth becomes more crucial when the primary database is running in high data protection modes. As mentioned in the previous chapters, the high data protection modes, MAXIMUM PROTECTION and MAXIMUM AVAILABILITY, require a synchronous transfer of redo records. In these cases, a transaction on the primary database is not complete until at least one standby database participating in the data protection mode receives redo records. It is not recommended that a standby database be configured to participate in a high data protection mode connected using a WAN.

In order to calculate the optimal network bandwidth for a Data Guard environment, it will be necessary to determine the amount of data the Oracle Net will carry in the busy period. In other words, the amount of redo generated on the primary database during the busy period will have to be known. Oracle provides several methods for determining the rate of redo generation during peak time. For example, the output of *STATSPACK,* an Oracle supplied package to monitor performance of the database, can be used to get the amount of redo generated per second.

In this text, the information stored in the view *v$archived_log* will be used to find the largest archived redo log file created over a period of few days. That file size will be used to estimate the volume of data that may be carried over Oracle Net to standby sites during peak activity periods. The script, *Network_BW.sql,* can be used to determine the optimal bandwidth for the network based on size of archived redo log files.

The script is based on assumption that the primary database has been running for last *n* days where *n* is an input parameter to the script. It determines the size of largest archived redo log file and the average size of archived redo log files in the last *n* days. If the largest file is five times or more larger than the average file size, the average file size is used to do the further calculations.

This assumes that the largest archived redo log file in the last *n* days has been a result of a heavy, but temporary, transaction on the database. If no such phenomenon exists, the largest file will be used.

The script assumes an overhead of approximately 25% data in transporting data over Net. These overheads are mostly related to network information required to carry packets from source to destination. The output of the script is the bandwidth of the network in Megabits per second that is required for timely transfer of archived redo logs using Oracle Net.

It is recommended to execute this script using *n=8 and n=32*. These two values of *n* will take care of extra redo logs generated by any weekly or monthly batch jobs.

🖫 Network_BW.sql

```
-- *************************************************
-- Copyright © 2004 by Rampant TechPress
-- This script is free for non-commercial purposes
-- with no warranties.  Use at your own risk.
--
-- To license this script for a commercial purpose,
-- contact info@rampant.cc
-- *************************************************

-- This script will calculate a suitable bandwidth required
-- For an acceptable performance of log transfer process.

Set linesize 100
Column MaxSize Format 99999999999
Column AvgSize Format 99999999999
Column BandWidth_Mbps Format 99999

Select
   Max(SizeOfFile) MaxSize,
   Avg(SizeOfFile) AvgSize,
   Ceil((Decode(Sign(Max(SizeOfFile)-5*Avg(SizeOfFile)),1,
   Avg(SizeOfFile)*(1+0.25),
   Max(SizeOfFile)*(1+0.25))*8)/(3600*1024*1024)) BandWidth_Mbps
From (
     Select
       to_char(COMPLETION_TIME,'YYYY-MON-DD HH24') Completion_Hour,
       Sum(BLOCK_SIZE*(BLOCKS+1)) SizeOfFile
     From
       V$ARCHIVED_LOG
     Where
       trunc(COMPLETION_TIME) Between
       trunc(Sysdate - &NumDays) And
       trunc(Sysdate)
     And
       Dest_id = 1
```

```
   Group By
      to_char(COMPLETION_TIME,'YYYY-MON-DD HH24')
);
```

A sample output from the script *Network_BW.sql* is shown below:

```
MAXSIZE          AVGSIZE          BANDWIDTH_MBPS
-------          -------          --------------
802862592        111223948                     1
```

This calculation will help in the specification of a network topology to connect the primary and standby sites. Usually, a standby database located within the LAN is not an issue as much as a standby site connected over WAN. The use of ATM, T-3 (USA) or E-3 (Non USA) network topology must be considered in order to provide an optimal network bandwidth for Data Guard configuration transferring redo data over WAN. In nutshell, for a smooth working of the log transfer service, a network has to provide high bandwidth and low latency.

Gathering Oracle Net Related Statistics

Collecting performance statistics for Oracle Net can be a very tedious task due to the fact that Oracle does not provide specific data dictionary tables that hold data pertaining to Oracle Net. In most circumstances, it will be necessary to depend on operating system utilities to diagnose network issues. The view, *v$system_event,* keeps event and wait statistics for Oracle databases since instance startup.

It can therefore be used to obtain the average wait related to SQL*Net. If there is a high value in the AVERAGE_WAIT column for SQL*Net events, consider using a trace route or sniffer to find the network latency and performance of intermediate network components between the source and destination. The following SQL statement can be used to find the average wait from the *v$system_event* view:

```
Select
   Sum(AVERAGE_WAIT)
From
   V$SYSTEM_EVENT
Where
   Upper(EVENT) like 'SQL*NET%';
```

Network Tuning for the Log Transport Service

The Session Data Unit (SDU) parameter of TNS and listener governs the size of packets transported over Oracle Net. The default value of SDU is 2KB, and the default value of archive log buffer is 1MB. Thus, 1MB archived redo logs will be transferred in 512 packets. This will require 512 round trips on the network.

If the latency is high a round trip will significantly impact the overall performance of Oracle Net. In order to reduce the number of packets, the SDU size can be increased in the *tnsnames.ora* file and *listener.ora* file for services identifying standby sites. The maximum value for SDU is 32KB. The following example shows a new SDU size for service stdby1:

Example *tnsnames.ora* file:

```
stdby1 =
  (DESCRIPTION =
    (SDU = 32768)
    (ADDRESS_LIST =
      (ADDRESS = (PROTOCOL = TCP)(HOST = jrsp01 )(PORT = 1521))
    )
    (CONNECT_DATA =
      (SID = appsdb )
    )
  )
```

Example *listener.ora* file:

```
SID_LIST_LISTENER =
  (SID_LIST =
    (SID_DESC =
      (SDU = 32768)
      (SID_NAME = appsdb)
```

```
      (ORACLE_HOME = /sw/oracle/product/9.2.0)
  )
  (SID_DESC =
    (SDU = 32768)
    (SID_NAME = meddb)
    (ORACLE_HOME = /sw/oracle/product/9.2.0)
  )
)
```

Very few parameters can influence the performance of Oracle Net, and SDU is one of the most significant one that can. If network throughput is not sufficient, consider upgrading the network topology; however, in some cases it may not be easier to upgrade the network topology. In these circumstances, the DBA must evaluate the potential performance gain that can be achieved by reducing the network traffic.

How can the network traffic be decreased? In a Data Guard environment, transfer all the archived redo records to the standby site. This cannot be compromised. One possible solution is to compress the archived redo log files before sending them over to the standby site.

To some extent, Secure Shell port forwarding and compression can be used to reduce the size of archived redo log files. Since archived redo log files are in binary format, it may not be possible to achieve a huge compression ratio using Secure Shell. Moreover, the extra overhead in compression may outweigh the benefits achieved by reduction in network traffic. This option must be evaluated in the configuration before reaching a conclusion.

The Secure Shell port forwarding technique enjoys varied degrees of success depending on the size of redo log files and the nature of data protection mode. More information about using Secure Shell port forwarding in a Data Guard environment is available on Oracle's Metalink site at metalink.oracle.com. More information about Secure Shell can be obtained from www.ssh.com.

I/O Activity on the Standby Host

The performance of the log transfer service to a standby site depends on the I/O subsystem and the speed of I/O activity on the disk where archived redo logs are being written. To determine if the I/O on the standby host is the bottleneck in the log transfer process, the *iostat* operating system utility, or a variant of it depending on the operating system, can be used. The *iostat* utility shows a detailed map of the I/O activity on the disks. The important columns for log transfer service are:

- Kw/S (Average KB written per second)

- Wait

- %w (Occupancy of wait queue)

- %b (device busy)

- asvc_t (average service time)

If there is a lot of I/O wait in the system, the disks should be configured properly, using RAID or any other technology, to boost the efficiency of I/O activity.

The following is sample output from iostat –xn 5 30 that shows I/O statistics collected every 5 seconds for 30 intervals. Note a %w and asvc_t for the device c0t0d0. This disk contains the log archive destination for the physical standby database "appsdb". This I/O wait will result in a delay in completion of the transfer of archived log files to the standby host.

```
DBA@jrsp01 iostat -xn 5 20

    r/s    w/s    kr/s    kw/s wait actv wsvc_t asvc_t  %w  %b device
   56.6  382.8 1079.1 3991.9  3.3  1.9    7.6    4.3  81  97 c0t0d0
    0.0    0.0    0.0    0.0  0.0  0.0    0.0    0.0   0   0 c0t2d0
    0.0    0.0    0.0    0.0  0.0  0.0    0.0    0.0   0   0 c0t3d0
```

Tuning the Data Guard Log Apply Services

The log apply service is the slowest phase in the process of data synchronization in a Data Guard environment. If the log transfer service is well tuned, the DBA should divert attention to tuning the log apply service. On a logical database, the log apply service uses the SQL apply method. On a physical standby database, it uses a block-per-block media recovery.

For this reason, the log apply service on a physical standby database is more efficient than on the logical standby database. In this section, the collection of data needed for performance tuning of the log apply service will be presented. Interpreting this information and applying corrective measures will also be discussed.

Gathering Log Apply Service Related Statistics

Performance data gathering on physical and logical standby databases will be covered in this section. For this chapter, the information will start with the physical standby database.

Physical Standby Database

As mentioned earlier, the log apply services on a physical standby database rarely cause performance issues. However, run some periodic checks to ensure that it is not falling behind. Querying the dynamic performance table *v$managed_standby* will reveal if the log apply is not coping with the amount of redo generated by the primary database.

The script, *MngStandby.sql,* from the code depot can be used for this purpose. Execute this script on the physical standby database:

```
-- ***************************************************
-- Copyright © 2004 by Rampant TechPress
-- This script is free for non-commercial purposes
-- with no warranties.  Use at your own risk.
--
-- To license this script for a commercial purpose,
-- contact info@rampant.cc
-- ***************************************************

-- Script to monitor the log apply service performance on
-- physical standby database.

Set Linesize 90
Column Process Format a7
Column Status Format a12
Column Sequence# Format 9999999999
Column Block# Format 99999999
Column Blocks Format 99999999

Select
    Process,
    Status,
    Sequence#,
    Block#,
    Blocks
From
    V$MANAGED_STANDBY;
```

The following is a sample output from the script:

```
PROCESS STATUS        SEQUENCE#    BLOCK#    BLOCKS
------- ------------  -----------  --------- ---------
ARCH    CONNECTED            0          0          0
ARCH    CONNECTED            0          0          0
RFS     RECEIVING         1965       2046       2046
RFS     ATTACHING         1964       2046       2046
MRP0    WAIT_FOR_LOG      1948       2044       2046
```

The SEQUENCE# column indicates the archived log file sequence number being processed. A significant difference between the SEQUENCE# of RFS and MRP0 shows a poor performance of the log apply service.

Logical Standby Database

In order to find the overall progress of the log apply service on a logical standby database, the *dba_logstdby_progress* view can be queried. The view provides read and applied SCN. The script named *log_progress.sql,* from the code depot, can be executed on a logical standby database in order to find the overall progress of the log apply service. This should be the starting point in the diagnosis of performance issues with SQL apply operation. A sample output from the *log_progress.sql* is shown below:

```
APPLIED_SCN       READ_SCN        NEWEST_SCN
-------------    -------------    ---------------
    2187154          1987779          2187417
```

If the APPLIED_SCN and NEWEST_SCN are the same, the SQL apply operation has applied all the available transactions. In cases where these two values are not equal, further investigation into the level of individual processes involved in the SQL apply operation is required.

Querying the dynamic performance *v$logstdby* on a logical standby database will provide the performance of individual processes involved in the SQL apply operation. The script, *sql_apply_progress.sql,* from the code depot can be used to gather data from *v$logstdby*.

🖫 **sql_apply_progress.sql**

```
-- ****************************************************
-- Copyright © 2004 by Rampant TechPress
-- This script is free for non-commercial purposes
-- with no warranties.  Use at your own risk.
--
-- To license this script for a commercial purpose,
-- contact info@rampant.cc
-- ****************************************************

-- Script to find out the progress of individual process
-- involved in SQL Apply operation
```

```
Column Type Format a12
Column Status Format a40 Trunc
Column High_Scn Format 999999999
Select
    Type,
    Status,
    High_Scn
From
    V$LOGSTDBY;
```

A sample output from the script is shown below:

```
TYPE          STATUS                                   HIGH_SCN
------------  ---------------------------------------  ----------
COORDINATOR   ORA-16116: no work available
READER        ORA-16127: stalled waiting for additiona
BUILDER       ORA-16127: stalled waiting for additiona  2187196
PREPARER      ORA-16116: no work available              2187196
ANALYZER      ORA-16117: processing                     2187196
APPLIER       ORA-16117: processing                     2187156
```

The HIGH_SCN column will give an estimate of the progress of the individual process. From the above output, it is apparent that the APPLIER process is falling behind.

Statistics Related to Log Mining Engine and Memory Usage

A dynamic performance view called *v$logstdby_stats*, provides useful information about the log mining engine and memory usage during the SQL apply operations. Understanding the data presented by this view will help isolate the performance related issues. This view will not have any statistics when the SQL apply service is not running.

Query the view, *logstdby_stats.sql*, from the code depot and congregate the results into four bands. These bands are: LogMiningEngine; Memory Wait; Unsuccessful Handling of Low Memory; and Total Pageouts. Based on the output of this script, the determination can be made as to whether the log-mining engine or the *shared_pool_size* on a logical standby database need to be tuned.

💾 logstdby_stats.sql

```
-- ****************************************************
-- Copyright © 2004 by Rampant TechPress
-- This script is free for non-commercial purposes
-- with no warranties.  Use at your own risk.
--
-- To license this script for a commercial purpose,
-- contact info@rampant.cc
-- ****************************************************

-- Script to gather statistics from v$logstdby_stats DPT
Set linesize 82
Column logMiningEngine format 9999999999
Column MemWait format 9999999999
Column UnsuccHandleLowMem format 99999999
Column PageOuts format a10

Select
   a.Value logMiningEngine,
   b.Value MemWait,
   c.Value UnsuccHandleLowMem,
   d.Value PageOuts

From
   (Select
       sum(Value) Value
    From
       V$LOGSTDBY_STATS
    Where
       Name like '%committed txns%') a,
   (Select
       sum(Value) Value
    From
       V$LOGSTDBY_STATS
    Where
       Name in ('preparer memory alloc waits',
                'builder memory alloc waits')) b,
   (Select
       (v1.Value - v2.Value) Value
    From
       V$LOGSTDBY_STATS v1,
       V$LOGSTDBY_STATS v2
    Where
       upper(v1.Name) = 'ATTEMPTS TO HANDLE LOW MEMORY'
    And
       upper(v2.Name) = 'SUCCESSFUL LOW MEMORY RECOVERY') c,
   (Select
       Value
    From
```

```
        V$LOGSTDBY_STATS
    Where
        Name = 'pageouts') d;
```

A sample output of the script is shown below:

```
LOGMININGENGINE    MEMWAIT UNSUCCHANDLELOWMEM PAGEOUTS
--------------- ----------- ------------------ ---------
          1234        263                 8 76
```

A high value in LOGMININGENGINE suggests there are plenty of transactions ready for the APPLIER process, so the log-mining engine is not a bottleneck. The other three columns in the output of the *logstdby_stats.sql* script present data related to memory usage from the shared pool of the logical standby database. More about tuning the log apply service will be provided in next the section.

Tuning Tips for the SQL Apply Operation

In the previous section, information was presented on the methods and the use of the Oracle data dictionary to diagnose performance issues and determining the bottlenecks. This section will focus on the changes required on a logical standby database or in some cases on the primary database to alleviate the performance problems.

- Uniquely identifying a row in the table and avoiding full table scans can optimize the performance of the SQL apply operation. It is necessary to verify that there are no tables in the primary database without a primary key or unique index defined to them. If there are any such tables, adding a Primary Key RELY constraint will minimize the amount of work required by the SQL apply process to uniquely identify rows from these tables. If the SQL apply operation is doing lots of full table scans, consider adding indexes on these tables in the logical standby database.

- Reducing the level of *transaction_consistency* will always result in better performance. Evaluate the requirements of transaction consistency based on the usage of the logical standby database. If the logical standby database is used only for disaster recovery purposes and no other processes such as reporting services are accessing the logical standby database, consider setting the *transaction_consistency* to NONE. This will not guarantee any read consistent data until all the logs are applied. If the database is used for reporting, consider setting the *transaction_consistency* to READ_ONLY. Full transaction consistency should be avoided wherever possible. This is the default value, so it is important to remember to change it after creating a logical standby database.

- In general, increasing the shared pool size improves the performance of the log apply service, subject to the page out of SGA from memory. If the output of the *logstdby_stats.sql* script shows a significant "Memory wait" or "Unsuccessful Handling Of Low Memory", consider changing the memory allocation for the log apply service. Before increasing the size of shared pool, check the "free memory" from the shared pool. By default, the SQL apply service can use only up to 25% of the shared pool size. If the "free memory" in shared pool is not enough, considering increasing the size of shared pool through the initialization parameter *shared_pool_size*. The amount of memory that the SQL apply process can consume can be changed using the *dbms_logstdby.apply_set* procedure. For example, the following statement will set a 100MB reserve for the SQL apply process from shared pool:

```
EXEC DBMS_LOGSTDBY.APPLY_SET('MAX_SGA',100);
```

- Increasing the memory allocated for the SQL apply process will certainly reduce the unsuccessful handling of low memory conditions. The benefits gained by the increase in memory should be weighed against the pageout count.

Oracle Data Guard

- If the APPLIER process is falling behind in the SQL apply operation, consider increasing the number of parallel servers.

- During the heavy transaction period, the output of the script *sql_apply_progress.sql* may indicate that the SQL apply process is not making any progress. ORA-16127 will appear in the output of the *sql_apply_progress.sql* script. Oracle suggests reducing the value for the *eager_size* parameter and the *max_transaction_count* parameter using the procedure, *dbms_logstdby.apply_set*. The *eager_size* parameter should be in the range of 100 and the *max_transaction_count* parameter should be around 12.

```
EXEC DBMS_LOGSTDBY.APPLY_SET
            ('_MAX_TRANSACTION_COUNT',12);
EXEC DBMS_LOGSTDBY.APPLY_SET('_EAGER_SIZE',100);
```

 These two parameters are not documented in Oracle documentation and can change without any prior notice. However, Oracle's support site provides more information on these two parameters.

Configuring Data Guard for High Performance

So far in this book, various "Do's and Don'ts" about standby database implementation in the creation of a well-tuned Data Guard configuration have been presented. The following is a list of consolidated points used in this section as a set of guidelines to achieve better performance from Data Guard:

- LAN and WAN topologies should provide a suitable bandwidth for timely delivery of archived redo logs to remote destinations. Consider a Gigabit Ethernet for LAN applications and a T-3/E-3 topology for WAN applications.

- Standby databases participating in high data protection modes such as MAXIMUM PROTECTION should be carefully chosen. A standby database should not be connected over a

WAN to participate in maximum data protection. This will significantly impact the performance of the primary database.

- Consider using a cascaded standby database configuration for standby sites connected over WAN. In this configuration, a remote archival destination on a LAN will receive archived redo log files from the primary database and distribute to standby sites connected over WAN. This will reduce the load on the archiver process of the primary database.

- Any reporting requirements and backup activities should be offloaded to a suitable standby database.

- On the remote archiving destination, use a fast disk and RAID technology to improve the I/O of the log transfer service.

- Consider using Secure Shell port forwarding to compress the archived redo logs before sending to the remote destination. Secure Shell port forwarding may not always result in better performance; therefore, this option must be evaluated in conjunction with the data protection mode of the Data Guard configuration.

- Regularly monitor the log apply process on standby databases, especially the logical standby databases. The logical standby databases are more likely to be hit by performance problems than a physical standby database.

- Physical standby databases should have redo logs configured to minimize the time required for role transfer during switchover or failover.

Conclusion

This chapter on performance tuning of standby databases and processes involved in Data Guard configuration covered the following topics:

- The requirement for performance tuning in a Data Guard environment.

- Details of dynamic performance views that can be used to collect the statistics related to performance of log management services.

- The network bandwidth requirement for a timely delivery of archived log files to standby sites.

- Tuning tips for Oracle Net, I/O activity and SQL apply operation in a Data Guard environment.

- Consolidating all the tuning tips into guidelines to configure Data Guard to achieve maximum performance.

More techniques used to collect and use statistics for performance improvement using Data Guard Broker will be presented later in this book.

"It might be an overloaded CPU."

Data Guard Broker

"Miss Jones, we need Oracle Data Guard Broker.
Please find out what Data Guard Broker is."

Introduction to Data Guard broker

Data Guard Broker is a tool supplied with Oracle database server software that is designed to ease the processes used in the creation and management of a Data Guard configuration. It is comprised of a server side component known as the DMON process and a client side component known as the CLI or GUI console. In Chapter 2, "Data Guard Architecture", a brief description on server side and client side components along with the management model was presented.

In this chapter, information will be presented about the broker management model in Oracle10g, which is slightly different from the one in Oracle9i. The main focus of this chapter is to provide practical details on the use of the Data Guard Broker command line interface to create and manage a configuration. It does not present detailed information on using the Data Guard GUI interface, which is integrated with Oracle Enterprise Manager. There are genuine reasons for focusing on CLI interface and not GUI interface. These reasons are:

- GUI interface integrated with OEM provides brilliant online help, so it is very easy to use.

- To use GUI interface, Oracle Enterprise Manager 9i Release 2 or later will have to be installed. This is a separately licensed product and may not be available to all users.

- CLI statements can be imbedded in custom scripts and toolkits. Doing so will prove to be very useful at times.

On the disadvantage side, the CLI interface cannot be used to create a physical or logical standby database. They are a prerequisite for using CLI interface of the Data Guard manager.

The difference in the broker management model between Oracle9i and Oracle10g has resulted in significant modifications in the CLI statements between these two releases. Throughout this chapter, wherever applicable, relevant statements from both releases will be provided.

Broker Concept

As described in chapter 2, "Data Guard Architecture", Data Guard Manager (GUI or CLI), DMON process, and site configuration files are the necessary components of Data Guard Broker. Using GUI or CLI interface, commands can be sent to the primary or standby sites, and the DMON process running on the site executes the command on behalf of the Data Guard manager.

In addition to executing the command, the DMON process updates the configuration file if the command modifies any properties or state of the site. Change in the configuration file is communicated to the DMON processes running on other sites, such that a consistent copy of the configuration file can be maintained across the entire Data Guard environment.

The broker management model defines the layers in a Data Guard configuration that can be managed individually through Data Guard broker. The management model varies between Oracle9i and Oracle10g. The management model of Oracle9i has already been presented in chapter 2. The following section presents an overview of the management model in Oracle10g.

Broker Management Model in Oracle10g

Oracle10g reduced the complexity of the management model by combining the site and resource layers into one database object layer. As a result, there are only two object layers in the model. These are:

- **Configuration Layer** – A configuration layer in the management model is a logical grouping of database objects identified by their profile. A profile contains state, status, and properties of the database. There can be one primary and up to nine standby databases in a configuration. The standby databases could be either physical or logical.

- **Database Object Layer** – A database object layer identifies a single database in the configuration. Each database object has its own exclusive profile.

States and Properties

These two terms will appear several times in this text; therefore, the definition for each term is listed below:

State

A state defines the condition of a database such as whether the database is open, closed, open for query only, etc. A primary database can be in the ONLINE, LOG-TRANSPORT-OFF or OFFLINE state. In the LOG-TRANSPORT-OFF state, the primary database will suspend the log transport services to the standby databases. The archiver process will continue to archive to local archiving destinations.

A physical standby database can be in the ONLINE, READ-ONLY, LOG APPLY-OFF, or OFFLINE state. In the ONLINE state, the physical standby database is in managed recovery mode. Similarly, in the READ-ONLY state, the database is open for query. In the LOG-APPLY-OFF state, the database is mounted in physical standby mode, but the recovery is not started.

A logical standby database can be in the ONLINE, LOG-APPLY-OFF or OFFLINE state. In the LOG-APPLY-OFF state, the logical standby database is open for read-only queries. In the OFFLINE state, the broker shuts down the database, stops the managed recovery process and disables the site in the configuration. Both the primary and the standby site have similar behaviour in the OFFLINE state.

Properties

Properties are the atomic level attributes of a database. There are two types of properties: monitorable and configurable. Monitorable properties can only be viewed, but configurable properties can be modified and controls the behaviour of the database.

Preparing to Use Data Guard Broker

Before going into the details of management and administration using Data Guard broker, please read the following pre-requisites and the starting up of Data Guard broker. Set the following parameters in initialization parameter file:

- *dg_broker_config_file2='filespec1'*

- *dg_broker_config_file2='filespec2'*

These two parameters specify the location of the broker configuration files. In absence of these parameters, the broker configuration files are created in an operating system dependent location with an operating system dependent file naming convention.

On Sun Solaris and other UNIX operating systems, these files are created in the $ORACLE_HOME/dbs directory. Oracle uses two configuration files to keep the last good known configuration settings during the modification of the configuration properties or state by the DMON process.

- Create a server parameter file for each database in the configuration.

- This is required because the DMON process can restart a database when its state is changed from offline to online or after role transition. The parameters required to start up a database are recorded in the server parameter file, which the DMON process can read to start the database.

- Use the parameter *dg_broker_start* to start and stop the Data Guard broker process.

- To start the broker, set this parameter to TRUE in the initialization parameter file and restart the database.

- To start the broker for a database that is already up and running, use the following statement:

```
ALTER SYSTEM SET DG_BROKER_START=TRUE;
```

- After executing this statement, a DMON process will start. On UNIX operating systems, it can be verified using the ps – ef command.

- To stop the DMON process, set this parameter to FALSE.

- Use DGMGRL to start the CLI environment. The following statement on a UNIX operating system will start the CLI environment:

```
DBA@jrpr01 dgmgrl
```

Managing Data Guard Using DGMGRL

Data Guard manager greatly simplifies the otherwise complicated tasks of log management, role management, and data protection modes. It can be used to monitor the overall health of the entire configuration as well as an individual site. This section will investigate the use of the CLI interface of Data Guard manager to administer a configuration.

The information presented will start with the creation of a configuration followed by more complicated tasks such as log management, switchover, failover and manipulating data protection modes. As always, Oracle documentation remains the largest single source of information on this topic.

Data Guard Configuration Management

As explained earlier, a configuration contains the primary and standby sites. In this section, the pre-requisites and procedures to create a configuration will be presented.

One requirement of creating a configuration using the CLI interface is that the standby databases participating in the configuration should exist. CLI interface cannot be used to create a standby database.

Assume that the primary database "appsdb", physical standby database "stdbydb" and logical standby database "logstdby" already exist. To create a configuration, ensure that the broker is running on the primary and all participating standby databases. On the primary site, start the CLI environment and connect to the primary database.

```
DGMGRL>connect sys/<sys password>
```

An account with the SYSDBA privilege will have to be used.

Use the CREATE CONFIGURATION command to create a configuration. The following code snippet shows the usage of this statement in Oracle9i:

```
CREATE CONFIGURATION 'appsconfig' AS PRIMARY SITE IS 'appsdb'
RESOURCE IS 'appsdb' HOSTNAME IS 'jrpr01' INSTANCE NAME IS 'appsdb'
SERVICE NAME IS 'appsprimary' SITE IS MAINTAINED AS PHYSICAL;
```

Oracle will validate the HOSTNAME and INSTANCE NAME from the *v$instance* view. Arguments Configuration, Site and Resource are user–defined labels. The service name should match the Net8 service name for the primary database on all hosts participating in the configuration. There should be an identical

---

service-naming scheme on all the host machines within a configuration.

The last argument, SITE MAINTAINED AS, signifies the type of standby database that this primary database will assume after the switchover operation. When a primary database is marked as physical, it cannot be turned into a logical standby database by switching it over with a standby database. The CREATE CONFIGURATION statement has been simplified in Oracle10g:

```
CREATE CONFIGURATION 'appsconfig' AS
PRIMARY DATABASE IS 'appsdb'
CONNECT IDENTIFIER IS 'appsprimary';
```

The PRIMARY DATABASE identifier should match the initialization parameter *db_unique_name*, exactly.

After creating a configuration, the next step is to add sites to the configuration. This is achieved by using the CREATE SITE statement for Oracle9i and ADD DATABASE for Oracle10g. Usage of the CREATE SITE statement is similar to the CREATE CONFIGURATION statement, except that the primary site name does not have to be specified. This statement does not require the name of the configuration, which implies that there can only be one configuration per primary site. The following script shows an example of adding a site in the configuration. These statements should be executed after connecting to the primary database using DGMGRL. Here is the statement as it would appear in Oracle9i syntax.

```
CREATE SITE 'stdbydb' RESOURCE IS 'stdbydb' HOSTNAME IS 'jrpr02'
INSTANCE NAME IS 'stdbydb' SERVICE NAME IS 'appsstdby'
SITE IS MAINTAINED AS PHYSICAL;
```

Here is it as it would appear in Oracle10g Syntax:

```
ADD DATABASE 'stdbydb'
CONNECT IDENTIFIER IS 'appsstdbydb'
MAINTAINED AS PHYSICAL;
```

The keyword MAINTAINED AS identifies the present type of database and not the type it will assume after switchover. In the above example, the standby site added to the configuration is a physical standby database.

By default, a newly created configuration will be in a disabled state. The configuration will have to be enabled so that the Data Guard broker can manage it. The ENABLE CONFIGURATION statement can be used to enable a configuration and all of its dependents. The syntax is identical for Oracle9i and Oracle10g. Similarly, the DISABLE CONFIGURATION statement can be used to disable a configuration and all the sites and databases included in the configuration.

A configuration can be completely removed using the REMOVE CONFIGURATION statement.

Data Guard broker writes its log file in the location specified by the *background_dump_dest* initialization parameter. In addition to the DMON process log file, there will be a *drc<primary site>.log* file, which contains detailed messages regarding the Data Guard broker.

Viewing Configuration and Site Attributes

Data Guard manager's CLI interface provides several commands to view the state and properties of various components of the broker management model. Due to the differences in the management model between Oracle9i and Oracle10g, the commands to view the properties are not identical. The following commands are valid in Oracle9i:

- Configuration level attributes can be viewed using the SHOW CONFIGURATION command. Optionally, a keyword, VERBOSE, can be used to retrieve a detailed report. The example below shows the use of this command:

```
DGMGRL> SHOW CONFIGURATION VERBOSE
Configuration
  Name:              'appsconfig'
  Enabled:           'yes'
  Default state:     'ONLINE'
  Intended state:    'ONLINE'
  Protection Mode:   'MaxPerformance'
  Number of sites:   2
  Sites:
    Primary Site: appsdb
    Standby Site: stdbydb
Current status for "appsconfig":
Warning: ORA-16608: one or more sites have warnings
```

- The SHOW SITE command can be used to view the attributes of individual sites. The usage of this command is:

```
SHOW SITE VERBOSE 'Site Name';
```

- Again, the use of VERBOSE is optional.

```
DGMGRL> SHOW SITE VERBOSE 'appsdb';
Site
  Name:                       'appsdb'
  Hostname:                   'jrpr01'
  Instance name:              'appsdb'
  Service Name:               'appsdb'
  Standby Type:               'physical'
  Number Built-in Processes:  '2'
  Number Generic  Processes:  '0'
  Enabled:                    'yes'
  Required:                   'yes'
  Default state:              'PRIMARY'
  Intended state:             'PRIMARY'
  PFILE:                      ''
  Number of resources:  1
  Resources:
    Name: appsdb (default) (verbose name='appsdb')
Current status for "appsdb":
SUCCESS
```

- To view the value of individual resources such as the database running on a site, use the command SHOW RESOURCE 'resource name' ON SITE 'site name'; as shown below:

```
DGMGRL> SHOW RESOURCE VERBOSE 'appsdb' ON SITE 'appsdb';
Resource
  Name:            appsdb
  Manager Type:    internal
   Standby Type:    PHYSICAL
Online States:
  ONLINE
  PHYSICAL-APPLY-READY
  PHYSICAL-APPLY-ON
  READ-ONLY
  LOGICAL-APPLY-READY
  LOGICAL-APPLY-ON
  READ-WRITE
  READ-WRITE-XPTON
Properties:
  INTENDED_STATE            = 'READ-WRITE-XPTON'
  ENABLED                   = 'yes'
  IGNORE_STATUS             = 'no'
  LogXptMode                = 'ARCH'
  Dependency                = ''
  Alternate                 = ''
  DelayMins                 = '0'
  Binding                   = 'OPTIONAL'
  MaxFailure                = '0'
  ReopenSecs                = '300'
  AsyncBlocks               = '2048'
  LogShipping               = 'ON'
  ApplyNext                 = '0'
  ApplyNoDelay              = 'NO'
  ApplyParallel             = '1'
  StandbyArchiveDest        =
'LOCATION=/oracle/appsdb/archstd'
  LogArchiveTrace           = '255'
  StandbyFileManagement     = 'AUTO'
  ArchiveLagTarget          = '0'
  LogArchiveMaxProcesses    = '2'
  LogArchiveMinSucceedDest  = '1'
  DbFileNameConvert         = ''
  LogFileNameConvert        = ''
  LogArchiveFormat          = 'appsdb_%t_%s.dbf'
  InconsistentProperties    = '(monitor)'
  InconsistentLogXptProps   = '(monitor)'
  SendQEntries              = '(monitor)'
  LogXptStatus              = '(monitor)'
  SbyLogQueue               = '(monitor)'
Properties for 'PRIMARY' state:
  DEFAULT_STATE    = 'READ-WRITE-XPTON'
  EXPLICIT_DISABLE = 'no'
  REQUIRED         = 'yes'
Properties for 'STANDBY' state:
  DEFAULT_STATE    = 'PHYSICAL-APPLY-ON'
  EXPLICIT_DISABLE = 'no'
  REQUIRED         = 'yes'
Current status for "appsdb":
SUCCESS
```

In the above command output, the value for each monitorable and configurable properties of the resource is shown.

- An individual property of a resource can be viewed by using the following command:

```
SHOW RESOURCE VERBOSE 'resource name' property name
```

- For example:

```
SHOW RESOURCE VERBOSE 'appsdb' ApplyNoDelay;
```

Due to the differences in the broker management model, the site and resource specific commands have been replaced with the SHOW DATABASE commands in Oracle10g. Additionally, Oracle10g has added the SHOW INSTANCE command to support Data Guard in RAC environment. Conceptually, these commands are not much different from the ones existing in Oracle9i.

Administration of Log Management Services

Log management service is a combination of the log transport service and the log apply service. The log transport service manages the transfer of redo data from the primary database to standby databases. The log apply service operates solely on standby databases and is responsible for applying the changes from the primary database onto the standby database.

It is recommended that the log management services remain running without any interruption to avoid any data loss. However, in certain circumstances such as scheduled maintenance work, it may be desirable to stop the log management services to a specific site or all sites in a configuration. In the next section, information about administrating log transport services and log apply services using CLI commands will be presented.

Log Transport Services

In order to stop log transport services to all standby sites, the sub-state of the primary database needs to be altered to READ-WRITE in Oracle9i and to LOG-TRANSPORT-OFF in Oracle10g. The following statement can be used to modify the sub-state in order to stop log transport service:

Oracle9i Syntax:

```
ALTER RESOURCE 'appsdb' ON SITE 'appsdb' SET STATE='READ-WRITE';
```

Oracle10g Syntax:

```
EDIT DATABASE 'appsdb' SET STATE='LOG-TRASPORT-OFF';
```

In this sub-state, the archiver process will not transmit any redo data to the standby archival destination. The local archival destinations will continue to receive archived redo logs without any interruption. To restart the log transport service to all sites, put the primary database back into the READ-WRITE-XPTON sub-state in Oracle9i and to ONLINE state in Oracle10g as shown below.

Oracle9i Syntax:

```
ALTER RESOURCE 'appsdb' ON SITE 'appsdb'
SET STATE='READ-WRITE-XPTON';
```

Oracle10g Syntax:

```
EDIT DATABASE 'appsdb' SET STATE='ONLINE';
```

The log transport service to a specific site is controlled by the property LogShipping. The default value of LogShipping is "ON". It must be set to "OFF" in order to stop sending redo

---

data to a specific site. In the following example, the log transport to the standby site "stdbydb" is being stopped:

Oracle9i Syntax:

```
ALTER RESOURCE 'stdbydb' ON SITE 'stdbydb'
SET PROPERTY LogShipping='OFF';
```

Oracle10g Syntax:

```
EDIT DATABASE 'stdbydb' SET PROPERTY LogShipping='OFF';
```

Log Apply Services

The log apply services can be controlled by modifying the sub-state of the standby database. On a physical standby database running on Oracle9i database software, the log apply service can be stopped by putting the database in the PHYSICAL-APPLY-READY state.

When the database is in the READ-ONLY mode, the redo logs will not be applied. Similarly, on a logical standby database, setting the sub-state to LOGICAL-APPLY-READY will achieve the same result.

Oracle10g introduced a new state called LOG-APPLY-OFF, which is applicable to both physical and logical standby databases. In this state, as the name suggests, the log apply services will not apply redo data from the primary database.

Role Transition using Data Guard Broker

Role transition is a complicated activity in a Data Guard environment. Data Guard broker has significantly simplified the task of switchover and failover by internally combining the steps required to transition a standby database into the primary role.

Role transition management using Data Guard manager's CLI interface is identical in both Oracle9i and Oracle10g. This section will present the switchover and failover operation using CLI commands.

Switchover Operation

In order to switchover a standby database to the primary role and vice-versa, the following pre-requisites should be met before issuing the SWITCHOVER command:

- The intended state of the primary database should be READ-WRITE-XPTON for Oracle9i and ONLINE for Oracle10g.

- The intended state of the target physical standby database should be PHYSICAL-APPLY-ON for Oracle9i, and ONLINE for Oracle10g.

- If the target standby database is a logical standby database, its intended state should be LOGICAL-APPLY-ON for Oracle9i, and ONLINE for Oracle10g.

- There should be no blocking error on the participating standby database. Usually, the blocking issues are any error in log management services or data file identifications. If the broker finds any blocking issues, it terminates the switchover operation leaving the primary and standby databases in their original state.

These pre-requisites are no different than the requirements for manually switching over a standby and primary database.

To switchover a standby database into the primary role, execute the following statement. It can be executed in the CLI environment after connecting to the primary database or the target standby database using an account having SYSDBA privilege.

```
SWITCHOVER TO 'stdbydb';
```

The broker will restart the primary and standby database after the switchover. In some cases, usually due to privilege or incorrect setting of initialization parameters, the broker may not be able to restart the databases. In those circumstances, the database needs to be manually started after the switchover operation is complete. Then, run the SHOW SITE command to verify the state and role of the databases after the switchover operation.

Failover Operation

The first step in a failover operation is to evaluate the best available standby database for failover. This is explained in Chapter 6, "Switchover and Failover". The FAILOVER command should be executed on the standby database that is selected for the failover operation. The GRACEFUL or FORCED keyword can be used with the FAILOVER command. GRACEFUL failover is always preferred in order to minimize any data loss.

```
FAILOVER TO 'stdbydb' GRACEFUL;
```

Data Guard broker will restart the new primary database. After the failover, the appropriate SHOW commands should be executed in order to validate the failover operation.

Managing Data Protection Modes

From previous chapters, a Data Guard configuration must have a defined protection mode. By default, the protection mode of a configuration is MAXIMUM PERFORMANCE. In order to change the protection mode of a configuration, execute the following steps:

- Modify the log transport mode for each standby database that is participating in the new protection mode. The Data Guard broker property, LogXptMode maps to the attributes of the *log_archive_dest_n* parameter managing the log transport mode. Hence, the value of the LogXptMode property must be altered for each site participating in the new protection mode. Assume that the goal is to change the protection mode from MAXIMUM PERFORMANCE to MAXIMUM PROTECTION, and the standby database "stdbydb" will be participating in this new protection mode. Create standby redo log files on the stdbydb database and modify its LogXptMode to SYNC as shown below:

Oracle9i Syntax:

```
ALTER RESOURCE 'stdbydb' ON SITE 'stdbydb' SET PROPERTY
LogXptMode=SYNC;
```

Oracle10g Syntax:

```
EDIT DATABASE 'stdbydb' SET PROPERTY LogXptMode=SYNC;
```

- The protection mode of a configuration should be modified as follows:

Oracle9i Syntax:

```
ALTER CONFIGURATION SET PROTECTION MODE AS MAXPROTECTION;
```

Oracle10g Syntax:

```
EDIT CONFIGURATION SET PROTECTION MODE AS MAXPROTECTION;
```

The primary database will need to be restarted for the new protection to take effect. Data Guard broker restarts the primary database if the configuration is enabled.

Protecting your Oracle database can be a battle

Conclusion

In this chapter, the administration of Data Guard configuration using the command line interface of Data Guard manager was presented. The following topics were covered in detail:

- The Data Guard broker concept has been presented with detailed information building on that provided in Chapter 2. The difference in the management model between Oracle9i and Oracle10g has been the main focus of this section.

- A brief description of the pre-requisites and preparations for the use of Data Guard manager has been covered.

- Details on how to create and manage a Data Guard configuration have been provided.

- Administrating log management, role transitions and Data Guard protection modes have been discussed.

More information on this topic can be found in the following Oracle documentations:

- Oracle9i Data Guard Broker Release 2(9.2)
- Oracle Data Guard Broker 10g Release 1(10.1)

Recovery Manager and Data Guard

*"I hear that RMAN can be installed by a 12-year old.
Please line-up some interviews"*

Introduction

Recovery Manager (RMAN) is a backup and recovery tool that is packaged and shipped with Oracle Database software. RMAN provides a flexible and scalable backup solution that can be integrated with media management sub-systems to facilitate end-to-end backup and recovery policies. The key task in creating a Data Guard configuration is to obtain a backup of the primary database along with all the necessary archived redo logs required to recover the database to the last SCN.

RMAN can be used to create this backup and duplicate the primary database as a standby database. In addition, RMAN can recover the newly created standby database to the last SCN, after which, the managed recovery process can keep the standby database in sync with the primary database. In a nutshell, the standby database creation process uses all three functionalities of the Recovery Manager: backup; restore; and recovery.

RMAN can be used to create various types of Data Guard configurations such as a physical standby database on the same host, a physical standby database on a separate host, a cascaded standby database, etc. However, RMAN cannot be used to create logical standby databases.

RMAN provides a functionality of incremental backup. This can be very useful when a DBA needs to create a standby database from a very large, in the range of terabytes, primary database. Creating a conventional backup using operating system utilities may take several hours for this type of database. In those circumstances the DBA can use the advantages offered by Recovery Manager. RMAN always compresses data files in a backup set such that the files in the backup set are a true representative of the amount of data in the database and not the size of the data files. The compression feature can be very useful when the need exists to transfer the backup set to a remote destination over Oracle Net in order to create a physical standby database.

A backup set, image copies, or a combination of both can be used to create a standby database. In this chapter, the information will focus on using RMAN to create standby databases. First, the procedure for creating a physical standby database using a backup set will be presented. This will be followed by the creation procedure using image copies. The text in this chapter will present the step-by-step process of creating these standby databases. An example in each section will be used to illustrate the complexities of configuring Data Guard using RMAN.

Additionally, this chapter will present the details on how to create a backup of the standby database using Recovery Manager. Familiarity with Recovery Manager prior to reading this chapter will be extremely useful. Oracle manual, *Oracle9i Recovery manager User's Guide Release 2 (9.2)*, provides more information on the working of Recovery Manager. The first step will be to cover some of the RMAN terminology that will be used throughout this chapter.

Explanation of RMAN Terminology

This section presents definitions of the RMAN terms used in the subsequent sections of this chapter:

- **TARGET DATABASE** – A Target Database is the primary database that will be backed up for standby database creation. In RMAN's terminology, the term target database identifies the database that is undergoing a backup, restore or recovery operation by Recovery Manager.

- **AUXILIARY DATABASE** – An Auxiliary Database is a standby database that will be created as a result of the duplication of the target database. In RMAN's terminology, Auxiliary instance identifies an instance which RMAN connects in order to execute the duplicate command.

- **CHANNEL** – A Channel is a communication pipeline between a RMAN executable and a target or auxiliary database. A channel consists of a server session on the target or auxiliary database and a data stream from the database to the backup device or vice-versa. RMAN console sends commands to the database using this channel, and the server session running on the database executes the command on behalf of Recovery Manager. Some degree of parallelism during the backup or restore operation can be achieved using multiple channels.

- **AUTOMATIC CHANNEL ALLOCATION** – RMAN Channels can be configured to use a set of default attributes for each operation when a channel is not allocated manually. This set of channels is persistent and can be configured using the CONFIGURE command. When such a set of channels is pre-defined, it is called automatic channel allocation. By default, RMAN configures a channel of device type, DISK, to be used for automatic channel allocation.

- **MANUAL CHANNEL ALLOCATION** - As the name suggests, a channel can be configured manually for special needs such as increasing the degree of parallelism. Channels can be allocated manually by using the ALLOCATE CHANNEL command in the RUN block of RMAN statement.

- **DUPLICATE COMMAND** – To restore a backup set or image copy, the DUPLICATE command can be used. The duplicate command always performs a complete restoration of the target database. Using this command, a database can be restored on the local host sharing with the target database or on remote host. A recovery catalog is not needed to use the duplicate command. It can be used with the control file of the target database serving as the repository.

- **BACKUP SET** – Recovery Manager backs up the datafiles, control file, archived log files, and server parameter files in a RMAN specific format called backup pieces. A set of one or more such backup pieces makes up a backup set. A backup set is created using the BACKUP command.

- **IMAGE COPY** – As opposed to the backup set, an image copy is not a RMAN specific format. It is a replica of an actual file. Image copies are created using the COPY command.

- **SET NEWNAME** – This command can be used to rename the data files to be restored to a new location. It is equivalent to the *db_file_name_convert* parameter of the server initialization parameter file. Combination of the SET NEWNAME and SWITCH command is the equivalent of the ALTER DATABASE RENAME FILE statement.

- **CONFIGURE AUXNAME** – CONFIGURE AUXNAME is equivalent to the SET NEWNAME command, except that the CONFIGURE AUXNAME is persistent, whereas, the SET NEWNAME command must be used every time the DBA wants to rename a data file. It is necessary to connect to the recovery catalog in order to use the CONFIGURE AUXNAME command.

- **DORECOVER** – When the DUPLICATE command is specified with the DORECOVER option, it starts recovery after restoration. The recovery is performed using all available archived redo logs and incremental backups. This is the recommended option while creating standby databases using recovery manager. This will save the extra step of recovering the standby database once it is created.

- **NOFILENAMECHECK** – It is an option for the DUPLICATE command. When NOFILENAMECHECK is used with the DUPLICATE command, RMAN does not validate the filenames during restoration. If the primary database and the standby database are on the same host, this option should not be used.

Creating Physical Standby Databases using RMAN

In this section, the details of creating physical standby databases using Recovery Manager will be presented. It will cover the backup requirements and the step-by-step guide to creating physical standby databases. Standby database creation cannot be completely automated using RMAN as it can by using Data Guard Broker.

Before the creation of the standby database using RMAN can be started, the server parameter file and Oracle net configuration files will have to be modified manually to suit the Data Guard configuration.

What needs to be Backed Up for a Standby Database Creation?

The first step in creating a standby database, using any method, is to identify a suitable backup to use. To use RMAN for standby database creation, there should always be a backup containing the following components:

- Control file
- All data files
- Archived redo log files
- Server initialization file

The control file, data files and archived redo log files can be backed up as a backup set or image copies. The backup of the server parameter file does not have to be using RMAN. This file can simply be copied to another file using the operating system utility and then the necessary changes made.

The changes required in the server parameter file are similar to the ones presented in Chapter 3. To create a standby database, any of the following can be used: a backup set containing all the required files; a set of image copies of the required files; or a heterogeneous set containing some files as the backup set and some as image copies.

In a scenario where the primary and the standby database are residing on the same host, a backup of the archived redo log files is not required. This is due to the fact that the control file or recovery catalog of the primary database will have information about the archived redo log files location. Therefore, during the recovery operation of the DUPLICATE command, RMAN can make use of this information. In this case, during the initial recovery, RMAN will read and apply archived redo log files from the local archival destination of the primary database onto the standby database.

Similarly, for a standby database creation on a remote host, if the file system containing archived redo log files on the primary site can be mounted to the remote host machine, a backup of the archived redo log files is not required.

In summary, if the local archival destination of the primary database can be made available to the standby host machine, a backup of archived redo logs is not required.

Creation Using a Backup Set

This section will provide a step-by-step guide to creating a physical standby database using a backup set of the target database. The standby database will share the same host with the primary database. As a consequence, the directory structure will not be exactly the same as the primary database. The change in directory structure can be accommodated using the *db_file_name_convert* and *log_file_name_convert* parameters or the SET NEWNAME command of Recovery Manager.

The example used in this section assumes that the name of the primary database is "appsdb" and the standby database is called "stdbydb".

Integrity Check of the Primary Database

Before creating an actual backup set containing data files of the primary database, the data files can be checked for any physical and logical corruption using the BACKUP VALIDATE command. This step is not essential; however, it will ensure that the primary database is free from errors and all the files required are in the correct location.

The BACKUP VALIDATE DATABASE command can be used to check the integrity of all data files. The ARCHIVELOG ALL keyword can be included to check the validity of archived logs as well. The following example shows the usage of these commands. Start the RMAN command line interface and connect to the primary database as the target. On the RMAN prompt, execute the following command to validate the data files of the primary database:

```
RMAN> BACKUP VALIDATE DATABASE;

Starting backup at 07-MAR-04
using channel ORA_DISK_1
channel ORA_DISK_1: starting full datafile backupset
channel ORA_DISK_1: specifying datafile(s) in backupset
including current controlfile in backupset
input datafile fno=00002 name=/oracle/appsdb/data/undotbs01.dbf
input datafile fno=00001 name=/oracle/appsdb/data/system01.dbf
input datafile fno=00007 name=/oracle/appsdb/data/logstdby02.dbf
input datafile fno=00003 name=/oracle/appsdb/data/userdata01.dbf
input datafile fno=00004 name=/oracle/appsdb/data/indxdata01.dbf
input datafile fno=00005 name=/oracle/appsdb/data/logstdby.dbf
input datafile fno=00006 name=/oracle/appsdb/data/userdata02.dbf
channel ORA_DISK_1: backup set complete, elapsed time: 00:01:16
Finished backup at 07-MAR-04
```

From the output, it is clear that the primary database is free from any physical or logical corruption. To check the integrity of archived redo logs, use the following statement:

```
RMAN> BACKUP VALIDATE ARCHIVELOG ALL;

Starting backup at 07-MAR-04
current log archived
using channel ORA_DISK_1
RMAN-00571:
============================================================
RMAN-00569: =============== ERROR MESSAGE STACK FOLLOWS
===============
RMAN-00571:
============================================================
RMAN-03002: failure of backup command at 03/07/2004 12:13:56
RMAN-06059: expected archived log not found, lost of archived log
compromises recoverability
ORA-19625: error identifying file
/oracle/appsdb/arch/appsdb_1_716.dbf
ORA-27037: unable to obtain file status
SVR4 Error: 2: No such file or directory
Additional information: 3
```

From the output, all the archived redo log files since the last backup are not available on the system. Therefore, the validate command terminates with the error RMAN-03002/RMAN-06059. In this case, to create a standby database a new backup should be created first as all of the required archived redo logs needed to recover the database are available.

Creating a Backup Set of the Primary Database

Since the primary database and the standby database share the same host, a back up of archived redo log files will not be created. The following sample script, *rman_backup*, creates a backup of all the data files and the control file for the standby database:

```
#Script: rman_backup
run {
    allocate channel fs1 type disk
            format= '/oracle/appsdb/bkp/%u.%p';
    backup
        incremental level = 0
        filesperset = 3
        database
        include current controlfile for standby
        tag = 'level0backup_ForStandby';
        sql "ALTER SYSTEM ARCHIVE LOG CURRENT";
}
```

Multiple channels can be allocated to parallelize the back up process. To execute this script, set the *ORACLE_SID* to *sid* of the target database, connect using RMAN and call the script.

On a host running the UNIX operating system, do the following:

```
DBA@jrbk01; export ORACLE_SID=appsdb
DBA@jrbk01; rman target /
RMAN>@rman_backup
```

This script will create a backup of the data files and the control file of the primary database "appsdb" in the location */oracle/appsdb/bkp directory*.

Server Parameter and Oracle Net Configuration

The modifications required in the server parameter file and the Oracle Net configuration file are the same as those described in Chapter 3. The following changes are required in the server parameter file. It is only a sample, and the actual list of parameters requiring modification will vary depending on the configuration.

```
#Extract from server parameter file of standby database.
CONTROL_FILES=("/oracle/stdbydb/control/standbycontrol.ctl")
STANDBY_ARCHIVE_DEST=/oracle/stdbydb/arch
LOG_ARCHIVE_FORMAT=appsdb_%t_%s.dbf
LOG_ARCHIVE_START=TRUE
LOG_ARCHIVE_TRACE=255
LOG_ARCHIVE_DEST_1='LOCATION=/oracle/stdbydb/archlocal'
LOG_ARCHIVE_DEST_2='SERVICE=appsdb'
```

```
LOG_ARCHIVE_DEST_STATE_2=ENABLE
REMOTE_ARCHIVE_ENABLE=TRUE
STANDBY_FILE_MANAGEMENT=AUTO
DB_FILE_NAME_CONVERT=('/oracle/appsdb','/oracle/stdbydb')
LOG_FILE_NAME_CONVERT=('/oracle/appsdb','/oracle/stdbydb')
INSTANCE_NAME=stdbydb
LOCK_NAME_SPACE=stdby2
```

The Oracle Net configuration file must be modified to create a service for the new standby database.

Duplicate and Recover as the Standby Database

Once the initialization parameter file and Oracle Net files are modified, the process of duplicating the primary database as the standby database can be started. The first step in this process is to start the standby database without mounting it. After starting the standby database, connect the standby database as auxiliary and the primary database as target using the following statement:

 To create a standby database on remote host, copy all the backup pieces of the set to the remote host in the same directory structure. If the same structure cannot be created, use a symbolic link to simulate the structure.

```
DBA@jrbk01; export ORACLE_SID=stdbydb
DBA@jrbk01; rman auxiliary / target sys/change_on_install@appsdb
```

On the RMAN prompt, start duplicating the database as shown below:

```
RMAN> DUPLICATE TARGET DATABASE FOR STANDBY DORECOVER;
```

The output of this statement shows that RMAN first restores the file from the most recent backup and then recovers the database.

```
# Extract from the output of duplicate command:

Starting Duplicate Db at 07-MAR-04
using target database controlfile instead of recovery catalog
allocated channel: ORA_AUX_DISK_1
channel ORA_AUX_DISK_1: sid=11 devtype=DISK

printing stored script: Memory Script
{
   restore clone standby controlfile to clone_cf;
   replicate clone controlfile from clone_cf;
   sql clone 'alter database mount standby database';
}
executing script: Memory Script

Starting restore at 07-MAR-04

using channel ORA_AUX_DISK_1
.  .  .  .  .
.  .  .  .  .
Finished restore at 07-MAR-04

replicating controlfile
input filename=/oracle/stdbydb/control/standbycontrol.ctl

sql statement: alter database mount standby database
.  .  .  .  .
.  .  .  .  .
datafile 7 switched to datafile copy
input datafilecopy recid=24 stamp=520184020
filename=/oracle/stdbydb/data/logstdby02.dbf

printing stored script: Memory Script
{
   set until scn  3126804;
   recover
   standby
   clone database
    delete archivelog
   ;
}
executing script: Memory Script

executing command: SET until clause

Starting recover at 07-MAR-04
using channel ORA_AUX_DISK_1

starting media recovery

archive log thread 1 sequence 2032 is already on disk as file
/oracle/appsdb/arch/appsdb_1_2032.dbf
archive log filename=/oracle/appsdb/arch/appsdb_1_2032.dbf thread=1
sequence=2032
media recovery complete
Finished recover at 07-MAR-04
Finished Duplicate Db at 07-MAR-04
```

From the output, it is apparent that RMAN uses the archived redo log file *appsdb_1_2032.dbf* required for recovery from the local archival destination of the primary database. At this point the standby database is created and is ready to be put into managed recovery mode.

The standby database must always be recovered when it is created using RMAN. This is due to the fact that when RMAN is used to create the backup, the primary or target database has been open for read-write, so the backup is not consistent. This is similar to creating a standby database using a hot backup of the primary database.

Starting the Managed Recovery Process

The next step in creating the standby database is to start the managed recovery process. Connect to the standby database using the SYSDBA account and execute the following statement:

```
Sql> ALTER DATABASE RECOVER MANAGED STANDBY DATABASE DISCONNECT FROM
SESSION;
```

This statement can also be executed within the RMAN environment. Connect to the standby database as the target database using RMAN and execute the following statement:

```
RMAN> sql "ALTER DATABASE RECOVER MANAGED STANDBY DATABASE
DISCONNECT FROM SESSION";
```

Testing the Standby Database

Once the standby database is created and managed recovery is started, check the alert log file of both the primary and the standby database for any errors. Additionally, the standby database can be put in read-only mode and few database queries executed to ensure that the standby database has been created successfully. Chapter 3 provides more details on verifying a newly created physical standby database.

Creation Using Image Copies

As mentioned earlier in this chapter, an image copy of data files of the target database is similar to the backup created using operating system utilities. In order to use image copies to create the standby database, the use of RMAN may not be needed. However, in one scenario in which the goal is to create and recover a standby database, RMAN should be used to simplify the creation process.

This section will describe the use of an image copy to create and recover a standby database using RMAN. Some steps from the previous section remain valid. These steps are Server Parameter and Oracle Net Configuration, Starting Managed Recovery Process and Testing the Standby Database.

One of the requirements for using an image copy is that the primary database should be closed cleanly, then it should be mounted but not open. This limitation may make the use of image copies for a standby creation a less attractive option compared to the use of a backup set.

The following is a step-by-step guideline on creating physical standby databases using image copies. Use of the procedure described below assumes that a server parameter file has been created for the standby database and the Oracle Net files have been configured to create a service for the standby database.

Creating an Image Copy of the Primary Database

To create an image copy of the primary database, shutdown the primary database then cleanly, start and mount it; however, the primary database should not be opened. Once the database is started, connect to the target database using RMAN as shown below:

```
DBA@jrbk01; rman target sys/change_on_install@appsdb
```

On the RMAN prompt, execute the script *rman_image*. This will create an image copy for each of the data files and the control file of the primary database. This script will have to be modified to suit individual requirements. The *v$datafile* view can be used to get the file number information.

```
#Script: rman_image
# Copy the datafiles to backup area
  Copy
  Datafile 1 to '/oracle/appsdb/bkp/system01.dbf',
  Datafile 2 to '/oracle/appsdb/bkp/undotbs01.dbf',
  Datafile 3 to '/oracle/appsdb/bkp/userdata01.dbf',
  Datafile 4 to '/oracle/appsdb/bkp/indxdata01.dbf',
  Datafile 5 to '/oracle/appsdb/bkp/logstdby.dbf',
  Datafile 6 to '/oracle/appsdb/bkp/userdata02.dbf',
  Datafile 7 to '/oracle/appsdb/bkp/logstdby02.dbf',

# Copy the control file
  CURRENT CONTROLFILE FOR STANDBY TO
            '/oracle/appsdb/bkp/standbycontrol.ctl';
```

After this script is executed, exit from RMAN, open the primary database and execute the following statement to archive the latest SCN:

```
ALTER SYSTEM ARCHIVE LOG CURRENT;
```

Duplicate and Recover as Standby Database

Use the following command to duplicate the primary database from an image copy and recover it. The duplication process will create the standby database. Before starting the duplication process, the standby database should be started, but it should not be mounted. Then, connect to the auxiliary and target database using RMAN and issue the duplicate command as shown below:

```
DBA@jrbk01; rman auxiliary / target sys/change_on_install@appsdb
RMAN> DUPLICATE TARGET DATABASE FOR STANDBY DORECOVER;
```

> If the standby database is on remote host, copy the image copies to the remote host in the same directory structure. The file system mount option can be used to facilitate it.

Once the database is duplicated, start the managed recovery process and test the newly created standby database as described in the previous section.

Backup of a Standby Database Using RMAN

According to the information presented in earlier chapters, it is clear that a standby database can take the load of the backup operation from the primary database. In fact, offloading the backup operation to the standby site is a preferred solution to reducing the computing resource consumption on the primary database. The data files and archived redo log files can be backed up on the standby site, and those backed up files can be used to recover the primary database. However, the control file of the standby database cannot be used to recover the primary database.

This section will present the steps required to create a backup of the physical standby database. When backing up the standby database, it should be treated as the primary database and connections to it should be made using RMAN as the target database. Ideally, connect to the recovery catalog, as well, during the backup operation.

In the case where the recovery catalog cannot be used during the backup operation, use the standby control file as the repository. In this case, the recovery catalog should be refreshed as soon as possible. If the recovery catalog is not updated with the backup information, that backup set cannot be used to recover the primary database.

Either a consistent or inconsistent backup of the standby database can be created. If an inconsistent backup for recovery is used, a media recovery will certainly have to be completed. As a result, it is advisable to do a consistent backup of the standby database to avoid any complication during recovery.

To create a consistent backup, shutdown the standby database, start it and mount it as a standby database. Do not start the managed recovery process or open it for read-only queries. Doing so will result in an inconsistent backup. Once the standby database is mounted, execute the following two steps to create a backup set containing all the data files and archived redo log files:

- Set the ORACLE_SID to the standby *dbsid* and connect using RMAN as target:

```
DBA@jrbk01 export ORACLE_SID=stdbydb
DBA@jrbk01 rman target /
```

- This will not use the recovery catalog as the repository.

- Execute the following script to create a backup set in the */oracle/stdbydb/bkp* directory. This script will need to be modified to suit the environment:

```
# Script: Create backup of standby database
run {
    allocate channel fs1 type disk
format='/oracle/stdbydb/bkp/%u.%p';
    backup
        incremental level = 0
        filesperset = 3
        database plus archivelog
        tag = 'level0Backup_OfStandby';
}
```

- The script will complete with the following warning:

```
"RMAN-06497: WARNING: controlfile is not current, controlfile
autobackup skipped released channel: fs1"
```

- This warning shows up because the control file is a standby control file. This warning can be ignored because a backup of the standby control file is not usable in any sense for recovery.

To learn more about the backup of a standby database using RMAN, refer to *Oracle 9i Recovery Manager User's Guide Release 2 (9.2)*, which provides a great deal of information on this subject.

Conclusion

The primary focus of this chapter was to introduce the concept of using Recovery Manager for physical standby database creation. The following topics were discussed in detail:

- Key Recovery Manager concepts and the explanation of RMAN terminology used throughout this chapter have been provided.

- Details on creating a physical standby database using a backup set or image copies of the primary database were included.

- A step-by-step guide and a few sample scripts have been provided to assist when creating a physical standby database using RMAN.

- The backup procedure for standby databases using RMAN was detailed.

Refer to *Oracle 9i Recovery Manager User's Guide Release 2 (9.2)*, which provides much more additional information on this subject.

Oracle 10g: New Features of Data Guard

"I'm not sure, but it looks like a server failure".

Introduction

With the introduction of the grid computing model, Oracle10g brings a whole new concept in database architecture and management. In addition to the dynamic resource allocation feature built into the database server, Oracle10g promises various improvements in other areas such as high availability.

Introduction

271

In this chapter, information will be presented on the enhancements specific to the Data Guard technology. Most of the improvements are in the creation and management of logical standby databases. From information in previous chapters, it was not difficult to conclude that the limitations of the logical standby database did not make it a very useful option in Oracle9i. Oracle Corporation has worked to lift some of these restrictions in Oracle10g to make it more attractive to the administrators and system architects.

Moreover, the Data Guard architecture has been fine tuned to support the standby redo logs in all protection modes in order to strike a balance between data loss and performance in the Data Guard environment.

Before delving into the details of Data Guard feature improvements in Oracle10g, a quick overview of upgrades to Oracle10g Data Guard from a previous version will be presented.

Oracle10g Data Guard Enhancements

Oracle Data Guard is one of the popular options available to DBAs for setting up disaster recovery of a database or an alternate database for secondary uses. With the dual option of physical standby and logical standby databases, administrators have more choices in setting up near-real time synchronized secondary databases.

Oracle10g goes further in enhancing the Data Guard database environment. In this section the new features that expand data guard capabilities and improve ease of use will be presented.

Overview of Oracle 10g New Data Guard Features

The improvements include the introduction of real time apply, enabling of redo encryption, integrity sum-checking and authentication, specifying role-based destinations, setting service provider's name, automatic and remote archiving, and better support for a RAC environment.

New features for Logical Standby include the simplified creation of a logical standby database with a logical standby control file, support for standby redo log files for logical standby databases, support for additional data types, IOT, tables with unused columns, and an improved command set. There are also some new columns added to certain *dba* views to enhance diagnosis and trouble shooting capability.

In the case of the Data Guard broker, the configuration model has been simplified. Many commands in the DGMGRL have been improved. Data Guard Manager, which is a part of the Enterprise Manager, has a new interface and a new look. It extends support for Oracle RAC environments also. The next section contains details on these topics.

Real Time Apply

Data Guard Log Apply Services can automatically apply information from redo logs to standby databases, keeping data synchronized with the primary database. In general, log apply services wait for the full archived redo log to arrive to the standby database host before applying to the standby database.

Redo data is received by the remote file server process (RFS) on the standby system, where the RFS process writes the redo data to either archived redo logs or optionally to a standby redo log. However, if a standby redo log is used, real time apply can be enabled, which allows Data Guard to recover redo data from the current standby redo log as it is being filled by the RFS process. This facility of real time apply is a new feature introduced in Oracle database 10*g*.

It has the benefit of quicker switchover, instantly updating results after a physical standby database is changed to read-only with up-to-date reporting from a logical standby database.

The ALTER DATABASE statement can be used to enable the real-time apply feature. For example, in physical standby databases, issue the statement,

```
ALTER DATABASE RECOVER MANAGED STANDBY DATABASE USING CURRENT
LOGFILE;
```

For logical standby databases, issue the statement,

```
ALTER DATABASE START LOGICAL STANDBY APPLY IMMEDIATE;
```

To determine if real time apply is enabled, the *recovery_mode* column in the *v$archive_dest_status* view can be queried. It will display MANAGED REAL TIME APPLY when real time apply is enabled.

If a delay is defined on a destination, with the DELAY attribute, and Real Time Apply is used, the delay is ignored.

When, for any reason, the apply service is unable to keep up, the apply service will automatically go to the archive log files as needed. It will also try to catch up and go back to reading the current standby redo log file as soon as possible.

Authentication and Encryption

Data Guard log transport services can now use authenticated network sessions to transfer redo data between the members of a Data Guard configuration. If the Oracle Advanced Security option is also installed, using encryption can increase security further and integrity checksums on network transmission of redo data.

Authentication is now required for all redo shipments. The *remote_login_passwordfile* parameter must be set to SHARED or EXCLUSIVE mode at all sites in the configuration. The password for SYS must be identical at all databases.

In order to enable encryption of the redo information, follow these requirements:

- Install Oracle Advanced Security option at both the primary and standby database.

- Set up the appropriate *sqlnet.ora* parameters as documented in the Oracle Advanced Security manual to allow Oracle Net to encrypt and integrity checksum the redo traffic shipped to the standby.

Oracle documentation should be consulted for information on setting up the encryption.

Using *sp-name*

The *sp-name* initialization parameter specifies the unique service provider name for the standby database. Data Guard identifies all the databases in its configuration from their service provider names. A service provider name can be assigned with the *sp_name*. When the database identifiers are assigned with this parameter, keep names that are unique for each database. The *sp_name* value must remain constant for a given database.

Each *sp_name* value can be up to 30 characters long and should be the same for all instances in a RAC database. *sp_name* replaces *lock_name_space*, which is now deprecated. *lock_name_space* can still be used and it will not halt the startup of the instance. However, *sp_name* takes precedence over *lock_name_space*. The default is the database name. If the Data Guard Manager GUI is used to create a standby, it will set this to a unique value for the new standby.

Using *sp_name*, the configuration can be defined with the initialization parameter *log_archive_config*.

Simplified creation of logical standby in 10g

In earlier releases, it was difficult to create the logical standby database without shutting down the primary database. If the online backup was used to create the logical standby, a quiesce of the database at the end of backup is needed, which also required the resource manager. The SCN must also be recorded. These actions necessitated the primary database shutdown.

With Oracle Database 10*g*, there is no need to quiesce the primary database. The required information is read through the logical standby control file. Oracle recommends the use of a new method to create a logical standby database that is explained next.

This new method will allow the DBA to achieve 'zero down time instantiation' by using an online backup of the primary database and the logical standby control file.

The suggested steps are as follows:

1. Take an online backup of the primary database. Optionally, the offline backup of the primary database can be used. If the offline backup is used, all the archive log files from the time of the backup are needed.

2. After the backup is obtained, create a logical standby control file with the newly provided CREATE LOGICAL CONTROL FILE command. For example, use the following statement:

```
ALTER DATABASE CREATE LOGICAL STANDBY CONTROL FILE AS
'mylogicalstandby.ctl';
```

The logical standby control file is similar to the physical control file but has additional information.

3. Copy all the backup files, archive files, and logical standby control files to the standby host.

4. After restoring all the files, mount the standby database with the logical standby control file.

5. Set up the log transport services on the primary.

6. Start the managed recovery on the standby database. Execute the following statement.

```
ALTER DATABASE RECOVER MANAGED STANDBY DATABASE;
```

7. Then, begin applying the redo logs. To start the log apply services, execute the statement:

```
ALTER DATABASE START LOGICAL STANDBY APPLY;
```

Using the Standby Redo Log Files

The concept of the standby redo log files was introduced in Oracle9i. However, this was confined to the physical standby databases only.

With the introduction of support for standby redo logs for logical standby databases in Oracle10g, it is possible to have a logical standby database be a part of a Data Guard configuration running in maximum protection mode. In this way, the Data Guard SQL Apply method offers complete zero-data-loss support.

The archiver process (ARCn) or the log writer process (LGWR) on the primary database can transmit redo data directly to remote standby redo logs. Thus, this process eliminates the need to register partial archived redo logs. Standby redo logs can also be multiplexed using multiple members, improving reliability over archived redo logs.

To create a new group of standby redo logs, use the ALTER DATABASE statement with the *add standby logfile group* clause. The size of a standby redo log must exactly match the primary database online redo logs.

The following benefits accrue from the standby redo log files:

- During a failover, standby redo logs enable Data Guard to apply more redo data than what is available in the archived redo logs alone.

- Standby redo logs are required to implement the maximum protection and maximum availability levels of data protection (no-data-loss) disaster recovery solutions.

- Standby redo logs are required to implement real time apply.

- Standby redo logs are required for cascaded redo log destinations.

With the help of this method, it becomes possible to eliminate the potential need to register partial archived redo logs, and it allows as the configuration of as many cascaded redo log destinations as are needed.

Data Guard Broker improvements

The DGMGRL CLI command set is used to configure the standby configuration. Oracle Database 10*g* has introduced many improvements to the command set and has also added extra functionality. Many of the commands have been simplified.

The CREATE CONFIGURATION COMMAND is highly simplified and only three arguments need to be provided.

- The *configuration-name* is a name provided for the broker configuration.

- The *database-name* is the name that will be used by the broker to refer to the primary database object.

- The *connect-identifier* can be a fully specified connect-descriptor or a name to be resolved via an Oracle Net naming method, such as TNS, to the primary database.

The Data Guard Broker has several new commands to manage. They are as follows: ADD DATABASE, EDIT DATABASE, REMOVE DATABASE, DISABLE DATABASE, ENABLE DATABASE, EDIT INSTANCE, and EDIT CONFIGURATION.

Some of these commands are replacements for obsolete commands.

- DISABLE DATABASE replaces DISABLE RESOURCE

- ENABLE DATABASE replaces ENABLE RESOURCE

- EDIT DATABASE replaces ALTER RESOURC

- EDIT CONFIGURATION replaces ALTER CONFIGURATION

The Data Guard broker has added support for RAC databases. RAC databases allow multiple instances to access a single, shared database.

A RAC database can be configured and supported in a Data Guard configuration using the GUI or the command line interface. The DGMGRL commands and GUI pages can be used for a RAC database, just as they are used for a single instance database.

The broker only supports the sending of all redos to one instance on the standby database. The standby database can be a single instance database or a RAC database, but in either case, only one instance will act as the receiving instance and the apply instance.

10g Data Guard Supplemental Logging

Supplemental Logging enhancements are aimed at improving streams and other data sharing facilities.

Oracle Database 10*g* introduces two new options for identification key logging at the database level. With database-level identification key logging, the DBA can enable database-wide before image logging for all updates. In addition to PRIMARY KEY and UNIQUE INDEX, the following two new identification keys can also be used:

- **ALL** - This option specifies that when a row is updated, all the columns of that row, except for columns of type LOB, LONG, LONG RAW, and user-defined types, are placed in the redo log file.

- **FOREIGN KEY** - This option causes the Oracle database to place all columns of a row's foreign key in the redo log file, if any column belonging to the foreign key is modified.

When identification key logging is enabled at the database level, minimal supplemental logging is enabled implicitly.

Table supplemental logging specifies, at the table level, which columns are to be supplementally logged. Identification key logging or user-defined conditional and unconditional supplemental log groups can be used to log supplemental information.

Identification of key logging at the table level offers the same options as those provided at the database level: all, primary key, foreign key, and unique index. However, when identification key logging is specified at the table level, only the specified table is affected.

Starting with Oracle Database 10g, supplemental logging statements are cumulative. For example, if two consecutive ALTER DATABASE ADD SUPPLEMENTAL LOG DATA commands are issued, each with a different identification key, both keys are supplementally logged.

Upgrading to Oracle10g Data Guard

Upgrading to Oracle10g database software in a Data Guard environment involves the following activities:

- If the Data Guard configuration is managed by Data Guard broker, the broker configuration needs to be removed using the existing version of database software. In other words, remove the Oracle9i configuration before upgrading to Oracle10g. Execute the following command after connecting to any site in the configuration using DGMGRL to remove the configuration:

  ```
  REMOVE CONFIGURATION;
  ```

- Install Oracle10g database software. The Data Guard feature is not available with the Standard edition, so the Enterprise edition must be installed. Additionally, install Oracle Enterprise Manager (OEM) 10.1 in order to manage the configuration using Data Guard Manager GUI interface, which is tightly integrated with OEM.

- The primary and standby databases should be upgraded to Oracle10g. The log management services should be stopped during the primary database upgrade. All of the redo logs generated during the database upgrade should be applied manually on each standby database. For more information on upgrading to Oracle10g, refer to the documentation, "Oracle Database Upgrade Guide 10g Release 1(10.1)".

- Update the initialization parameter files or server parameter files on the primary database and all the standby databases to include the parameter *db_unique_name*. The database unique name must be identical on all the databases in a configuration.

- Once all the databases in the Data Guard configuration are upgraded to Oracle10g, the broker configuration file will have to be created in order to manage it using Data Guard broker. Execute the following command, connecting to the primary database using DGMGRL, to recreate the broker configuration file and to add standby databases:

```
CREATE CONFIGURATION '<ConfigName>' AS PRIMARY DATABASE IS
'<Primary Database Name>' CONNECT IDENTIFIER IS <Service name>;
ADD DATABASE '<Standby Database Name>' AS CONNECT IDENTIFIER IS
<Service Name> MAINTAINED AS PHYSICAL;
```

Architectural Changes

Data Guard architecture has been fine tuned in Oracle10g to support some of the previously unsupported features. These architectural modifications have primarily been around log management services. Moreover, the integration of Data Guard technology and Flashback database has resulted in a couple of useful techniques available to database administrators. This section looks further into these changes and their impact.

Standby Redo Logs

The following features related to standby redo log files are new in Oracle10g:

- Oracle10g supports the standby redo logs on a logical standby database, which was not feasible in the previous version of

Oracle. As a result, the logical standby database can now be configured in maximum data protection modes such as MAXIMUM PROTECTION and MAXIMUM AVAILABILITY. The "ALTER DATABASE ADD STANDBY LOGFILE" statement can be used to add standby redo log files on the logical standby database. The usage of this SQL statement is the same for physical and logical standby databases and is described in detail in Chapter 5, "Log Management Services".

- In Oracle10g, the ARCn process can be configured as the archiving agent when using standby redo log files on remote sites. In this scenario, the archiver process keeps sending the redo logs to remote sites as a redo log is generated on the primary site. As a result, in case of disaster and complete loss of the primary database, the entire redo log worth of data will not be lost because the standby redo log file on standby site will contain some or all of the transactions contained in the lost redo log file. This has been one of the most useful enhancements in Data Guard technology, as it minimizes the loss of data while operating in MAXIMUM PERFORMANCE mode.

- In the previous version of Oracle database, the standby redo log file needed to be archived before the transactions embedded in those log files could be applied onto the standby database. Oracle10g provides the ability to configure the log apply service to immediately apply the redo log transaction directly from the standby redo log files. This improves the reporting capabilities from the logical standby database and reduces the down time required for switchover or failover operation. Real-time apply is not the default behavior. The following statements can be executed on the standby site to enable the real-time redo apply feature:

On Physical Standby Database

```
ALTER DATABASE RECOVER MANAGED STANDBY DATABASE USING CURRENT
LOGFILE;
```

On Logical Standby Database

```
ALTER DATABASE START LOGICAL STANDBY APPLY IMMEDIATE;
```

Flashback Database

Flashback database is an alternate solution to point-in-time recovery. It allows the restoration of a database from the flashback logs and archived redo log files. This is not a default feature, so the primary and standby databases will need to be configured to use the flashback database functionality.

Once configured, any change made on the primary database is recorded in the flashback recovery area in the form of change vectors or flashback logs. There are two important advantages of using the flashback database in conjunction with Data Guard. The two advantages are as follows:

- It removes the necessity of adding delay in the log apply service in order to avoid any corruption of the standby database due to user errors. If a data error is propagated to a standby database, the standby database can be re-created to a point in time just prior to when the error occurred, and a switchover can be performed to recover the overall situation. Similarly, the primary database can be flashed back to a point in time in order to remove the transactions containing data error. In the previous version of Oracle database, correcting this situation would have required a switchover and re-creation of the primary database.

- Configuring the flashback database feature on the primary database removes the need for recreating the database after a failover operation. It can simply be flashed back to a point in time just prior to the failover and all archived redo log files applied to roll forward.

> In case of media failure, it may not be possible to flashback without recovering the affected data files. In this scenario, a combination of traditional tablespace point-in-time recovery and flashback database technology will be very useful to achieve a fast recovery.

For more information regarding flashback technology, refer to the documentation, "Oracle Database Backup and Recovery Advanced User's Guide 10g Release 1 (10.1)".

Creating Standby Databases Using Oracle10g

Oracle10g has expanded the data type support in logical standby databases and has simplified the task of logical standby database creation. This section presents a list of new data types supported in Oracle10g logical standby database and a step-by-step guide to creating a logical standby database by transitioning the physical standby database.

This method of creating a logical standby database is not possible in Oracle9i, because Oracle9i does not support the logical control file.

> There is no change in the procedure for creating a physical standby database.

Enhanced Data Type Support

The following data types and table storage are supported in the logical standby database in Oracle10g; however, they were not supported in Oracle9i:

- NCLOB

- LONG and LONG RAW

- Index-Organized Tables. The index-organized tables should not contain any LOB columns and should be defined without any overflow clause.

The SQL statements required to find the unsupported type and objects that remain unchanged are described in detail in Chapter 3, "Implementing Standby Databases".

Creating Logical Standby Databases

A logical standby database in Oracle10g is transitioned from a physical standby database. In order to create a logical standby database, a physical standby database must be created. This is a much simpler task.

In this section, it is assumed that the primary database and the standby database reside on separate hosts. A quick review of the standby database creation concepts explained in Chapter 3, "Implementing Standby Databases," is good preparation for this section, as most of the concepts presented here are similar to those of Oracle9i that are described in great detail in that chapter.

Following is the step-by-step guide that is used to create a logical standby database:

- Enable the forced logging to capture all database changes in the redo log file. To enable the FORCE LOGGING, execute the following statement on primary database:

```
ALTER DATABASE FORCE LOGGING;
```

- Enable the supplemental data logging to capture additional information that assists the SQL apply operation on the logical standby database. Supplemental logging can be enabled by executing the following statement on the primary database:

```
ALTER DATABASE ADD SUPPLEMENTAL LOG DATA (PRIMARY KEY, UNIQUE
INDEX) COLUMNS;
```

- Create a physical standby database and start the managed recovery mode so that the primary database and the standby database are in sync. The method of creating a physical standby database is explained in detailed in Chapter 3 of this book.

- Once the physical standby database is recovered to the last available archived redo log file, start the process of transitioning it to a logical standby database. Modify the initialization parameter file to support the logical standby database. A logical standby database has its own online log file, which will be archived to one of the local archived destination. As a result, a log archival destination preferably, *log_archive_dest_1* should be configured to handle it. Also, in order to have an efficient log apply service, increase the *parallel-max_server* parameter from the default value of five to the default value of nine which is the setting recommended by Oracle. The following is an extract of the *init.ora* parameter file from a standby database showing the log management parameters:

```
# Archive
STANDBY_ARCHIVE_DEST=/oracle/stdby10g/arch/
LOG_ARCHIVE_DEST_1='LOCATION=/oracle/stdby10g/archlocal'
LOG_ARCHIVE_DEST_STATE_1=ENABLE
LOG_ARCHIVE_FORMAT=apps10g_%t_%s_%r.dbf
LOG_ARCHIVE_DEST_2='SERVICE=apps10g'
LOG_ARCHIVE_DEST_STATE_2=DEFER
LOG_ARCHIVE_TRACE=255
REMOTE_ARCHIVE_ENABLE=TRUE
PARALLEL_MAX_SERVERS=9
```

- Stop the managed recovery process and shutdown the physical standby database.

- Create a logical standby control file using the following statement on the primary database. Copy this control file to the location specified by the *control_files* parameter:

```
ALTER DATABASE CREATE LOGICAL STANDBY CONTROLFILE AS 'FILESPEC';
```

Creating Standby Databases Using Oracle10g **287**

For Example

```
ALTER DATABASE CREATE LOGICAL STANDBY CONTROLFILE AS
'/oracle/stdby10g/control/control01.ctl';
```

- The create control file statement also creates the LogMiner dictionary; hence, it may take few minutes to create, depending on the availability of the computing resources. LogMiner dictionary creation can be verified from the *v$archived_log* view.

- The primary database generates redo data during the LogMiner dictionary build. The redo data needs to be applied on the physical standby database before activating it as the logical standby database. In order to apply these log files, mount the physical standby database and start the recovery. The control file used to mount the database is a logical control file, so it is not essentially a physical standby database; however, this database is still in the PHYSICAL STANDBY database role as evident from the *v$database* view. The statement shown below will start the recovery of standby database:

```
STARTUP MOUNT;
ALTER DATABASE RECOVER MANAGED STANDBY DATABASE;
```

- Once all the archived redo logs have been applied onto the standby database, control will return to the user. At this point, the standby database can be activated as the logical standby database using the following statement:

```
ALTER DATABASE ACTIVATE STANDBY DATABASE;
```

- The next step is to change the name of database using *nid* utility and reflect the new name in the initialization parameters file. After changing the database name, mount and open it using RESETLOGS. Create temp files for the temp tablespace, and start the log apply service. These steps are identical to the steps used for Oracle9i, and are explained in Chapter 3 of this text.

- The verification techniques remain same as explained for Oracle9i.

Oracle10g has greatly improved the logging messages in the alert log file. The alert log file gives the warning message and hints on how to resolve the issue.

In the next section the enhancement in administration and management of standby databases will be presented.

Improvements in Data Guard Management

There are a few enhancements to further ease the administration and management of Data Guard configuration. These improvements are summarized in this section.

Administration of Standby Database

Startup statements for the physical standby database have been modified in Oracle10g. A summary of these changes is listed below:

- To start a physical standby database and put it in managed recovery mode, execute the following statements:

  o Connect using SYS or any other account having SYSDBA privilege.

  ```
  STARTUP MOUNT;
  ALTER DATABASE RECOVER MANAGED STANDBY DATABASE
  DISCONNECT FROM SESSION;
  ```

- To start a physical standby in READ ONLY mode, issue the STARTUP statement after connecting using SYS or any other account having SYSDBA privilege.

- To put a physical standby database in READ ONLY mode from Managed Recovery mode, issue the following statements:

  o Connect using sys or any other account having SYSDBA privilege.

```
ALTER DATABASE RECOVER MANAGED STANDBY DATABASE CANCEL;
ALTER DATABASE OPEN;
```

The next section provides information on the Oracle10g improvements to log management.

Improved Log Management Services

Data Guard technology in Oracle9i poses the challenge of maintaining valid database initialization parameters during and after role changes. For example, when a standby database is transitioned into the primary role, the log management related parameters need to be updated to suit the new role of the database.

VALID_FOR Attribute

One method of approaching this challenge was by using the symmetrical initialization parameter file as explained in Chapter 3, "Implementing Standby Databases". Some DBAs keep two versions of the initialization parameter file to cater different database roles. Oracle10g has removed the need to alter the log management related initialization parameters during role transition by introducing a new attribute of the *log_archive_dest_n* parameter called VALID_FOR. This attribute is defined using two arguments *redo_log_type* and *database_role* as shown below:

```
LOG_ARCHIVE_DEST_n='SERVICE=service_name
VALID_FOR=(redo_log_type,database_role)'
```

These two arguments identify the role of the database specified by the *log_archive_dest_n* parameter and the type of redo log file used at that destination.

The valid values of *redo_log_type* are ONLINE_LOGFILE, STANDBY_LOGFILE and ALL_LOGFILES.

The second argument, *database_role*, can take the value of the PRIMARY_ROLE, the STANDBY_ROLE or ALL_ROLES.

Combining these two arguments give nine possible values for the attribute VALID_FOR. However, the combination (STANDBY_LOGFILE, PRIMARY_ROLES) is not acceptable, because there cannot be active standby redo log files on the primary database. The default combination is (ALL_LOGFILES, ALL_ROLES). The following snippet from the *init.ora* file shows an example of the VALID_FOR attribute:

```
LOG_ARCHIVE_DEST_1='LOCATION=/oracle/appsdb/arch
VALID FOR=(ONLINE LOGFILE, ALL_ROLE)'
LOG_ARCHIVE_DEST_2='SERVICE=phystdydb VALID_FOR=(ONLINE_LOGFILE,
PRIMARY_ROLE)'
LOG_ARCHIVE_DEST_3='SERVICE=logstdbydb VALID_FOR=(ONLINE_LOGFILE,
PRIMARY ROLE)'
LOG_ARCHIVE_DEST_4='LOCATION=/oracle/appsdb/archSRL
VALID_FOR-(STANDBY_LOGFILE,STANDBY_ROLE)'
```

In the example given above, *log_archive_dest_1* is valid only for the primary database role and the logical standby database role.

On the logical standby site, the redo data generated from the logical standby database will be archived in this location. It will not contain the archived standby redo log files.

On the physical standby site, this destination will not play any part because the RFS process decides the archival destination based on the *standby_archive_dest* parameter, and the MRP uses the archived log files from this location. *log_archive_dest_2* and *log_archive_dest_3* are only valid when the database is operating in the primary role.

A proper Oracle Net configuration as detailed in Chapter 3, "Implementing Standby Databases", is the key to the seamless use of the VALID_FOR attribute during role transition. *log_archive_dest_4* is only valid if the standby databases have standby redo log files configured.

> Do not use (ALL_LOGFILES, ALL_ROLES) for log archival destination that is a logical standby database. This may overwrite the online log files local to the logical standby database.

Secure Redo Data Transmission

Oracle10g supports the secure transmission of redo data by the log transport service using a password file based authentication. To use this feature, the following instructions must to be executed on all databases participating in Data Guard configuration:

- Set the *remote_login_passwordfile* initialization parameter to EXCLUSIVE or SHARED.

- Create a password file using the *orapwd* utility on all databases involved in Data Guard configuration. The password for the SYS account should be identical on all the databases.

Once these two changes are made, the log transport service on the primary database authenticates the remote archival destination using the SYS password before transmitting the redo data. In Oracle10g, the log transport services will not work if a password file is not configured on all the sites and if the SYS password is not identical for all the participating databases.

SGA Buffer Size for an Asynchronous Redo Transfer

In order to transmit redo data asynchronously, buffer blocks within SGA should be allocated to keep the redo data in memory during the transmission to remote archival destinations. In Oracle10g, the upper limit of network buffer blocks has been raised to 102,400 blocks of 512-bytes. This alleviates the performance issue in asynchronous redo transmission on very high transaction intensive databases. The following snippet from the *init.ora* parameter file shows an asynchronous transfer using the largest network buffer size:

```
LOG_ARCHIVE_DEST_3='SERVICE=stdby2 LGWR ASYNC=102400'
```

Data Guard Performance Improvement

Standby databases in a Data Guard environment can be configured to operate in MAXIMUM PERFORMANCE mode. This setup is common in systems where performance is of the utmost importance, and a small amount of data loss is acceptable in case of disaster and complete loss of the primary database. In such an environment, the primary database uses the ARCn process as the archiving agent.

In Oracle9i Data Guard, the archiver process, ARCn, is triggered on a log switch. It simultaneously initiates the archiving to local and remote archival destinations. The redo log group on the primary database will not be marked for reuse until archiving to all destinations is complete. As a consequence, a Data Guard configuration containing a standby database connected over a wide area network may suffer a significant impact on performance, and negate the meaning of term MAXIMUM PERFORMANCE.

Oracle10g addresses this issue by splitting local archiving from remote archiving when configured in MAXIMUM PERFORMANCE mode. The default behavior is to archive the online redo log file to local destinations and then start archiving to remote destinations. Archival to a remote destination will not begin until the online redo log file is written completely to at least one local destination.

At this point, the redo log group is marked for reuse with the result of minimizing impact on the primary database performance. The benefit of this feature is obvious in transaction intensive databases, in which a few hundred megabytes of redo is generated every minute.

This new behavior of log transport service is controlled by the *log_archive_local_first* parameter. It is a boolean parameter and can be set to TRUE or FALSE. The default value is TRUE. Setting it to FALSE will emulate the Oracle9i archiving behavior.

Conclusion

The main purpose of this chapter was to introduce the new Data Guard features of Oracle10g. In most of the sections, the functionality of Oracle10g has been compared with that provided in Oracle9i. The following salient Data Guard features of Oracle10g have been covered:

- Guidelines on upgrading to Oracle10g Data Guard from previous releases.

- Architectural changes such as standby redo logs and flashback databases to enhance the performance and ease the administration and management of Data Guard configuration.

- Creating a logical standby database by transitioning the physical standby database. This reduces the complexity in the logical standby database creation.

- Enhancements in the log management service and improvements in Data Guard performance.

Book Conclusion

This book is the result of many years of working with Oracle standby database and using Oracle Data Guard on a daily basis.

As a working Oracle professional, it has been my intent to deliver a practical book that shows you all of the steps and procedures for succeeding in your disaster recovery and Oracle failover endeavors.

I'm always seeking new techniques and approaches. I invite you to share any ideas or techniques that I might use to improve my book.

Please feel free to e-mail me at info@rampant.cc with "Bipul Kumar" in the subject line. I sincerely hope that you enjoyed this book as much as I did writing it.

Data Guard Reference

Oracle Data Recovery demands the latest technology.

Data Guard Reference

This appendix introduces the initialization parameters, dynamic performance views and PL/SQL package relevant to Data Guard technology. It only presents the more important parameters, views and package references. Readers are encouraged to refer to Oracle manual "Oracle Data Guard Concepts and Administration Release 2(9.2)", "Oracle9i Database Reference Release 2(9.2)", "PL/SQL Packages and Types References 10g

Release 1(10.1)" and other Oracle documentation for more information on these parameters, views, and packages.

Initialization Parameters

In this section, the initialization parameters that control the behavior of Data Guard are presented. For these initialization parameters, a brief description, the default value and a recommended value will be provided wherever applicable.

The *db_file_name_convert* parameter

This parameter is used when the file path on primary database and standby database is not identical. It is only applicable to physical standby database. This parameter must be set in the initialization parameter file and the database restarted. It is a static parameter and cannot be modified using the ALTER SYSTEM statement. More than one file path pattern can be specified in the argument list as shown below.

```
DB_FILE_NAME_CONVERT= ('string1','string2','string3','string4')
```

Where string1 and string 3 are the file path patterns on the primary database and string2 and string4 are the corresponding file path patterns on the standby database.

For example:

```
DB_FILE_NAME_CONVERT=('/oracle/appsdb','/oracle/stdbydb')
```

This parameter does not have any default value.

The *fal_client* parameter

This parameter specifies the Oracle Net service name of physical standby database on primary site. This is used for the automatic gap resolution using the FAL (Fetch Archive Log) method. It can be set in the initialization parameter file on physical standby database or can be modified using ALTER SYSTEM statement. The following example shows the usage of *fal_client* parameter.

```
FAL_CLIENT=stdby1
```

stdby1 is the Oracle Net service name defined on the primary site pointing to this physical standby database.

The *fal_server* parameter

The *fal_server* is the Oracle Net service name of the server defined on a physical standby site that can be used for archive gap resolution. This is a dynamic parameter and can be set either in the initialization parameter file or modified using ALTER SYSTEM statement. Typically, this is set to the service name pointing to primary database. The following example shows its usage:

```
FAL_SERVER=primary1
```

primary1 is the service name of the primary database defined on the standby site.

The *log_archive_dest_n* parameter

This is the most important parameter in the working of Data Guard, especially the log management services. It has several attributes that can be used to fine control the log transport process serving various archival destinations identified by *n*, which can take values between 1 through 10. It can be set in the initialization parameter file as a list of strings separated by space or using ALTER SYSTEM statements as shown below. Some of the attributes can be set at session level as well. Refer to Oracle documentation, "Oracle Data Guard Concepts and

Administration Release 2(9.2)" for more information on these attributes.

```
LOG_ARCHIVE_DEST_1='LOCATION=/oracle/appsdb/arch MANDATORY
REOPEN=10'
ALTER SYSTEM SET LOG_ARCHIVE_DEST_1='LOCATION=/oracle/appsdb/arch'
ALTER SYSTEM SET LOG_ARCHIVE_DEST_1='MANDATORY REOPEN=10'
```

Setting the LOCATION attribute using ALTER SYSTEM statement resets all the previously set attributes for an archival destination. The following table lists these attributes along with their description and possible values.

Attribute Name	Description	Possible Values
LOCATION	Specifies the directory on local disk where redo logs will be archived. This is a mandatory parameter.	A valid directory on disk accessible to the host machine.
SERVICE	Specifies the Oracle Net service name of the standby database where redo logs will be remotely archived.	A valid Oracle Net service name of a standby database.
MANDATORY	An archival destination when marked as MANDATORY must receive archived redo logs on log switch. The online redo logs on the primary database cannot be reused if archival to a mandatory destination fails.	MANDATORY

Attribute Name	Description	Possible Values
OPTIONAL	It sets an archival destination as an OPTIONAL destination. The primary database will not be impacted if archival to an optional destination does not succeed.	OPTIONAL
REOPEN	Specifies the number of seconds before the archiver process will retry archiving to a previously failed destination.	Time in number of seconds. Minimum delay between retry is 60 seconds i.e. the rate of heartbeat.
NOREOPEN	Archiver process will not retry to open the archival destination marked as NOREOPEN.	NOREOPEN
DELAY	Specifies the time delay between the log transfer service and the log apply service.	Number of minutes. The default value is 30 minutes.
NODELAY	Specifies no delay between the log transfer and log apply services.	NODELAY
REGISTER	Specifies that the name and location of the archived redo logs to be recorded in the control file of the standby database.	REGISTER is the default value for *log_archive_dest_n* parameter.

Attribute Name	Description	Possible Values
NOREGISTER	Specifies that the name and location of archived redo logs should not be recorded in the control file of the standby database.	NOREGISTER
ALTERNATE	Specifies the alternate location for archiving if the archiving to the original destination fails.	A valid log archiving destination specified by *log_archive_dest_n* parameter.
NOALTERNATE	Archiver process will not try to archive to any alternate destination in case archiving to the original destination fails.	NOALTERNATE
TEMPLATE	Specifies the location and log archive format for remote arching at the standby site.	Valid location and log file naming format.
NOTEMPLATE	Does not specify any location and file name format. The location and file name format in this case will be determined from the *standby_archive_dest* and *log_archive_format* parameter.	NOTEMPLATE

Attribute Name	Description	Possible Values
DEPENDENCY	Specifies a parent-child relationship between two archival destinations. The destination acting as the parent should be defined as LOCATION and the child destination as SERVICE.	Valid local log archival destination defined in the initialization parameter file.
NODEPENDENCY	Specifies no parent-child relationship between two destinations. In this case, the archiver should archive to all enabled destinations.	NODEPENDENCY
ARCH	Specifies ARHC process as the archiver agent.	ARCH
LGWR	Specifies log writer as the archiver agent. Required for high data availability mode.	LGWR
SYNC	Specifies that the log transport process should synchronously perform the network I/O activity.	SYNC=PARALLEL SYNC=NOPARALLEL
ASYNC	Specifies that the log transport process should asynchronously perform the I/O activity.	ASYNC=[Size of SGA network buffer to use]

Attribute Name	Description	Possible Values
AFFIRM	Specifies that the disk I/O on the remote archival site should be performed synchronously. Redo log file on the primary database is not used unless the redo log is completely archived on the remote destination.	AFFIRM
NOAFFIRM	Specifies that the disk I/O on the remote archival destination can be performed asynchronously, i.e. the redo log file on the primary database can be used without waiting for disk I/O to complete on the remote site.	NOAFFIRM
MAX_FAILURE	Specifies the number of consecutive retry log transport service will make to a failed destination. This should be specified with REOPEN.	MAX_FAILURE= [Number of retries]
NOMAX_FAILURE	Specifies unlimited number of attempts to archive to a previously failed destination.	NOMAX_FAILURE

Attribute Name	Description	Possible Values
QUOTA_SIZE	Size of physical device allocated for redo log archival to a local destination. This is specified in 512-byte blocks.	QUOTA_SIZE=[Size in K,M or G]
NOQUOTA_SIZE	Specifies no limitation on the disk usage by the archiver process to the local archival destinations.	NOQUOTA_SIZE
QUOTA_USED	Actual usage of local archival destination. This attribute is determined by Oracle and cannot be set.	
NOQUOTA_USED	Same as NOQOUTA_SIZE. This attribute is determined by Oracle and cannot be set.	
NET_TIMEOUT	Specifies the number of seconds the log writer of the primary database will wait before breaking the Oracle net connection to the standby site, if the standby site does not respond to parallel synchronous or asynchronous log transfer.	NET_TIMEOUT= [Number of Seconds]. Default is NONET_TIMEOUT. This should be set to a small value to avoid any stalling of the primary database.

Attribute Name	Description	Possible Values
NONET_TIMEOUT	Specifies that the log writer process of the primary database should wait until it receives acknowledgement of network I/O from the standby site.	NONET_TIMEOUT
VERIFY[10g]	Specifies that the archiver process should verify the correctness of archived redo log files after completing the disk I/O. This attribute is not available when LGWR is used as archiver agent.	VERIFY
NOVERIFY[10g]	Specifies that the archiver process need not verify the correctness of archived redo log files after completing the disk I/O.	NOVERIFY
VALID_FOR[10g]	Controls the transmission of redo data to the standby site based on the role of the database and the state of the redo log files.	VALID_FOR= (redo_log_type, database_role)

Attribute Name	Description	Possible Values
DB_UNIQUE_NAME[10g]	Specifies the unique db name for standby database. This should match the value defined by *db_unique_name* parameter. Log transfer service cannot communicate if the *db_unique_name* is not set correctly.	DB_UNIQUE_NAME= string
NODB_UNIQUE_AME [10g]	Log transfer service does not verify the database name.	NODB_UNIQUE_ NAME

[10g] - These attributes are applicable with Oracle 10g Release 1(10.1)

The *db_unique_name* parameter

This parameter specifies a name that uniquely identifies the databases in the Data Guard configuration. The *db_unique_name* attribute specifies the unique database unique name for this destination. The *db_unique_name* attribute must match the value that was defined originally for this database with the *db_unique_name* initialization parameter. There is no default value for this attribute.

The *db_unique_name*=NAME attribute must match the *db_unique_name* initialization parameter of the database identified by the destination. If the *log_archive_config*=*db_config* parameter is not specified, the *db_unique_name* attribute is optional. If the *log_archive_config*=*dg_config* parameter is specified, the *db_unique_name* attribute is required for remote destinations, specified with the *service* attribute, and must match one of the *db_unique_name* values in the *dg_config* list. Furthermore, log transport services validates that the *db_unique_name* of the database at the specified destination matches the *db_unique_name* attribute or the connection to that destination is refused

This parameter is required for remote destinations, specified with the *service* attribute, and must match one of the *db_unique_name* values in the *dg_config* list. Furthermore, log transport services validates that the *db_unique_name* of the database at the specified destination matches the *db_unique_name* attribute or the connection to that destination is refused.

This parameter is optional for local destinations, specified with the *location* attribute. However, a local destination is specified, the name specified with the *db_unique_name* attribute must match the name specified for the database's *db_unique_name* initialization parameter.

The *log_archive_dest_state_n* parameter

It is a corresponding parameter to *log_archive_dest_n* specifying the state of individual archival destinations. The valid values are ENABLE, ALTERNATE and DEFER. The default value is ENABLE. This parameter should be set on the database that is acting as the source of the archived redo logs to the archival destinations. The archiver process will not archive to a destination if this parameter is set to DEFER.

Using ALTERNATE, the dependency of one log archival destination upon other can be set. For example, if the goal is to have the archiver process to archive redo log files to destination #3 only if archiving to destination #2 does not succeed, the parameters should be set as follows:

```
LOG_ARCHIVE_DEST_STATE_2=ENABLE
LOG_ARCHIVE_DEST_STATE_3=ALTERNATE
```

The *log_file_name_convert* parameter

This parameter is similar to the *db_file_name_convert* parameter. It is used to map the file path patterns for redo log files when the directory structure of the primary database and the standby database is not identical. It can be set in the initialization parameter file of the physical standby database as shown below. It is not applicable to logical standby databases.

```
LOG_FILE_NAME_CONVERT=('/oracle/appsdb','/oracle/stdbydb'
```

The *remote_archive_enable* parameter

This parameter controls the sending and receiving of archived redo logs. The valid values are TRUE, FALSE, SEND and RECEIVE. The default value is TRUE. This parameter applies to both the primary and the standby database.

The *standby_archive_dest* parameter

This parameter is used to determine the location of archived redo log files delivered by the archiver process. It needs to be set on the standby database. The usage of this parameter is

```
STANDBY_ARCHIVE_DEST='/oracle/stdbydb/arch'
```

The *standby_file_management* parameter

This file management parameter controls propagation of changes made in datafiles or tablespaces on the primary database. The valid values are MANUAL and AUTO. The default value is MANUAL. It is recommended to set this parameter to AUTO to ease the administration of the standby database. This parameter must be set on the primary database. Its usage is shown in the following example:

Now that the basic parameters have been covered, the next step is to move on to take a look at the Oracle *v$* views that are used to monitor Data Guard configuration and performance.

Dynamic Performance Views

This section presents the dynamic performance views used for monitoring the Data Guard configuration. In this section, there will be a short description of the view and its useful columns. The views are categorized on the type of standby database. The views and columns marked with "10g" are not available for Oracle database software prior to Oracle10g Release 1.

Common Views

The following views contain information about both logical and physical standby database:

v$database

The following table presents the definition of the *v$database* view. This view can be queried on the primary, the physical, or the logical standby database and will provide information relevant to the database where it is being queried.

COLUMN_NAME	DATA_TYPE	DATA GUARD COLUMNS
ACTIVATION#	NUMBER	
ARCHIVELOG_CHANGE#	NUMBER	
ARCHIVE_CHANGE#	NUMBER	
CHECKPOINT_CHANGE#	NUMBER	
CONTROLFILE_CHANGE#	NUMBER	
CONTROLFILE_CREATED	DATE	
CONTROLFILE_SEQUENCE#	NUMBER	

COLUMN_NAME	DATA_TYPE	DATA GUARD COLUMNS
CONTROLFILE_TIME	DATE	
CONTROLFILE_TYPE	VARCHAR2	This indicates the type of control file. For standby databases the possible values are: STANDBY – For physical standby database. LOGICAL - For logical standby database.
CREATED	DATE	
DATABASE_ROLE	VARCHAR2	Specifies the database role. The possible values are: PHYSICAL STANDBY LOGICAL STANDBY
DATA GUARD_BROKER	VARCHAR2	Indicates if the DG Broker manages Data Guard configuration. The possible values are: ENABLED DISABLED
DBID	NUMBER	
FORCE_LOGGING	VARCHAR2	

COLUMN_NAME	DATA_TYPE	DATA GUARD COLUMNS
GUARD_STATUS	VARCHAR2	Specifies if the data in the logical standby database is protected by Data Guard. The possible values are: ALL STANDBY NONE
LOG_MODE	VARCHAR2	
NAME	VARCHAR2	
OPEN_MODE	VARCHAR2	
OPEN_RESETLOGS	VARCHAR2	
PRIOR_RESETLOGS_CHANGE#	NUMBER	
PRIOR_RESETLOGS_TIME	DATE	
PROTECTION_LEVEL	VARCHAR2	Specifies the aggregate data protection level across entire Data Guard configuration.
PROTECTION_MODE	VARCHAR2	Specifies the data protection mode.
REMOTE_ARCHIVE	VARCHAR2	
RESETLOGS_CHANGE#	NUMBER	
RESETLOGS_TIME	DATE	
SUPPLEMENTAL_LOG_DATA_MIN	VARCHAR2	
SUPPLEMENTAL_LOG_DATA_PK	VARCHAR2	
SUPPLEMENTAL_LOG_DATA_UI	VARCHAR2	

COLUMN_NAME	DATA_TYPE	DATA GUARD COLUMNS
SWITCHOVER_STATUS	VARCHAR2	Specifies the switchover status of the standby database. Refer to chapter 6 for more information on data provided by this column.
VERSION_TIME	DATE	

v$dataguard_status

The following table presents the definition of the *v$dataguard_status* view. This view can be queried on the primary, the physical, or the logical standby database. All columns of this view are relevant for Data Guard.

COLUMN_NAME	DATA_TYPE	DATA GUARD COLUMNS
CALLOUT	VARCHAR2	
DEST_ID	NUMBER	
ERROR_CODE	NUMBER	
FACILITY	VARCHAR2	Specifies the process that encountered the event.
MESSAGE	VARCHAR2	
MESSAGE_NUM	NUMBER	
SEVERITY	VARCHAR2	Severity of event.
TIMESTAMP	DATE	

v$logfile

Following table presents the definition of *v$logfile* view:

COLUMN_NAME	DATA_TYPE	DATA GUARD COLUMNS
GROUP#	NUMBER	
MEMBER	VARCHAR2	
STATUS	VARCHAR2	
TYPE	VARCHAR2	Indicates the type of redo log file. Possible values are: STANDBY ONLINE

v$standby_log

The following table presents the definition of the *v$standby_log* view. It contains data only if standby redo logs are created on the database.

COLUMN_NAME	DATA_TYPE	DATA GUARD COLUMNS
ARCHIVED	VARCHAR2	
BYTES	NUMBER	
FIRST_CHANGE#	NUMBER	
FIRST_TIME	DATE	
GROUP#	NUMBER	
LAST_CHANGE#	NUMBER	
LAST_TIME	DATE	
SEQUENCE#	NUMBER	
STATUS	VARCHAR2	Indicates the status of the standby redo log files.
THREAD#	NUMBER	
USED	NUMBER	

v$archived_log

The following table presents the definition of the *v$archived_log* view.

COLUMN_NAME	DATA_TYPE	DATA GUARD COLUMNS
ACTIVATION#	NUMBER	
APPLIED	VARCHAR2	
ARCHIVAL_THREAD#	NUMBER	
ARCHIVED	VARCHAR2	
BACKUP_COUNT	NUMBER	
BLOCKS	NUMBER	
BLOCK_SIZE	NUMBER	
COMPLETION_TIME	DATE	
CREATOR	VARCHAR2	
DELETED	VARCHAR2	
DEST_ID	NUMBER	
DICTIONARY_BEGIN	VARCHAR2	Indicates if the archived redo log file contains the start of logminer dictionary. Used for the Logical Standby Database creation.
DICTIONARY_END	VARCHAR2	Indicates if the archived redo log file contains the end of logminer dictionary. Used for the Logical Standby Database creation.
END_OF_REDO	VARCHAR2	
FIRST_CHANGE#	NUMBER	
FIRST_TIME	DATE	
NAME	VARCHAR2	

COLUMN_NAME	DATA_TYPE	DATA GUARD COLUMNS
NEXT_CHANGE#	NUMBER	
NEXT_TIME	DATE	
RECID	NUMBER	
REGISTRAR	VARCHAR2	
RESETLOGS_CHANGE#	NUMBER	
RESETLOGS_TIME	DATE	
SEQUENCE#	NUMBER	
STAMP	NUMBER	
STANDBY_DEST	VARCHAR2	Contains the service name of the standby database specified as the remote archival destination.
STATUS	VARCHAR2	
THREAD#	NUMBER	

v$archive_dest

The following table presents the definition of the *v$archive_dest* view. The columns correspond to the attributes setting for *log_archive_dest_n* initialization parameter. All columns are relevant for Data Guard configuration:

COLUMN_NAME	DATA_TYPE	DATA GUARD COLUMNS
AFFIRM	VARCHAR2	
ALTERNATE	VARCHAR2	
ARCHIVER	VARCHAR2	
ASYNC_BLOCKS	NUMBER	
BINDING	VARCHAR2	
DB_UNIQUE_NAME[10g]	VARCHAR2	
DELAY_MINS	NUMBER	
DEPENDENCY	VARCHAR2	

COLUMN_NAME	DATA_TYPE	DATA GUARD COLUMNS
DESTINATION	VARCHAR2	
DEST_ID	NUMBER	
DEST_NAME	VARCHAR2	
ERROR	VARCHAR2	
FAILURE_COUNT	NUMBER	
FAIL_BLOCK	NUMBER	
FAIL_DATE	DATE	
FAIL_SEQUENCE	NUMBER	
LOG_SEQUENCE	NUMBER	
MAX_FAILURE	NUMBER	
MOUNTID	NUMBER	
NAME_SPACE	VARCHAR2	
NET_TIMEOUT	NUMBER	
PROCESS	VARCHAR2	
QUOTA_SIZE	NUMBER	
QUOTA_USED	NUMBER	
REGISTER	VARCHAR2	
REMOTE_TEMPLATE	VARCHAR2	
REOPEN_SECS	NUMBER	
SCHEDULE	VARCHAR2	
STATUS	VARCHAR2	This column Is useful in the troubleshooting of the log transfer service.
TARGET	VARCHAR2	
TRANSMIT_MODE	VARCHAR2	
TYPE	VARCHAR2	
VALID_NOW[10g]	VARCHAR2	
VALID_TYPF[10g]	VARCHAR2	
VALID_ROLE[10g]	VARCHAR2	
VERIFY[10g]	VARCHAR2	

v$archive_dest_status

The following table presents the definition of the v$archive_dest_status view. All columns are relevant from the Data Guard perspective:

COLUMN_NAME	DATA_TYPE	DATA GUARD COLUMNS
APPLIED_SEQ#	NUMBER	
APPLIED_THREAD#	NUMBER	
ARCHIVED_SEQ#	NUMBER	
ARCHIVED_THREAD#	NUMBER	
DATABASE_MODE	VARCHAR2	
DB_UNIQUE_NAME[10g]	VARCHAR2	
DESTINATION	VARCHAR2	
DEST_ID	NUMBER	
DEST_NAME	VARCHAR2	
ERROR	VARCHAR2	
PROTECTION_MODE	VARCHAR2	
RECOVERY_MODE	VARCHAR2	
SRL	VARCHAR2	
STANDBY_LOGFILE_ACTIVE	NUMBER	
STANDBY_LOGFILE_COUNT	NUMBER	
STATUS	VARCHAR2	
TYPE	VARCHAR2	

v$archive_gap

The following table presents the definition of the v$archive_gap view. All columns are relevant from the Data Guard perspective:

COLUMN_NAME	DATA_TYPE	DATA GUARD COLUMNS
HIGH_SEQUENCE#	NUMBER	
LOW_SEQUENCE#	NUMBER	

COLUMN_NAME	DATA_TYPE	DATA GUARD COLUMNS
THREAD#	NUMBER	

v$dataguard_config [in Oracle 10g only]

The following table presents the definition of the *v$dataguard_config* view. It provides a view of the Data Guard environment from any site in the configuration:

COLUMN_NAME	DATA_TYPE	DATA GUARD COLUMNS
DB_UNIQUE_NAME	VARCHAR2	Shows the unique name of the current database and other databases in the configuration,

Physical Database Only Views

The *v$managed_standby* view contains information about the physical standby database only.

v$managed_standby

The following table presents the definition of the *v$managed_standby* view. It can be queried on the primary database and the physical standby database. On the primary database, it contains information about the archiver process. On the physical standby database it holds data related to the Remote File Server (RFS) and Managed Recovery Process (MRP). All columns are relevant to the Data Guard environment.

COLUMN_NAME	DATA_TYPE	DATA GUARD COLUMNS
ACTIVE_AGENTS	NUMBER	
BLOCK#	NUMBER	
BLOCKS	NUMBER	
CLIENT_DBID	VARCHAR2	
CLIENT_PID	VARCHAR2	
CLIENT_PROCESS	VARCHAR2	
DELAY_MINS	NUMBER	
GROUP#	VARCHAR2	
KNOWN_AGENTS	NUMBER	
PID	NUMBER	
PROCESS	VARCHAR2	
SEQUENCE#	NUMBER	
STATUS	VARCHAR2	
THREAD#	NUMBER	

Logical Database Only Views

The following views hold useful data relevant to the logical standby database.

v$logstdby

The following table presents the definition of the *v$logstdby* view. It should be queried on the logical standby database when the log apply service is running:

COLUMN_NAME	DATA_TYPE	DATA GUARD COLUMNS
HIGH_SCN	NUMBER	This column shows the progress of the log apply service.
LOGSTDBY_ID	NUMBER	

COLUMN_NAME	DATA_TYPE	DATA GUARD COLUMNS
PID	VARCHAR2	
SERIAL#	NUMBER	
STATUS	VARCHAR2	Status of processes involved in SQL Apply operation.
STATUS_CODE	NUMBER	
TYPE	VARCHAR2	

v$logstdby_stats

The following table presents the definition of the *v$logstdby_stats* view. It should be queried on the logical standby database when the log apply service is running. It is useful for performance monitoring of the log apply service:

COLUMN_NAME	DATA_TYPE	DATA GUARD COLUMNS
NAME	VARCHAR2	Name of the statistics
VALUE	VARCHAR2	Value of the statistics

dba_logstdby_events

The following table presents the definition of the *dba_logstdby_events* view. It contains information about the transactions applied on the logical standby database by the log apply service. It should be queried on the logical standby database. All the columns are relevant for the Data Guard environment.

COLUMN_NAME	DATA_TYPE	DATA GUARD COLUMNS
COMMIT_SCN	NUMBER	
CURRENT_SCN	NUMBER	

COLUMN_NAME	DATA_TYPE	DATA GUARD COLUMNS
EVENT	CLOB	
EVENT_TIME	DATE	
STATUS	VARCHAR2	
STATUS_CODE	NUMBER	
XIDSLT	NUMBER	
XIDSQN	NUMBER	
XIDUSN	NUMBER	

dba_logstdby_log

The following table presents the definition of the *dba_logstdby_log* view. It contains information about the archived redo logs applied on the logical standby database. It should be queried on the logical standby database. All the columns are relevant for the Data Guard environment.

COLUMN_NAME	DATA_TYPE	DATA GUARD COLUMNS
APPLIED[10g]	VARCHAR2	Indicates whether all the redo logs received by the RFS have been applied or not.
DICT_BEGIN	VARCHAR2	
DICT_END	VARCHAR2	
FILE_NAME	VARCHAR2	
FIRST_CHANGE#	NUMBER	
FIRST_TIME	DATE	
NEXT_CHANGE#	NUMBER	
NEXT_TIME	DATE	
SEQUENCE#	NUMBER	
THREAD#	NUMBER	
TIMESTAMP	DATE	

dba_logstdby_not_unique

The following table presents the definition of the *dba_logstdby_not_unique* view. It contains information about the tables that do not have a primary key or non-null unique key defined. It should be queried on the primary database prior to creating the logical standby database.

COLUMN_NAME	DATA_TYPE	DATA GUARD COLUMNS
BAD_COLUMN	VARCHAR2	
OWNER	VARCHAR2	
TABLE_NAME	VARCHAR2	

dba_logstdby_parameters

The following table presents the definition of the *dba_logstdby_parameters* view. It contains information about the parameters used by the log apply service. It should be queried on the logical standby database.

COLUMN_NAME	DATA_TYPE	DATA GUARD COLUMNS
NAME	VARCHAR2	Name of Parameter. Oracle 10g introduces three new parameters namely PREPARE_SERVERS APPLY_SERVERS APPLY_SCN
VALUE	VARCHAR2	Value of Parameter.

dba_logstdby_progress

The following table presents the definition of the *dba_logstdby_progress* view. It can be queried on the logical standby database to check the progress of the log apply service. Thread# and Sequence# columns have been introduced in Oracle10g to support the logical standby database in the Real Application cluster environment. All columns are relevant for the Data Guard environment.

COLUMN_NAME	DATA_TYPE	DATA GUARD COLUMNS
APPLIED_SCN	NUMBER	
APPLIED_TIME	DATE	
APPLIED_SEQUENCE# [10g]	NUMBER	
APPLIED_THREAD# [10g]	NUMBER	
NEWEST_SCN	NUMBER	
NEWEST_TIME	DATE	
NEWEST_SEQUENCE# [10g]	NUMBER	
NEWEST_THREAD# [10g]	NUMBER	
READ_SCN	NUMBER	
READ_TIME	DATE	
READ_SEQUENCE# [10g]	NUMBER	
READ_THREAD# [10g]	NUMBER	

dba_logstdby_skip

The following table presents the definition of the *dba_logstdby_skip* view. It contains the table names that will be skipped by the log apply service. It should be queried on the logical standby database. All columns are relevant for the Data Guard environment.

COLUMN_NAME	DATA_TYPE	DATA GUARD COLUMNS
ERROR	VARCHAR2	
ESC[10g]	VARCHAR2	To support the regular expression feature.
NAME	VARCHAR2	

COLUMN_NAME	DATA_TYPE	DATA GUARD COLUMNS
OWNER	VARCHAR2	
PROC	VARCHAR2	
STATEMENT_OPT	VARCHAR2	
USE_LIKE[10g]	VARCHAR2	To support the regular expression feature.

dba_logstdby_skip_transaction

The following table presents the definition of the *dba_logstdby_skip_transaction* view. It contains information about the individual transaction that will be skipped by the log apply service. It should be queried on the logical standby database. All columns are relevant for the Data Guard environment.

COLUMN_NAME	DATA_TYPE	DATA GUARD COLUMNS
XIDSLT	NUMBER	Slot Number
XIDSQN	NUMBER	Sequence Number
XIDUSN	NUMBER	Segment Number

dba_logstdby_unsupported

The following table presents the definition of the *dba_logstdby_unsupported* view. It contains information about the tables on the primary database containing data types that is unsupported in the logical standby database.

It should be queried on the primary database prior to creating the logical standby database. All columns are relevant for the Data Guard environment.

COLUMN_NAME	DATA_TYPE	DATA GUARD COLUMNS
ATTRIBUTES[10g]	VARCHAR2	Indicates unsupported storage attributes for a given table
COLUMN_NAME	VARCHAR2	Name of unsupported column
DATA_TYPE	VARCHAR2	Data type of unsupported column
OWNER	VARCHAR2	
TABLE_NAME	VARCHAR2	Table name containing unsupported column.

PL/SQL Supplied Packages for Data Guard

The *dbms_logstdby* PL/SQL package can be used to manage the working of Data Guard. In this section, you will learn about the useful procedures of the *dbms_logstdby* package. A brief description of the procedures of this package and their usage will be provided. Oracle manuals "Oracle9i Supplied PL/SQL Packages and Types Reference Release 2 (9.2)", and "PL/SQL Packages and Types Reference 10g Release (10.1)" are the best source to get more information on this package and its procedures. The valid parameters for each argument will not be listed here in order to save some trees! Oracle documentation should be consulted in order to obtain this list.

dbms_logstdby Supplied Package

The following procedures are available in the *dbms_logstdby* package to assist in the management of the logical standby database.

APPLY_SET

This procedure can be used to set the parameters controlling the behavior of the log apply service.

Usage:

```
DBMS_LOGSTDBY.APPLY_SET(PARAMETER_NAME IN VARCHAR2,
                        PARAMETER_VALUE IN VARCHAR2);
```

APPLY_UNSET

It resets the value of the parameter previously set by the APPLY_SET procedure to the system default value.

Usage:

```
DBMS_LOGSTDBY.APPLY_SET(PARAMETER_NAME IN VARCHAR2);
```

BUILD

The Build Procedure is used to import the LogMiner dictionary information in the redo logs. This procedure should be used on the primary database during the creation of the logical standby database.

Usage:

```
DBMS_LOGSTDBY.BUILD;
```

GUARD_BYPASS_OFF

This procedure can be used to reset the Data Guard on. This should be used on the logical standby database.

Usage:

```
DBMS_LOGSTDBY.GUARD_BYPASS_OFF;
```

GUARD_BYPASS_ON

This procedure will remove any protection of the logical standby database provided by Data Guard. This procedure can be used on the logical standby database to perform maintenance activities.

Usage:

```
DBMS_LOGSTDBY.GUARD_BYPASS_ON;
```

INSTANTIATE_TABLE

This procedure can be used on the logical standby database to create and populate a table from the primary database. It connects to the primary database using a database link passed as an argument. The database link must be created before using this procedure.

Usage:

```
DBMS_LOGSTDBY.INSTANTIATE_TABLE(SCHEMA_NAME IN VARCHAR2,
                                TABLE_NAME IN VARCHAR2,
                            DBLINK_NAME IN VARCHAR2);
```

PREPARE_INSTATIATION

This procedure takes the name of the database link to be used for table instantiation and verifies whether communication with the primary database can be established using this database link.

Usage:

```
DBMS_LOGSTDBY.PREPARE_INSTANTIATION( DBLINK_NAME IN VARCHAR2 );
```

SKIP

Skip procedure can be used to defined filters to prevent the application of all SQL statements from the primary database onto the logical standby database. SKIP is an overloaded procedure.

Usage:

```
DBMS_LOGSTDBY.SKIP(STMT IN VARCHAR2,SCHEMA_NAME IN VARCHAR2,
                OBJECT_NAME IN VARCHAR2,PROC_NAME IN VARCHAR2);

DBMS_LOGSTDBY.SKIP(STMT IN VARCHAR2,SCHEMA_NAME IN VARCHAR2,
                OBJECT_NAME IN VARCHAR2);

DBMS_LOGSTDBY.SKIP(STMT IN VARCHAR2);
```

SKIP_ERROR

This procedure defines the exception handling for the log apply service while skipping a transaction defined by the SKIP procedure.

Usage:

```
DBMS_LOGSTDBY.SKIP_ERROR(STMT IN VARCHAR2,SCHEMA_NAME IN VARCHAR2,
                OBJECT_NAME IN VARCHAR2,PROC_NAME IN VARCHAR2);
```

SKIP_TRANSACTION

This procedure can be used to skip individual transactions on the logical standby database. It is used in situations when a particular transaction, such as a DDL statement, has caused the log apply service to fail. In that case, that transaction can be skipped and the log apply service restarted.

Usage:

```
DBMS_LOGSTDBY.SKIP_TRANSACTION(UNDO_SEG# IN NUMBER,
                SLOT# IN NUMBER, SEQ# IN NUMBER);
```

UNSKIP

The UNSKIP procedure will remove the filters set by the SKIP procedure.

Usage:

```
DBMS_LOGSTDBY.UNSKIP (STMT IN VARCHAR2,SCHEMA_NAME IN VARCHAR2,
                OBJECT_NAME IN VARCHAR2);

DBMS_LOGSTDBY.UNSKIP (STMT IN VARCHAR2);
```

UNSKIP_ERROR

It removes any exception-handling rules set by the SKIP_ERROR procedure.

Usage:

```
DBMS_LOGSTDBY.UNSKIP_ERROR(STMT IN VARCHAR2,SCHEMA_NAME IN VARCHAR2,
                    OBJECT_NAME IN VARCHAR2);
```

UNSKIP_TRANSACTION

Similar to the UNSKIP procedure, it removes any previously set SKIP TRANSACTION rule.

Usage:

```
DBMS_LOGSTDBY.UNSKIP_TRANSACTION(UNDO_SEG# IN NUMBER,
                        SLOT# IN NUMBER, SEQ# IN NUMBER);
```

Troubleshooting Guide

This appendix has been put together to provide guidance when it is most needed; that is, when things aren't going as planned! This section has analyses and solutions for common errors.

Appendix A of Oracle documentation, *Oracle Data Guard Concepts and Administration Release 2 (9.2)*, contains more specific problem scenarios and their solutions. Additionally, the Oracle support site metalink.oracle.com is a good source of information on Data Guard issues.

B.1

Resolving Issues Related to Log Transport Services

Problem Text:

The archived redo log files from the primary database are not shipped to the standby database.

Related Oracle Errors:

ORA-12505, ORA-12545, Other TNS related Oracle errors.

Problem Description and Detection:

This type of issue is observed during the initial set up of Data Guard configuration. The cause is usually the incorrect configuration of Oracle Net, which facilitates communication between the primary and the standby site. To find the error, the *v$archive_dest* view can be queried or the database alert log file can be checked as shown below.

Error observed when the listener on standby site is not running:

```
ORA-12505: TNS:listener could not resolve SID given in connect
descriptor
```

Error due to incorrect entry in host parameter:

```
ORA-12545: Connect failed because target host or object does not
exist
```

```
SQL> SELECT STATUS, ERROR FROM V$ARCHIVE_DEST WHERE DEST_ID = 2;

STATUS    ERROR
--------- -----------------------------------------------------------
ERROR     ORA-12545: Connect failed because target host or object
does not exist
```

Solution:

Once the error is encountered on the primary database, it marks the destination as ERROR [or invalid]. No further attempt will be made by the archiver process to send redo data to this destination. The error must be corrected in the Oracle Net layer, and the destination must then be validated as shown below. The FAL archive process will fill any archive gap created due to the error in Oracle Net layer.

```
SQL> ALTER SYSTEM SET LOG_ARCHIVE_DEST_STATE_2 = 'ENABLE'
SCOPE=BOTH;
```

System altered.

```
SQL> SELECT STATUS, ERROR FROM V$ARCHIVE_DEST WHERE DEST_ID = 2;

STATUS    ERROR
--------- ---------------------------------------
VALID
```

The following extract from the alert log file shows that the FAL archive process fills any archive gap:

```
ALTER SYSTEM SET log_archive_dest_state_2='ENABLE' SCOPE=BOTH;
Mon May 31 22:50:42 2004
ARC1: Begin FAL archive (thread 1 sequence 2079 destination stdby2)
Creating archive destination LOG_ARCHIVE_DEST_2: 'stdby2'
ARC1: Complete FAL archive (thread 1 sequence 2079 destination
stdby2)
Mon May 31 22:50:42 2004
ARC0: Begin FAL archive (thread 1 sequence 2080 destination stdby2)
Creating archive destination LOG_ARCHIVE_DEST_2: 'stdby2'
ARC0: Transmitting activation ID 27fa976d
```

B.2

SQL Apply Operation on the Logical Standby Database Stalls Due to Lack of Space in the Tablespace for LogMiner Dictionary.

Problem Text:

The SQL Apply operation on the logical standby database has stopped because there is not enough space in the tablespace used for re-creating SQL statements from the redo log file. This error is quite common and is specific for the logical standby database only.

Related Oracle Error:

ORA-01332, ORA-01119

Problem Description and Detection:

The SQL apply operation on the logical standby database uses a tablespace to re-create the SQL statements from redo log files. This functionality is achieved using LogMiner technology. During the period of intensive transaction, the LogMiner may exhaust all space allocated in its tablespace and not be able to continue any further. This results in termination of the SQL apply operation. The error message is registered in the alert log file of the logical standby database.

Solution:

The data file will need to be added to the tablespace used by the LogMiner tablespace. To keep the primary database and the logical standby database structurally identical, it is recommended that the data file be added to the affected tablespace on the primary database as well as on the standby database. Additionally, on the standby database the transaction will have to be skipped such that the SQL apply operation will not try to add the data file again. The step-by-step procedure to add data file and skip the transaction on the standby database is described below.

On Logical Standby Database:

Turn the Data Guard Off

```
SQL> EXECUTE DBMS_LOGSTDBY.GUARD_BYPASS_ON;
```

Add data file to tablespace

```
SQL> ALTER TABLESPACE 'TablespaceName' ADD DATAFILE 'filespce' SIZE
'filesize' REUSE;
```

Put the Data Guard back on

```
SQL> EXECUTE DBMS_LOGSTDBY.GUARD_BYPASS_OFF;
```

Find out the transaction ID using the following SQL

```
SQL> SELECT XIDUSN, XIDSLT, XIDSQN
     FROM DBA_LOGSTDBY_EVENTS
     WHERE EVENT_TIME = (
                  SELECT MAX(EVENT_TIME)
                  FROM DBA_LOGSTDBY_EVENTS);
```

Skip the transaction as identified by previous statement.

```
SQL> EXECUTE DBMS_LOGSTDBY.SKIP_TRANSACTION
     (<XIDUSN_id>, <XIDSLT_id>,<XIDSQN_id>);
```

Restart the SQL apply operation.

```
SQL> ALTER DATABASE START LOGICAL APPLY;
```

B.3

Log Apply Service Stops Due to Missing Temp files

Problem Text:

This error is specific to logical standby databases. It manifests as an error on the start up of the logical standby database or on executing query that requires a sort in the temporary tablespace. Sometimes this error causes the SQL apply service to abort.

Related Oracle Error:

ORA-25153, ORA-1652

Problem Description and Detection:

In order to sort a query result, Oracle uses memory specified by *sort_area_size*. If the value of *sort_area_size* is not sufficient for query result to fit in, the temporary tablespace is used for sorting. At this point, if the temporary files are missing, Oracle raises errors ORA-25153 or ORA-01652. Sometimes these errors are followed by the abrupt termination of the SQL Apply operation.

Solution:

Add temp files to the temporary tablespace using the following statement:

```
ALTER TABLESPACE TEMP ADD TEMPFILE 'filespec';
```

B.4

Upgrading the Protection Mode Causes the Primary Database to Shutdown

Problem Text:

The goal is to upgrade the overall protection mode of your Data Guard configuration from MAXIMUM AVAILABILITY to MAXIMUM PROTECTION. The statement to upgrade the protection mode succeeds without any error, but the primary database will not open.

Related Oracle Errors:

ORA-03113, ORA-16086, ORA-16072

Problem Description and Detection:

In order to upgrade the protection mode to MAXIMUM PROTECTION, configure LGWR to write archived redo records to at least one standby database. The standby database should have standby redo logs (SRL) created before the protection mode can be upgraded. If the standby redo log files are not created, the primary database will not start. The alert log file on the primary database contains more information about this error.

The following snippet from the alert log file shows that the standby database participating in MAXIMUM PROTECTION mode does not have standby redo log files configured:

```
LGWR: Error 16086 verifying archivelog destination
LOG_ARCHIVE_DEST_2
LGWR: Continuing...
Tue Jun  1 21:31:20 2004
Errors in file /oracle/appsdb/admin/bdump/appsdb_lgwr_21438.trc:
ORA-16086: standby database does not contain available standby log
files
LGWR: Error 16086 disconnecting from destination LOG_ARCHIVE_DEST_2
standby host 'stdby2'
```

```
LGWR: Minimum of 1 applicable standby database required
Tue Jun  1 21:31:20 2004
Errors in file /oracle/appsdb/admin/bdump/appsdb_lgwr_21438.trc:
ORA-16072: a minimum of one standby database destination is required
LGWR: terminating instance due to error 16072
Instance terminated by LGWR, pid = 21438
```

Solution:

Add the standby redo log files on the standby database and restart the primary database. More information about adding standby redo log files can be found in Chapter 5, "Log Management Services".

B.5

Error When Recovering from Partial Archived Redo Log File

Problem Text:

The primary database has suffered a major failure and is not recoverable. At the time of failure, the redo log files were being archived to the standby sites. Failover to a standby database is needed, and it needs to open as the primary database. The recovery process on the standby database would not complete gracefully, so it cannot be converted to the primary database.

Related Oracle Errors:

On physical standby database: ORA-283/ORA-261
On logical standby database: ORA-332

Problem Description and Detection:

This is one of the most common problems during failover. In this case, the standby databases will have partially archived redo log files. If the system is failing over to a physical standby database, initiate the failover procedure using the following SQL statement:

```
RECOVER MANAGED STANDBY DATABASE FINISH;
```

This statement will fail with Oracle error ORA-283 due to the fact that the RFS process, which is responsible to write archived redo log files on standby site, still has a lock on the last partially written log file.

In the case of the logical standby database, register the partial archived redo log file using the following statement:

```
ALTER DATABASE REGISTER LOGICAL LOGFILE 'filespec';
```

The statement above will return error ORA-332. The cause of failure is similar to the one for the physical standby database.

Solution:

Let the Operating System network layer clean up the dead connection. The time lag between failure of the primary database and clean up of the dead connection depends on the TCP/IP KEEPALIVE parameter. The RFS process on the standby site probes the connection between the primary database and the standby database. Frequency of this probe is determined based on the value of the KEEPALIVE parameter.

Once the RFS process detects a dead connection between the primary and the standby, it closes the partially archived redo log file and removes its lock from the file. After this, it should be possible to complete the recovery process or register the partial log file. This solution may take a good few minutes depending on the value of TCP/IP KEEPALIVE.

Another possible solution is to kill the RFS process. This will cause the RFS to close the partial log file and remove the lock from it.

Index

M

N

O

V

About the Author

 Bipul Kumar is a Senior Application Engineer for a Telecommunications company in St. Albans Hertfordshire, United Kingdom. His responsibilities include Oracle Database administration, Performance tuning, Recovery, and application development. He has more than six years of experience in creating and managing Oracle Databases of varying sizes, primarily on UNIX operating systems.

Mr. Kumar has a Masters degree in Science from the Indian Institute of Technology (IIT), Kharagpur, India and nearly nine years of experience in computing. In addition, he has acquired Oracle DBA certification for 7.3, 8.0, and 8i

About Mike Reed

When he first started drawing, Mike Reed drew just to amuse himself. It wasn't long, though, before he knew he wanted to be an artist.

Today he does illustrations for children's books, magazines, catalogs, and ads.

He also teaches illustration at the College of Visual Art in St. Paul, Minnesota. Mike Reed says, "Making pictures is like acting — you can paint yourself into the action." He often paints on the computer, but he also draws in pen and ink and paints in acrylics. He feels that learning to draw well is the key to being a successful artist.

Mike is regarded as one of the nation's premier illustrators and is the creator of the popular "Flame Warriors" illustrations at **www.flamewarriors.com**. A renowned children's artist, Mike has also provided the illustrations for dozens of children's books.

Mike Reed has always enjoyed reading. As a young child, he liked the Dr. Seuss books. Later, he started reading biographies and war stories. One reason why he feels lucky to be an illustrator is because he can listen to books on tape while he works. Mike is available to provide custom illustrations for all manner of publications at reasonable prices. Mike can be reached at **www.mikereedillustration.com**.

Free!
Oracle 10g Senior DBA Reference Poster

This 24 x 36 inch quick reference includes the important data columns and relationships between the DBA views, allowing you to quickly write complex data dictionary queries.

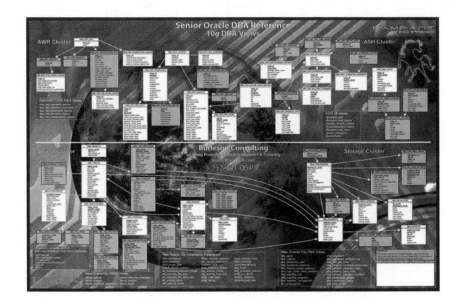

This comprehensive data dictionary reference contains the most important columns from the most important Oracle10g DBA views. Especially useful are the Automated Workload Repository (AWR) and Active Session History (ASH) DBA views.

WARNING - This poster is not suitable for beginners. It is designed for senior Oracle DBAs and requires knowledge of Oracle data dictionary internal structures. You can get your poster at this URL:

www.rampant.cc/poster.htm